Banking services and the consumer

**A report by the
National Consumer Council**

METHUEN & CO. LTD

First published 1983 for the National Consumer Council
18 Queen Anne's Gate, London SW1H 9AA
by Methuen & Co. Ltd
11 New Fetter Lane, London EC4P 4EE
© 1983 National Consumer Council

Typeset by Keyset Composition, Colchester, Essex
Printed in Great Britain by
Richard Clay (The Chaucer Press) Ltd, Bungay, Suffolk

British Library Cataloguing in Publication Data

National Consumer Council
Banking services and the consumer.
1. Banks and banking—Great Britain
I. Title
332.1 2 0941   HG2990
ISBN 0-416-35760-1
ISBN 0-416-35770-9 Pbk

Banking services
and the consumer

Contents

Introduction   *vii*

Note on terminology   *ix*

SECTION

1 / Conclusions and recommendations   1

2 / Banking services and the consumer   6

3 / Cash, cheques, credits, debits and charges   27

4 / Access to banking services   51

5 / New technology   64

6 / Banking services and the law   87

7 / The resolution of disputes between bank and customer   105

8 / Saving and borrowing   112

9 / Competition and regulation   129

10 / Northern Ireland and Scotland   143

11 / Executor and trustee services   151

APPENDIX

I / Some of the developments in consumer banking services during the time this report was in preparation   182

II / Research into consumers' attitudes to banking services, by Market Behaviour Ltd   185

III / Research into attitudes of consumers with bank accounts, by Market and Opinion Research International   201

IV / The economics of branch banking: a consumer perspective   231

V / Letter to Dr Gerard Vaughan, MP, Minister of State for Consumer Affairs, from Mrs Rachel Waterhouse, Chairman of the NCC Banking Services Working Party   240

VI / Cashless pay: the NCC's response to the Department of Employment's consultative paper   241

VII / Organisations which were consulted or gave written and/or oral evidence   244

Introduction

In the spring of 1982 the government asked the National Consumer Council to report on personal banking services, in these terms:

> . . . to collect and consider evidence on the banking services available to consumers in the United Kingdom; and, as appropriate, to make recommendations. The study should focus on personal banking services and should not of course address the wider role of banking in the economy.

Our remit speaks of banking services, not banks. We have therefore examined the services provided by institutions which either engage in one or more of the following activities or have aspirations to: deposit-taking; lending (excluding credit and hire purchase companies); and money transmission. Many aspects of lending to consumers were discussed in an earlier Council report to government *Consumers and Credit*, published in 1980. We have not gone again over the ground covered in that report; however, we have followed up some points from it.

We have seen the provision of finance specifically for house purchase as outside our remit. We have, however, considered building societies in their role as competitors for personal banking business.

During the eighteen months or so in which the report was prepared, it became clear that a central feature of the changing market place was the erosion of many familiar distinctions between banks and building societies. Essentially different types of institutions, operating within different legislative frameworks and emerging from different financial traditions, they were increasingly seen to be in competition for similar and in some cases identical business. Thus banks moved into the home mortgage market and some building societies began to make credit cards available to their depositors. In other respects too the pattern of competition to supply consumer financial services is changing rapidly, at times bewilderingly, and there is little sign of any slowing down of this process. (Appendix I lists some of the developments during the period – February 1982 to June 1983 – this report was being prepared.)

We collected evidence in three ways. Early in the project we invited formal submissions from a variety of individual London, Scottish, Irish and foreign banks, a selection of large, small and specialist building societies, finance houses, banking unions, consumer organisations, bodies representing lawyers and others (see Appendix VII). We asked those invited to give particular consideration in their submissions to the legal relationship between suppliers of banking services and their domestic customers, trends in the quality of personal banking services, and attitudes to changing competitive conditions. At the same time we were careful not to place any preconceived restriction on what the banks and others might wish to report to us; the impact of micro-technological change on customers and the application of the basic consumer principles of information and redress to banking services were both specifically mentioned in our letter of invitation as possible additional areas of comment.

We are very grateful to those who responded for the considerable trouble they took. No major financial institution declined to submit evidence: the Retail Consortium, however, felt unable to provide us with views. On legal issues, the London and Scottish clearing banks opted for collective replies which were produced for us by the Committee of London Clearing Bankers (CLCB) and the Committee of Scottish Clearing Bankers (CSCB) respectively. CLCB also submitted a paper on *Competition in Personal Banking*.

Once all the submissions had been examined, it became clear that we needed answers to a number of more detailed questions, notably on the operation of current accounts. We therefore sent a questionnaire to each of the London and Scottish clearing banks – again we are grateful for the detailed and helpful responses received. The response to this exercise, together with the earlier submissions, formed the basis of a series of meetings between members of the Council's Banking Services Sub-Committee and senior representatives of the banks, a number of their competitors, and the appropriate regulatory authorities. These meetings took place throughout the autumn, winter and spring of 1982 and 1983; they involved most of the major banks in England and Scotland, three major building societies, the Committee of London Clearing Bankers, the Bank of England, the Registrar General of Friendly Societies, the Office of Fair Trading, the Treasury, the Northern Ireland Bankers' Association and the Building Societies' Association. These submissions, answers to questionnaires and subsequent discussions, provided us with a substantial body of evidence on the workings of the UK retail banking sector.

The second major strand in our collection of evidence was an enquiry into what consumers think of the banks and their competitors, and an investigation of consumers' experiences. We carried out two types of research. First, we commissioned Market Behaviour Limited to carry out group discussions among a wide cross-section of consumers, some with bank accounts, some without. (These are described in Appendix II.) Before going on to the second, quantitative, stage of our research, we also asked the National Federation of Consumer Groups to arrange for four of its member consumer groups (in Aberdeen, Preston, South Humberside, and Winchester) to produce short local evaluations of banking services to help us ensure that no issues that are important to consumers were being overlooked.

In considering quantitative research, we were keen that, with limited resources, we should not go over well-trodden ground. We therefore commissioned Market and Opinion Research International (MORI) to examine the attitudes and experiences of a sample of the 'banked' population with particular reference to account holders of six or fewer years' standing, the object being to focus on the experiences of those customers who have opened bank accounts comparatively recently. (See Appendix III.)

The third strand in our research involved consultations with independent experts, particularly in law and in banking technology. A number of specialists were invited to act formally or informally as consultants and readers. We are grateful to them all for their help, but particularly to Patrick Frazer of the Banking Information Service. They, however, bear no responsibility for our conclusions.

This enquiry has been conducted by a sub-committee of the NCC chaired by Rachel Waterhouse CBE. The other members of the sub-committee were Sheila Black, Kate Foss, John Hatch, Elizabeth Hodder, Elizabeth Stanton, Ramindar Singh, Tom Quigley (Northern Ireland Consumer Council) and Douglas Williamson (Scottish Consumer Council).

Preparation of the research was directed by Martin Smith with assistance from Loveday Murley. The report was drafted by Martin Smith, Ann Foster, Richard Thomas and Jenny Potter, and edited by Maurice Healy and Jeremy Mitchell. The report was typed by Pip Baker, Robyn Fowler, Eldorna Mapp and Sally Pontin, and prepared for publication by Liz Dunbar.

Note on terminology

The phrases commonly used to describe the banks have become confusing due to some recent or impending changes of status as regards particular institutions. The following terms are employed in our text:

Traditional London clearing banks (or clearers)
Barclays, Coutts, Lloyds, Midland, National Westminster and Williams and Glyn's

Big four banks
Barclays, Lloyds, Midland and National Westminster

Newer London clearing banks
Co-operative, National Girobank and Trustee Savings Banks

Scottish clearing banks
Bank of Scotland, Clydesdale and Royal Bank of Scotland

High street banks
The London and Scottish clearing banks, plus Yorkshire, minus Coutts

Irish clearing banks
Allied Irish, Bank of Ireland, Northern and Ulster Banks

Ethnic banks

Banks whose main appeal is to members of the Indian, Pakistani, Bangladeshi, Cypriot and other communities; for example, Bank of India, Bank of Baroda and the Habib Bank

Section 1 / Conclusions and recommendations

In this report we have concentrated on the service which makes banks different from other financial institutions – the provision of a current account, and the payment services which go with it. We have considered more briefly savings and borrowing services and we have dealt in some detail with executor and trustee business, a very small part of banks' total relationship with their customers but one which seems to create particular problems.

The evidence of our research among bank customers is that they are, overall, highly satisfied with their banks. However they have substantial reservations about some aspects of bank services; bank customers do not find it easy enough to use banks. Many people do not understand bank charges and are dissatisfied with them. Bank customers who also have building society accounts tend to find building societies easier to deal with; significant numbers of them would like their building societies to offer payment services, like cheque books, which have traditionally been the exclusive preserve of banks.

This leads to the major thrust of our report – competition among banks and between banks and building societies. The last few years – including the time this report has been in preparation – have seen enormous changes in the banking services on offer to individual consumers. These have resulted from increasing competition between banks – both the traditional clearing banks and the Co-operative Bank, Trustee Savings Banks and National Girobank – and between banks and other institutions, most notably the large building societies. We very much welcome this growth in competition; our major recommendations are designed to encourage it and to see that the terms on which it takes place are as equitable as possible.

We seek more competition in current account services because we see the desire of the building societies to attract more depositors by offering a range of payment services as being a powerful instrument in encouraging the banks to improve their own payment services. If competition can be kept strong and strengthened further, then we hope that many of the improvements which we believe bank customers would like to see in banking services will emerge naturally.

This has led us to make some recommendations about the structure of building societies. We have already published in 1981 a more detailed report on building societies which we commissioned from the Mutual Aid Centre, *Building Societies and the Consumer*. Many of that report's recommendations were aimed at changing building society practice. We have supported their main thrust; some emerge again from this report.

Besides our recommendations about competition, we have also recommended a number of changes in banking practice. The most important of these are aimed at bank charges. We are strongly in favour of charging systems which make clear to consumers what they are paying for. We see competition as the best way of developing these, but we also see a need for better information for consumers about how their existing charges are made up.

Savings and borrowing facilities are important bank services. Our recommendations are aimed at improving the information that consumers get when choosing between offers and at improving the terms of competition between the different institutions. One of the institutions competing for consumers' savings is the government: some of our recommendations are therefore directed at it.

We have also considered the legal relationship between banks and their customers. We have seen no need to recommend a codification of banking law nor, on balance, do we favour a written contract between bank and customer. We do see a need for legislation to clarify the rights and obligations of banks and customers for electronic payments. We have also made some detailed recommendations to remove particular anomalies and for improving customers' knowledge of their rights and obligations.

Bank customers make relatively few complaints about banks. However, some complaints, particularly about trustee and executor business, are complex, deeply felt and touch matters of considerable importance to the person involved. We have therefore suggested that the banks should establish a Banking Ombudsman, on the same general principles as the Insurance Ombudsman.

The banking situation in Scotland and Northern Ireland is different in some respects from that in England and Wales. We have made specific recommendations about each country.

It is implicit throughout our report that consumers of banking services have much to gain by 'shopping around' for the services which best meet their individual needs. If competition is to work, as we hope it will, to develop banking services which more closely meet consumers' needs, then bank customers may need to be more prepared than they have been in the past, to move their account when they see a service which suits them better than their existing one.

Recommendations to government

1. The government should announce, as soon as possible, its intention to review the development of money transmission services within two to three years. If the institutions which wish to provide money transmission services have not been

able to enter the market on equitable terms, the government should then consider whether the joint ownership of the clearing systems for cheques and electronic payments by the members of the Committee of London Clearing Bankers in their present forms, is still appropriate.

2. The rights and obligations of banks and their customers for electronic payments and, in particular, for the operation of debit cards should be defined by legislation. This should ensure that the terms and conditions are not inferior to the terms and conditions of cheque and credit card use, so far as the comparison is practicable.

3. The Office of Fair Trading should reconsider whether the limit on cheque guarantee cards (£50 at the time of writing) is a suitable subject for collective agreement by the banks, when the banks have improved the fraud-resistance of their cards. We believe that it is not.

4. The composite rate of interest for building societies should be abolished. The Inland Revenue should make arrangements with banks, building societies and other savings institutions for interest payments to be made net of basic rate tax. Savers should be able to choose whether to receive their interest gross or net: if this is impractical for all savers, provision should certainly be made for non-taxpayers to receive interest without tax deduction.

5. The Secretary of State for Trade and Industry should ask the Director-General of Fair Trading to explore with institutions which seek personal savings ways of quoting rates of interest in a standard, comparable way. If voluntary agreement cannot be reached, government should be prepared to legislate. The government itself should comply with any solution that is reached.

6. Government should provide small savers with a no-strings-attached savings account which would guarantee small savers a rate of return equivalent to the rate of inflation plus, say, three per cent. Otherwise, government should not obscure the terms of competition for savings by offering tax-free concessions on particular types of saving.

7. Building societies should be given limited powers to lend without the security of a first mortgage, subject to appropriate prudential arrangements. Such powers should be reviewed after five years to see whether they should be extended or further limited.

8. All quotations for mortgages should be subject to the quotations regulations of the Consumer Credit Act.

9. The Inland Revenue should ensure that the corporation tax position of banks and building societies does not inappropriately favour either.

10. The exemption from restrictive practices legislation which allows the Northern Ireland Bankers' Association to operate a cartel covering opening hours, charging tariffs and interest rates should be withdrawn.

11. Section 53(2) of the Bills of Exchange Act 1882 should be amended so that the procedures for stopping cheques are the same in Scotland as in England and Wales.

12. Section 6 of the Statute of Frauds Amendment Act 1882 should be repealed. This piece of legislation has the effect that banks in England and Wales are

protected from the consequences of their employees giving fraudulent information about their customers' financial position.

Recommendations to the banks

13. We strongly welcome the development of interest-bearing current accounts which credit customers with the interest their money has earned and debit them with the charges for the work done on their behalf. We support charging systems which make it clear to consumers what they are paying for. We believe that, if our recommendations for encouraging competition in money transmission services are followed, such accounts should become more general. So far as current account practice is concerned we recommend that

    (i) banks should not take money for charges out of customers' accounts without telling them first;

    (ii) banks should radically improve the way in which charges are presented to customers.

14. All informal agreements on bank opening hours should cease. We welcome the gradual break-down in the standard pattern of bank hours, which many bank customers find inadequate.

15. All automated teller machines and future point-of-sale equipment should give a printed record of transactions.

16. Banks should give their customers better information about the costs of overdraft. They should inform customers of the annual percentage rate, calculated to a mutually agreed formula, when agreeing an arranged overdraft. They should also draw attention to the costs involved, when writing to customers about unarranged overdrafts.

17. Banks should give all new customers opening current or deposit accounts a simple, attractively designed statement outlining the rights and obligations which customers have.

18. Banks should inform all customers about the way their system for giving references on customers works. Customers should have the option to request their permission being sought whenever a reference is made to a banker. If this service imposes extra costs on the banks, banks should be able to charge for it, provided of course that this has been made clear to the customer.

19. Bank customers should have access to factual records about the operation of their account.

20. Banks should improve their internal procedures for dealing with trustee and executor work. Detailed suggestions are made on page 179.

21. The banks should collectively make arrangements for the creation and servicing of a Banking Ombudsman comparable to the Insurance Ombudsman. The Ombudsman should be empowered to consider and adjudicate upon all complaints of a personal banking nature, including executor and trust business, and should be requested to make and publish annual reports.

22. The Scottish clearing banks should consider offering their customers

opening hours which will serve them at least as well as banks serve their customers in England and Wales.

Recommendations to other organisations

23. The Building Societies Association should cease to recommend interest rates to its members. If it does not, the exemption it enjoys from restrictive practices legislation should be withdrawn.
24. No changes are necessary in the control of advertisements for savings. However the Independent Broadcasting Authority (IBA) and Advertising Standards Authority (ASA) should continue to scrutinise such advertisements carefully, and ASA should monitor them on a regular basis.
25. Financial advertising on satellite television and on cable should meet the standards set by the IBA and ASA.

Section 2 / Banking services and the consumer

From a consumer point of view the simplest definition of banking services would seem to be:

* a bank provides a safe home for your money
* a bank will make payments on your behalf
* a bank will lend you money.

To put it another way, banks can be seen to be in the market to provide consumers with savings services, money transmission services and credit services. These definitions bring us immediately to what is probably the most important issue that we have to deal with in this report: the fact that these services are not provided only by banks. A large number of different types of organisations compete for consumers' savings and a large number compete to lend money to consumers. Some organisations – most notably the building societies and money shops – provide, to a greater or lesser extent, the same three main services as banks. In this report, therefore, while we have concentrated primarily on the banks themselves, we have also considered the implications for consumers of competition from other financial institutions.

Of course these are not the only services which banks provide. Later in this section we describe the services which are on offer to consumers and how we have dealt with them in this report. Given the breadth of the issues that we have had to face, we have not felt obliged to deal in any detail with ancillary banking services unless we had some evidence that there were consumer problems. The main ancillary service we have dealt with has been trustee and executor work, covered in section 11.

In looking at any service we take into account a number of consumer criteria:

* can consumers get adequate access to the service?
* do consumers have effective choice and can this choice influence what is provided for them?
* have consumers adequate information on which to base their choices?
* have consumers adequate redress when things go wrong?
* is what is provided safe?

Access raises particular questions with banking services and these are dealt with in section 4. Choice and safety are discussed largely in section 9 which deals with competition and regulation. Our discussion of redress is largely in section 6 on banking services and the law and section 7 on the resolution of disputes. Information will be a common theme throughout the whole report.

The services provided by banks

Banks offer the personal consumer a wide range of services – in the case of the traditional clearers, over 120 individual services. We do not intend to provide an exhaustive list, but below we give an indication of the range of facilities which can be obtained through the branch network. Within each broad term, there will probably be several variations. For example 'personal loans' may well be sold to the customer as 'home improvement loans', 'car loans', 'boat loans', etc. Most people use the three basic services of deposit, money transmission and lending. Significant numbers also require foreign currency each year, but the banks' other services, such as investment management, are likely to be used only by a minority of bank customers.

The range of services

  (i) *Deposits and savings*
      current/cheque accounts
      automated teller machines (ATMs)
      deposit/savings accounts including investment and high interest deposit accounts
      special types of savings account e.g. mortgage deposit, holiday savings
      budget/credit account

  (ii) *Money transmission*
      cheques
      credit transfer
      standing orders
      direct debits
      bank drafts

  (iii) *Lending*
      overdrafts
      personal loans
      house purchase schemes
      bridging loans
      credit cards

  (iv) *Travel and foreign*
      foreign currency
      travellers' cheques
      international cheque-cashing arrangements
      international money transfer

(v) *Investment, trust and taxation*
safe deposit
executor and trustee
insurance
life assurance
pension plans
tax planning
investment e.g. unit trusts, share plans

(vi) *Specialised advice, information and services*
Often tailored to suit the needs of specific market segments, such as students, members of H.M. Forces, people working abroad.

Given the very wide range of issues involved in any report on banking services, we have to set a focus. The main thrust of our report is therefore about what seems to us the essential service provided by a bank – the operation of a current account. A current account embodies in one mechanism the three major banking services: it is home for the bank customer's money; it provides a way of making payments; and it is an opportunity for the customer to borrow money, through an overdraft. Certainly it is clear from our own research among consumers that it is the operation of a current account which they see as at the heart of a bank's services to individual consumers.

What consumers think of banks

We carried out two major pieces of research to investigate consumers' experience of banks. We asked Market Behaviour Limited (MBL) to carry out a series of group discussions (see Appendix II). We also asked Market and Opinion Research International (MORI) to carry out a sample survey (see Appendix III). We also received information from four local consumer groups (Winchester, Preston, Aberdeen, and South Humberside), all members of the National Federation of Consumer Groups (NFCG). They conducted surveys and reviewed their local banking facilities. Many individual consumers also wrote to us about their experiences.

The objectives of the group discussions were:

(i) to determine what consumers' perceptions are of their own needs for banking services and to discover what their perceptions are of the various different types of banking services now on offer;
(ii) to establish what specific problems people experience;
(iii) to establish whether specific ethnic groups differ in their needs and experience.

The purpose of the sample survey carried out by MORI was to establish the extent to which the perceptions and problems which we had identified were typical of banks' current account customers.

A technical account of the MBL research together with a summary of its main findings are given in Appendix II. MORI's detailed report of their research is given in Appendix III. The quotations from individual consumers in the text of this section are from the MBL report.

Opening an account

Over three-fifths of our sample have a personal current account, in either sole or joint name. More men than women have accounts and more men than women have accounts in their own names. People aged 25–54 are more likely to have accounts than those who are younger or older. There is a large difference by class: people in the upper socio-economic categories are far more likely to have a bank account than those in the lower ones.

For the majority of the people we surveyed who had an account, opening one seemed to be almost automatic and was usually connected with leaving school or starting a job, especially where the firm pays wages and salaries by bank transfer.

For these people, opening an account was such an intrinsic part of their adult life that it was not thought of in terms of the advantages and disadvantages it brings.

'It's second nature, isn't it?'
'Part of life.'

There is however a significant minority of people who would not have opened a bank account at all, but for their employer's virtual insistence.

'My husband changed his job within the firm, he went into the office and therefore his salary was paid through the bank. We've kept it even though he's now changed his job again.'

Then, we found a few respondents who were paid weekly in cash, but had made a positive decision to open a bank account, which they used mainly for paying bills.

'My husband used to give me cash each week and I had to put it away and pay the bills as well as the housekeeping, and the housekeeping wouldn't stretch and I used to take a bit out of the bill money, then when the bills came in there wasn't enough to pay them. So he stopped giving it to me and paid it into the bank which I preferred because if it's not there you can't touch it.'

A few women had specifically opened their own account, as opposed to having a joint one with their husband, when they returned to work after bringing up children. They talked about this account in terms of the feeling of independence it gave them and the extras which 'their money' could buy.

Without doubt, the majority of people with bank accounts, for whatever reason, would not now revert to being without one.

The majority of bank account holders had not given much thought or effort to choosing a bank. They did not appear to shop around, nor did they perceive much difference between one bank and another. Often they chose the bank and branch on the basis of convenience.

'I chose . . . bank because it was the nearest, on the opposite side of the road to where I live. I suppose my own personal opinion regarding different sorts of banks is that there is probably not a lot to choose between them.'

Or they chose to open an account with the same bank and possibly the same branch that their employer used.

'The only reason I've stayed with . . . bank is because it's the firm's bank and therefore I get wages on the day, I don't have to wait for transferral. They're no better than other banks'.

The recommendation of family and friends was also mentioned,

'One week I was £5 overdrawn, got a stinking letter, so I thought, right I'll take my money elsewhere, so I went to . . . bank and they're fantastic . . . people told me, they said if you have any trouble go to . . . bank, they're a fantastic bank.'

'My uncle had banked there and said it was a good bank and there hadn't been any problems on the couple of occasions they'd overdrawn.'

– as was the influence of particular deals which individual banks offered,

'I started off with . . . bank when I was a student because they had most free gifts.'

A very small minority of people do appear to 'shop around', looking for such things as lowest minimum balance required to avoid bank charges.

We also looked at 'new' account holders – people who had opened an account in the last six years – to discover their reasons for opening an account.

Inevitably, younger respondents are likely to have opened their accounts the most recently and 37 per cent of 15–24 year olds had opened their first account within the past two years (79 per cent within six years). However, it appears that the expansion in the number of bank accounts in the country has not been confined exclusively to the younger generation; ten per cent of over-65 year olds with accounts had held these accounts for no more than six years.

People in the lower socio-economic categories were also more likely to have opened an account recently. The banking habit appears to be spreading through all social classes. Although DE (generally, unskilled workers) respondents are less likely than higher social groups to have an account, they are noticeably more likely to have opened an account recently. Seventeen per cent of DEs had opened an account in the past two years and 33 per cent in the past six years.

The main reason why these new customers had chosen a particular bank or branch was convenience – either to home or work. Over half gave this as a reason. However, a quarter said their choice had been influenced by advertising, and nearly as many took out an account because their employer dealt with that bank. Particular attractions of the service offered by the bank seemed less important – only 15 per cent mentioned these.

Changing banks

Once with a particular bank, most people tended to stay with it, even if from time to time they were dissatisfied with the service they received. If they did change, it was usually because they had changed their job or house. Some people moved to get lower bank charges or more convenient opening hours and others moved as a result of a specific complaint about the bank.

'I wanted to get a loan for a car and the hassle I had to go to to get it. They nearly asked me what I had for breakfast. I said forget about it, close the account.'

However, generally, if bank customers did have complaints, they were not likely to go through the process of changing banks, which they often perceived as difficult and sometimes impossible.

It seems probable that the main reasons behind this apparent reluctance are a sense of obligation, especially if an overdraft or a loan is involved, a suspicion of the reference system and misgivings about the inevitable complications associated with changing banks such as informing employers and altering standing orders.

'It was too much trouble to change and get all the standing orders set up again.'

General attitudes and feelings towards banks and bank staff

There was a general acceptance that banks are in business to make money and that they offer services to the customer only if they can profit from them. There was some resentment that the banks are profiting from using other people's money, without giving anything in return.

'They've got your money and they've used it how they like but they don't do *you* a favour.'

Many consumers believe that the traditional clearing banks make their money from business accounts rather than from personal accounts and are therefore more likely to be interested in their commercial or well-to-do customers.

'. . . are very aloof. If you're in business OK, but if you're "Mr Man in the street" no!'

In comparison, non-traditional banks, such as the TSBs, are thought to show more interest in 'ordinary people'.

'It seems a different world somehow. It's not quite the same. How the other half lives. It's a different atmosphere altogether. You feel a bit of an intruder because they are more for business people, whereas the TSB is for the general public.'

Some of our respondents felt ill at ease inside banks and were critical of the general atmosphere and attitude, finding them hard, inhumane or sombre places. The relationship between counter staff and customer appears to be more important to women, many of whom expressed a preference for friendly, pleasant staff. But most people want a quick, efficient service and notice the staff only if they are inefficient or rude. Generally people appear to be satisfied with counter staff, although there were criticisms of post office staff

'They never smile or say good morning.'
'And they throw the things at you.'

Emotive judgments were also made about the bank manager who is clearly an influential figure. Some people tend to judge the branch on the strength of the relationship they may have established with the manager. People who have a good relationship with the manager appear to have the best opinion of the services that the banks offer. Judgments are often made on the basis of individual experience and managers who are accessible and approachable, who explain things clearly, who sanction loans with the minimum of fuss, or who are simply seen about the premises over a long period of time are judged to be 'good' managers;

'He seemed a normal sort of bloke.'

Unfavourable judgments stem from situations in which the customers see themselves in an inferior position, usually when they have to go 'cap in hand' to ask for the favour of a loan, when they are on the unfamiliar territory of the manager's office, or when they feel ill at ease.

'I think bank managers are frightening people; I don't like going to see mine at all. He seems to sit up at the other side of the desk and never smiles and makes me feel as though I'm begging for money. I just hate it.'

'I think it's about time bank managers stopped acting like gods.'

'They always look down at you, they frighten me.'

The old image of the bank manager as an older and wiser figure looking down from his (or, very rarely, her) pedestal still persists. The effect is that some customers are reluctant to approach the manager for advice.

Small personal touches are noticed and appreciated. The information we had from consumer groups indicated that people like to be addressed by name by the counter staff, especially as the information is readily available from cheque books and paying-in books.

In one MBL discussion group, none of the members knew the name of their manager. It was felt that the situation might be improved if the customer was at least introduced to the manager when the account was first opened. Conversely, respondents who had accounts in the National Girobank, where the manager is not on the premises, did not feel inconvenienced or upset by this lack at all.

Knowledge of bank services

Customers got to know about bank services in many ways: media advertising, newspaper features, information from friends, colleagues and relatives, leaflets and so on and, in rare cases, as a result of an approach by the manager. Television advertising appears to be particularly prominent in people's minds: many respondents were able to recall details of individual campaigns that were running at the time of the interview. However, it obviously does not give detailed information about the services banks provide.

Most respondents were aware of the range of services offered by their banks. Our MORI sample correctly identified nearly all services as being available: a few people did not know about the tax, investment and insurance advice and management services offered by banks. New account holders were slightly less well informed about bank services perhaps because a quarter of them reported that they had had no printed material from their bank describing the services on offer when they joined.

The various methods of obtaining information about bank services were discussed in greater depth with the MBL groups. The majority of customers felt that the responsibility to obtain information lay with themselves. Advertisement headlines or news items may catch the attention and create interest but obtaining further information required some form of action by the consumer, either asking at the counter, consulting the manager or reading the leaflets that might be available. Most respondents, when prompted, appeared to be aware in general terms of the services offered, but admitted to being uninformed about specific detail. Various reasons were offered to explain this. People had evolved a pattern of use of financial institutions which suited them and they saw no reason to change. In some cases, they were interested to know more about new services which might be beneficial to them although they thought that to make more use of their bank they needed to have large sums of money in the account. Others criticised the information leaflets and the staff for being too complicated, particularly in the explanation of interest rates when comparing the returns offered by various forms of accounts in banks (and building societies).

'They have a lot of leaflets and I think if you went to see your manager they're usually quite good. But they don't explain it in laymen's terms, it's gobble-degook. The same with a mortgage or anything, nobody explains it to you in simple terms, they talk in their terms.'

'Talking drivel means nothing to me but put it in pounds and I understand it.'

'I went to the bank for a car loan. The manager patted me on the head and thrust me out of the door with a leaflet in my hand. I went to the bus stop, read it, threw it in the bin and never bothered to go back. I couldn't understand it . . .'

Too much information or confusing information creates a barrier, and in the end many people resort to advice from a friend or a colleague when it comes to making a decision. People also feel embarrassed about revealing their ignorance or financial state in public and will more readily opt for hearsay or unreliable advice from peers instead of getting accurate details from the appropriate source. A general reticence to obtain more information in order to make greater use of the banks' services is more noticeable among lower socio-economic groups and women.

People generally quite liked the suggestion of positive advice from the bank. The financial information in the National Girobank's regular magazine was spoken about favourably. Another respondent described a visit from a TSB financial adviser:

> 'I had a letter from the TSB saying their financial adviser was in the area and could he come to see me . . . It was a service offering help on services that the TSB offer . . . when I finished paying for the washing machine he suggested investing money over five years, £20 a month. I'm glad I did it because I'd never thought about it.'

If the approach is personal, polite and relevant, and the advice is conveyed verbally in simple language, customers appear to appreciate this method of obtaining valuable and helpful information which otherwise they might never even hear of, let alone benefit from. Equally, if the customer felt that he was being pressurised by someone acting like a fast-talking doorstep salesman, then mistrust and suspicion would creep in.

> 'I think it would be a good thing but I would be a bit sceptical. Are they going to tell you how to use the account to your advantage or are they coming to tell you how to use it to their advantage? Because I don't believe the bank ever looks to the people first, they're looking to make the profits first.'

When talking about the availability of loans generally (and at the time of the survey loans were quite easily available) a small number of respondents were clearly unhappy about 'dangerous' services being imposed upon them, which might encourage them to spend beyond their means.

> 'Before I knew where I was, he was trying to give me credit up to the eyeballs. He scared me actually, I could have been right into debt. I suppose they wouldn't give you more than they thought you could cope with, but I didn't think I could cope with what he was offering me.'

Some respondents were unhappy about the way their banks had encouraged them to take credit cards.

Use of bank services

Nearly all bank current account holders use more bank services than simply writing cheques. The heaviest users of bank services tended to be male, in a high socio-economic group, aged between 25 and 44, account-holders of long standing and living in their own homes.

Advantages of having a bank account

Having a current account and a cheque book offers customers two major advantages – first, it does away with the need to carry around large amounts of cash and, secondly, it provides a convenient way of paying bills.

Many consumers are increasingly frightened of carrying around large sums of cash or keeping money in the house:

> 'I use cheques practically all the time. I used to carry £50 cash around but I don't carry more than £10 a week.'

Our respondents found a current account an easy way of paying bills, either by standing orders, direct debits, cheques through the postal system, giro transfer or occasionally some form of budget account. Some of our respondents were confused about the direct debit system of paying bills and consequently were less happy about its use:

> 'Well they confuse me . . . because I never quite understand what the difference is, except that one way or the other the company you're paying can change it. So I must admit I don't use them because I don't understand them.'

In correspondence, we were told of strong objections to being forced to make regular payments by direct debit. Some of our MBL respondents were surprised to discover that they had in fact authorised payments:

> 'I know once I signed a form for some insurance, I didn't even know what was happening, the next thing I knew it was being taken out of my bank account. I was so annoyed I cancelled my insurance policy. They don't actually tell you that they're going to take the money from the bank.'

Many respondents saw the overdraft facility, either pre-arranged or accidental, as a positive advantage of the banking system. People also liked using the 'float' – writing a cheque just before pay-day, knowing that there was no money in the account, but being certain that the money would be there before the cheque was cleared.

Errors

The MBL discussions revealed a variety of errors and 'misunderstandings' between bank and account holder. Mistakes on standing orders (either a failure to pay or making the same payment several times) and account mix-ups (money being paid into someone else's account) were mentioned. For some people, there is nothing worse than being branded as a 'bad payer' when they believe the fault lies with the bank.

'The Gas Board, we thought we'd pay monthly and we thought that that was a smashing idea. We started it last year and we've just been informed by the Gas Board that we haven't been paying it. It apparently never went through the bank. So we had a £289 gas bill to pay this last month because the bank hadn't put it through . . .'

'My bank made a big mess up with one of my standing orders recently, resulting in me receiving a nasty letter from someone else. But they wrote a letter themselves and explained that it was their mistake and that suited me. I don't mind people making mistakes as long as they admit and put it right which they did.'

The MORI research revealed that 29 per cent of account holders could recall having experienced an error, 15 per cent said that they had experienced such errors in the previous twelve months.

Inevitably a higher proportion of errors occurred with the more widely used services, and the more services customers used the more likely they were to have experienced an error. As standing orders are the most widely used service after cheques, one would expect to find a high incidence of errors associated with this facility. People who pay bank charges also appear to experience a higher incidence of errors, possibly arising out of an inability to understand how the charges are arrived at. We discuss this aspect in greater detail later.

The vast majority of those who had experienced an error in the previous twelve months had pointed it out to the bank. With most types of errors, about a third of bank customers were dissatisfied with the way the bank handled their complaint.

However, it appears that the majority of consumers are prepared to accept that errors occur, especially as banks operate complex systems, but it is important that they are dealt with quickly and efficiently.

Bank statements

There is no doubt that bank customers value regular statements. Some people in the group discussions criticised the banks for the move towards quarterly statements, apparently unaware that they could ask for more frequent statements. We asked the MORI sample about the frequency of their statements. Just under half of the respondents received a statement at least once a month. Younger respondents, 'heavy' users and those in higher socio-economic groups got their statements more often, as did bank customers in Scotland.

Three-quarters of customers were satisfied with the frequency with which they received their bank statements. Those who received their statements less frequently than once a month were more likely to express dissatisfaction with the arrangements, which does again suggest that people do not realise that they can request a more frequent service from their bank. People who have experienced an error were, not surprisingly, keener than others to have frequent statements.

Whilst 20 per cent of the sample were unhappy with the frequency with which they received their statements, only 10 per cent were dissatisfied with the amount of detail contained in their bank statement and only 3 per cent were dissatisfied about its accuracy. However, when the possibility of obtaining more information about bank charges was raised, customers were keen that their banks should provide this type of information on the statement.

Bank charges

The proportions of bank customers paying and not paying charges were roughly the same at the time our sample survey was carried out. Only 6 per cent admitted not knowing whether they had paid charges in the previous year. The more people used banks, the more likely they were to have paid charges.

We asked our MORI respondents if they knew how bank charges were calculated, whether they paid them or not. One third of the respondents had no idea how the charges figure was arrived at; even among those who had paid charges in the previous year a quarter did not know what factors the bank took into account in assessing charges.

Fifty-one per cent believed that charges were related to the amount of money kept in the account, and 22 per cent believed that they were related to the number of transactions.

We asked MORI respondents if their bank had ever explained to them the basis on which their charges are calculated. Almost three-quarters (73 per cent) could not recall ever having been given this information.

Satisfaction with bank charges

Many customers clearly resent paying bank charges for the services provided. Only 48 per cent of the MORI sample were satisfied with the amount of bank charges they paid (and 22 per cent were positively dissatisfied). Even fewer customers (39 per cent) said they were satisfied with the way in which bank charges are calculated.

The highest level of dissatisfaction, however, was with the lack of information given about the way bank charges are calculated. Nearly as high a proportion (32 per cent) of customers were dissatisfied with the information banks give on how bank charges are calculated as were satisfied (35 per cent). Those who had paid charges in the previous twelve months were particularly dissatisfied – with the amount they paid, the way in which these payments were calculated and the amount of information provided on this mode of calculation. In all, over half (51 per cent) of those who paid bank charges (in the past twelve months) felt that banks provided insufficient information in this area. Those who had experienced banking errors in the previous twelve months were even more critical; 56 per cent of this group were dissatisfied with the information provided on how their bank charges are calculated.

Bank charges were discussed in depth in the MBL interviews. It was clear that, rightly or wrongly, some customers felt aggrieved that they were being charged for using their own money, whilst the bank was making a profit out of it. They also regretted the 'waste' of the minimum balance money required to avoid charges, which some respondents could ill afford. Several people also complained about the general attitude of inflexibility which the bank displayed, mentioning letters about overdrafts involving small amounts (in one case 11p) and the rigidity of the minimum balance rule, which meant that one dip could incur charges for a whole period.

> 'You overdraw for a couple of days and you get a nasty letter through the post. Just 2 days and it's £10 yet you've been in the black with them for the last 6 months and they've been making money out of you all the time at top whack interest rate.'

> 'I was overdrawn 11p and the bank manager chased me to high heaven for 11p. It was that petty. He sent me a letter saying he wanted this 11p.'

If the majority of consumers do not know the basis on which the money is deducted from their account, then they are more likely to feel aggrieved. When the statement is received showing that bank charges have been deducted, the account holder is presented with a *fait accompli*, which he or she neither understands nor feels confident to challenge.

We asked the MORI sample whether banks should show the calculation of bank charges on bank statements. An overwhelming majority – 82 per cent – were in favour of this suggestion.

General satisfaction with banks and possible improvements

Most people, however, are satisfied with the level of service they receive from the bank. To the question 'Overall, how satisfied or dissatisfied are you with the service you receive from your bank?' 92 per cent of our MORI sample said they were very or fairly satisfied and only 5 per cent said they were dissatisfied. This is, we believe, a very high level of expressed satisfaction.

Levels of dissatisfaction were slightly higher among the young and those who had experienced an error in the last twelve months.

This very high level of overall satisfaction did not however mean that bank customers did not want to see improvements in the service they get.

We asked our MORI sample which changes, from a list of seventeen, they would like their bank to introduce. We then asked them to be more specific and confine their choice to three or four changes. Most of the seventeen elements of change can loosely be classified into three categories:

(i) easier and more convenient access to cash (for example, opening hours/ more tills/better queuing system);

(ii) more information (on banking charges and services, more detailed and frequent statements);

(iii) increased spending power (easier loans, increased limits, etc.).

It is clear from the results that the priority area for improvement is to obtain greater access to cash.

The most popular choices were those that would make the withdrawal of money from the banks more convenient. Half (51 per cent) of the respondents would like to see their bank open on Saturday, and for 41 per cent this would be one of the most welcome changes that their bank could introduce (with no significant difference between rural and urban respondents). A further 28 per cent wanted longer opening hours on weekdays, and 27 per cent would like to see more tills open at lunchtime. In all, 67 per cent of customers mentioned at least one of these changes. Consistent with the general desire for easier access to one's own cash were several other choices – an improved system of queuing, more cash dispensers and an end to the charge for cashing other banks' cheques. And 25 per cent of customers also wanted an increase in the £50 limit on cheque guarantee cards.

Of lesser importance was the desire for greater information from banks. A quarter (25 per cent) of customers would like details of how bank charges are calculated (although, as we have seen, when attention is focused on this aspect, the number of people who think the banks should provide such information jumps dramatically) and 21 per cent would welcome more frequent bank statements (the latter figure drops to 12 per cent amongst those receiving monthly statements).

There was comparatively little demand for changes which would give customers access to greater quantities of money. A few, however, wanted easier access to loans or higher credit limits. Undoubtedly the major desire is for greater access to existing money, not greater access to the ability to borrow.

'The banks should offer hours that the average working bloke earning a few hours' overtime can get to.'

'It's very difficult to get money out . . . it's getting down there in working hours.'

Banks compared with building societies

In spite of recent competition between the two types of institution, there is still a clear distinction between them in customers' minds. Building societies are primarily associated with saving and house purchase and banks with short-term money movement and paying bills.

We asked those people in our MORI sample who had both bank and building society accounts (64 per cent) to say which they thought had

* the most convenient opening hours
* the quickest counter service
* the friendliest staff.

Building societies were rated as having a clear advantage in opening hours;

though the difference was much smaller, people also preferred them for speed of service and friendliness of staff.

Opinions of the building societies were generally higher among the MBL groups as well. Many respondents also praised building societies for their ambience and décor compared with banks which were thought to be sombre and dull:

'Building societies tend to be brighter lights and a happier place to go into.'

'With a building society you feel you are a customer, you don't feel that when you go to a bank. I always feel that they're going to jump at me when I go in for a cheque book.'

Building societies were also considered to be more understanding places, compared with the businesslike briskness of the banks:

'I think the building societies are more friendly. I was out of work and I went to see the manager and he said no problem, pay me the interest and forget about the capital. If I'd had the loan with the bank I don't think they'd have looked with the same reality at the situation. I think they're looking for your monthly payments every month.'

'A building society is more friendly. It's a different sort of place to go into. I suppose it's my own attitude because when I go in it's usually to lodge money. I go into a bank to take it out.'

Given these feelings, it is not surprising that many bank account holders would like building societies to provide some of the services currently being provided by banks. We asked the MORI sample which of a list of services they would like from a building society.

Over half (56 per cent) would like their building society to offer cheque book facilities. Next, in order of priority, was payment of standing orders (39 per cent), cash dispensers (32 per cent), personal loans (28 per cent) and travellers' cheques (26 per cent) with overdraft facilities at the bottom of the list (20 per cent). Older people appeared less interested in seeing an extension of services by building societies.

The attitudes of the unbanked

We also held discussion groups with the unbanked. Much research has, of course, already been done with this group of consumers and our results reflect the now familiar set of attitudes that accompany the reasons for not having a bank account. Many cash-paid people saw no need to open a bank account – they thought they did not have enough cash to make it worth while – and could associate no advantage with it. Nor did they feel in any way at a disadvantage, not having a cheque book, cheque card or credit card. Indeed having a bank account was perceived as an inconvenience, involving problems with depositing and withdrawing cash and incurring unnecessary charges and a possible loss of control.

'Say I got paid by cheque. I'd never be able to get the money out. I can't see any time I'd be around to get it out. Even if they opened on a Saturday morning I'm never up.'

'It costs you money for banking.'

'I think that's all wrong. The money they're making out of your money already, I think that's disgusting.'

Bank accounts were associated with the method of payment of wages, responsibility for regular bills and the general arrangement of personal finances.

'With me being not married, no ties, there's no real advantage to it. I live at home with my folks, I haven't got to give out rent or anything.'

Many men felt that opening a bank account would mean loss of privacy, control and security, as knowledge of their affairs might reach the 'tax-man' or, even worse, 'the wife'. This latter fear seemed particularly prevalent in Scotland:

'A lot of wives in Scotland don't realise what their men are earning and if he's getting a statement every week [sic] the wife will see it . . . it still goes on.'

'That's why men want cash because only they know what they are getting.'

Many of the unbanked feared that their money would appear insignificant to the bank whose real purpose, they believed, was to serve the business community. If banks were for people like them, then it would be more obvious:

'There's nothing in the window of a bank, therefore it's not for the general public really. If they were applying to the general public to save with them, they'd have a window, same as the building society, it's covered with investment.'

'The bank is more like a dole office or social security. The same sort of windows, more official, all in there looking at you, all there with the typewriters at the back. . . .'

The majority of our unbanked respondents had a building society account which adequately served their limited financial requirements. They preferred the approach and atmosphere in a building society; they received a good rate of interest and they could have access to their money at convenient times.

'It doesn't cost you anything in a building society, does it, to save your money. It costs you money for banking.'

'You can walk into a building society and put £1 in and think nothing of it. I wouldn't walk in a bank with a £1. God!'

Indeed, it was pointed out that if they did want to pay a large bill, they could obtain a building society cheque, which was often regarded by retailers as superior to a bank cheque, as it meant that the customer was in funds. Household bills could also be paid by giro transfer at the post office.

Some of the younger unbanked respondents were considering opening a bank account at a future date, especially when they achieved a 'settled existence'.

Ethnic minorities

We carried out discussion groups with West Indians, Indians and Pakistanis, in order to establish any noticeable differences of opinion.

WEST INDIANS

In many ways the views displayed by West Indians reflected the main series of group discussions. When discussing the reasons for having a bank account, they expressed greater fear of being robbed of their cash. Their two major criticisms were the difficulties that they had experienced when applying for a loan and the reference system when opening an account which was felt to operate against people like them.

'The references you need now to open an account, you might as well forget about it.'

West Indian group members felt that they were meeting difficulty in getting loans because of their colour and not their overall financial status, especially as many felt that loans should be advanced automatically when requested by customers of long standing. (This view was shared by many respondents in the main part of the survey.)

'If you save with the bank for years and you want £250 to tide you over . . . it's a big *no*.'

The more relaxed and informal attitude of the building societies was undoubtedly preferred.

'You fill a form out, where do you work and that's it.'

'You can relax when you walk in.'

'They don't ask how you've got it, where you've got it, or where you're going to get it from . . . and if you want a house they will try their best. I tell you one thing, if the building societies give a cheque book, the bank is out of business.'

There appeared to be few significant differences in the way in which West Indians managed their financial affairs. Clearly they felt discriminated against and were more likely to join together to operate private money-lending and savings schemes, on a straightforward cyclical payment basis. No one seemed to mind not receiving interest on their money, as they appreciated not having to pay it on their advance.

INDIANS

Indians regarded a bank account as a safe, convenient method of storing money. Like the West Indians, they were worried about being mugged. They appeared to pay great attention to the detail of their finances and, of all the ethnic groups, were the most extensive users of bank services, especially standing orders which ensured that they were never behind with regular payments.

'I think it's very convenient to keep records – also it sorts out all your transactions rather than carrying cash around in your pocket. And also it makes life easier.'

The Indians did not complain of racial discrimination and mentioned much the same advantages and disadvantages as the main groups; although they had worse problems with opening hours, as they were more often paying in than drawing out. They displayed distrust of automatic machinery:

'You deposit money into this machine, you have no proof that you have done it. What if it's not there, it doesn't show up in your statement?'

Most of our Indian respondents also had a building society account, which they found convenient and more suitable for saving as well as being more friendly and, particularly, more polite.

The Indians also described lending within the community, sometimes involving large sums of money, including house purchase. Where the recipient is outside the close family circle, interest is usually charged.

'You leave out the middle man which is the bank or the building society and we help each other. You increase your prestige so next time you need some money he will help you.'

PAKISTANIS

Of all the ethnic groups interviewed, the Pakistanis seemed the least involved with the UK banking system. They also displayed slight confusion and misunderstanding over banking services. This may be because of language difficulties, their low wages and their colour.

'There is a lack of smile on the counter for coloured people, that's fact.'

It is possible that what some of the Pakistanis perceived as off-hand treatment or lack of explanations could have resulted from a communication problem. Furthermore, it was not in their upbringing to complain.

'A lot of Pakistan community are very polite, we don't like complaining, in several ways including banks I feel we don't get fair treatment, because of the colour of our skin.'

Like other minority groups, they found building societies friendlier and more polite. Community lending was also widespread.

'In our community, if you are buying a house, your close friend will come and ask you if you need any money.'

In conclusion, the majority of ethnic respondents still felt ill at ease in a bank, though less so if they actually held an account and had become more familiar with the system. We are unable to determine whether these attitudes are attributable to colour alone, or whether they reflect the views held by people in a similar social and economic position. In many cases, the disadvantages mentioned by the ethnic groups were identical to those already stated by the lower socio-economic groups and the unbanked. The ethnic groups were clearly happier dealing with building societies or operating their own community financial schemes.

Consumers in rural areas

Limited research was undertaken with consumers in rural areas. Of all groups interviewed, they appeared to be most satisfied with their banks. Their relationships with manager and staff alike were friendly, helpful and informal, often built up over years of mutual acquaintance.

'You are no longer a number, you are like a personal friend.'

Against this background, rural respondents were much more prepared to tolerate any disadvantages associated with transport or access. Moreover, alternative cheque-cashing facilities, using the local garage, village shop, pub or club, were well established. Although the post office was usually more convenient than the bank, none of our respondents had considered transferring to National Girobank, because in their opinion such an account offered neither the full range of services nor the guarantee of privacy from the post office staff.

Reactions to new technology, especially 'home banking', were sought. Whilst it was acknowledged that this could be an advantage for consumers in rural areas, it was also pointed out that home banking would deny them an important and much-valued point of contact provided by the banks.

Women and banks

We received little evidence that women are discriminated against. Account holding is slightly lower amongst women and they are less likely to be heavy users of bank services, but well over half our female respondents had a bank account in either sole or joint name. Women show themselves to be slightly less familiar with some of the complexities of banking, such as the basis for calculating bank charges or the relative tax position for standard rate investors in banks and building societies. Women also appear to be more sensitive to the personal relationship they have with the bank, taking greater notice of the attitude of the staff and the manager.

Consumers and the new technology

Amongst our groups there was a high level of awareness of recent developments involving computer technology in the financial world. Spontaneous mention was made of 'plastic money'. Such developments were regarded as inevitable, if not always welcome, and there was evidence of resistance towards further de-personalisation of banking and the concept of 'cashlessness'.

'I think it would be a shame if it started being too computerised, if you could only get money from cash points, because it's something else gone, some personal thing gone.'

Some respondents wanted to preserve the present range of choice, particularly if they felt suspicious of machinery.

'I wouldn't mind, it's just if they go wrong that they're a nuisance and they so often do at the moment.'

Particular reluctance and genuine mistrust about automatic paying-in was evident, especially if no immediate confirmation was to be available.

'We're looking for some sort of reassurance.'

'Confirmation that it's going into your account.'

'I think I'd like to see it marked in a book because they do make mistakes.'

Respondents were relatively unenthusiastic about the prospect of 'home banking' although some people could recognise potential advantages. They also expressed fears, relating to lack of privacy, loss of control, the unreliability of getting money through the post and, again, mistrust of machines.

'People would play about and get your account on the screen.'

'No way, I wouldn't be able to keep it away from my wife.'

On the whole, the younger age groups and more men than women were receptive to the forms of mechanised banking already in use. For others, the push-button armchair lifestyle of the future represented a science-fiction nightmare.

'It takes the enjoyment out of life, eventually you'll just be sitting around, everything will be done for you.'

'Oh my God, I'm sure it will come, but it's horrendous isn't it?'

Summary

Bank customers are highly satisfied with banks overall. However, there are significant detailed areas where they would like to see improvement.

Many of the improvements customers want are in the ease with which they can use bank services: better opening hours and less queuing, for instance. People would also like banks to be friendlier places.

Bank charging systems are also an important area of dissatisfaction. There is widespread ignorance and confusion about charges. Eighty-two per cent of our sample of bank customers would like to see, on their statements, an itemised account of how charges are calculated.

A significant minority of bank customers would like to see the £50 limit on the cheque guarantee card raised and the end of the practice of making charges for transactions carried out at branches of a bank not the customer's own.

Many of those without bank accounts still see a bank account as an inconvenient and expensive way of managing their money. This is connected with a social image of the banks held by people in the lower socio-economic groups: that the banks are less for individual customers with relatively low incomes than for businessmen and those with high incomes. This view is echoed among customers from ethnic minorities.

Many bank account holders who also have building society accounts would like their building societies to offer them the sort of money transmission services normally associated with banks.

A significant minority of respondents experience errors with some aspect of their bank account. It is clear that these people are more concerned with the bank's handling of these errors than with the fact that they occur.

Although developments in new technology are acknowledged as inevitable, there is widespread mistrust of the resultant changes in banking practice. Whilst improvements in speed and convenience are appreciated, many people fear the loss of personal contact, privacy and control of their financial affairs.

Section 3 / Cash, cheques, credits, debits and charges

To enable consumers to make payments, banks transmit money. In this section we discuss money transmission systems under six heads:

* customer access to cash and cash distribution;
* cheques and credit transfers;
* pre-authorised payments (standing orders and direct debits);
* credit cards;
* other methods of making payments;
* bank charges.

Newer and more advanced electronic forms of money transmission – some are already in use, others are on the horizon – are discussed in section 5.

Money transmission is overwhelmingly dominated by the traditional clearing banks. Almost all payments made in England and Wales depend, directly or indirectly, on the big four London clearers – Barclays, Lloyds, Midland and National Westminster. This is true both of paper vouchers like cheques, or bank notes and coin, and of the magnetic tapes on which automated debiting instructions are conveyed. Competition comes mainly from the newer clearers – the Co-operative Bank, the TSBs and National Girobank. In Scotland and Northern Ireland, the Scottish and Irish clearing banks play a similar role to that of the traditional London clearers, though on a much smaller scale.

It is estimated that over 50,000 million payments are made a year in Britain as a whole. In spite of the rapid growth in the use of paper instruments and plastic cards, cash is still used for a huge majority of these payments. In 1981 almost 90 per cent of all payments of a value of £1 or more were made in cash. Eighty-six per cent of all payments of £3 or more were made in cash. Although these percentages have fallen since 1976 (see Table 3.1) it is clear that in volume terms cash is still emphatically the dominant medium of exchange. The 'cashless society', of which much was heard in the 1960s, is still a remote prospect.

The banks are responsible for the circulation of bank notes and coins (see below). They are a direct source of cash to their customers, from whom they also undertake to receive cash deposits. They must ensure that the supply of cash meets the demand, not just in the banking system as a whole but at each of its

Table 3.1 How payments are made (1)*

	All adults		Current account holders	
	1976	*1981*	*1976*	*1981*
	%	%	%	%
Cash	94	88	88½	82½
Cheque	3½	6½	7½	10
Standing order/direct debit	1½	3	3	4
Others	1	2½	1	3½
	100	100	100	100

Source: Inter-Bank Research Organisation

* Numbered references are listed in full at the end of each section of the book.

thousands of branch outlets. Seasonal and geographical factors have to be taken into account. As one of the clearing banks put it in its evidence to us, they have to ensure 'that stocks of coin which "migrated" to our coastal resorts in summer are back in the "High Streets" before Christmas'. There is therefore much fetching and carrying of cash around the country in security vans.

People without bank accounts are equally dependent upon the banks for cash, though less directly so. They must usually get cash from their employer, by cashing state benefits or within the family (see Figure I). They cannot cash cheques or use cash dispensers; in effect they are dependent upon others who can.

It is clear from Figure I that large numbers of the adult population still depend upon their wage packets, most of which are paid weekly, for access to cash.

The proportion of all British employees paid in cash has declined sharply since 1976 but at 42 per cent (1981) this figure is still very high by international standards. In 1981, according to the Inter-Bank Research Organisation, only one per cent of US workers, and five per cent of Canadian and West German workers, were paid weekly in cash. (The figures may not be precisely comparable, but the difference is clear.)

Figure II shows how people receive their wages/salaries in Britain and the change that has taken place since 1976.

Figure II reflects the growth in current account holding during the years 1976–1981; the percentage of adults holding a bank current account increased from 45 to 61 per cent.

The high proportion of British workers still paid in cash puts heavy security and administration costs on employers. In recent years such employees have been encouraged to take out bank accounts in order to facilitate wage payment by bank giro credit. The major clearing banks have been involved in a joint campaign to this effect. Some parties, though interestingly not the banks themselves, have argued that the Truck Acts are an obstacle to more rapid

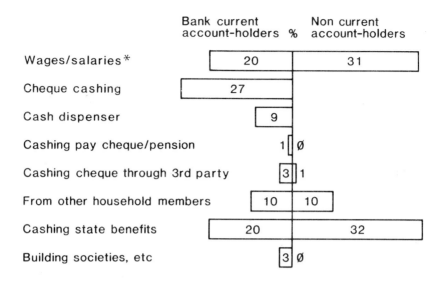

	Bank current account-holders	%	Non current account-holders
Wages/salaries*	20		31
Cheque cashing	27		
Cash dispenser	9		
Cashing pay cheque/pension	1		ø
Cashing cheque through 3rd party	3		1
From other household members	10		10
Cashing state benefits	20		32
Building societies, etc	3		ø

* At all (not necessarily in a week)
ø Negligible

Figure I *How people obtain cash: percentage using a method in an average week in 1981*

Source: Inter-Bank Research Organisation

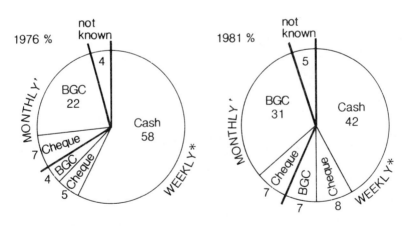

* including daily and 2-weekly
† including 4-weekly and other frequencies
BGC means Bank Giro Credit

Figure II *How people received their wages/salaries in 1976 and 1981*

Source: Inter-Bank Research Organisation

progress towards cashless pay. We have argued (see Appendix VI) that the continuing attachment of many workers to weekly pay in cash has much more to do with their view of the benefits and disbenefits of dealing with banks than with the continuing existence of antiquated legislation. There is a steady trend away from weekly cash pay in the UK.

Turning to non-cash payments (cheques, credit transfers, standing orders, direct debits, postal orders and credit cards), we can see from Table 3.2 that the cheque remains by far the most popular method of payment among ordinary consumers.

Table 3.2 Non-cash payments for goods and services by private individuals in the United Kingdom 1971–1981 (millions of transactions)

	1971	1976	1980	1981	Growth 1980/81	Average annual growth 1971/81
Cheque	450	650	1050	1080	3%	9.2%
Standing order	120	180	230	245	6½%	7.4%
Direct debit	40	100	160	180	12½%	16.2%
Postal order	270	150	125	90	−28%	−10.4%
Credit card	10	60	150	165	10%	32.0%
Credit transfer	40	60	100	100	0%	9.6%
Total	930	1200	1815	1860		

Sources: Inter-Bank Research Organisation and Battelle

All of these instruments except postal orders are bank operated, either directly or, in the case of credit cards, indirectly. One very obvious character-istic of the changing scene is the substantial decline in the use of postal orders.

Within the market for non-cash payments, the traditional London clearers exercise massive dominance. In 1976 they were responsible for 81 per cent of all non-cash payments, followed by the Scottish clearing banks (6 per cent), the Post Office and National Giro (8 per cent), the TSBs and the Co-operative Bank (1 per cent each) and others (2 per cent). The percentage share of the Post Office has since declined due to the marked trend away from postal orders.

Another way of looking at the importance of cheques in non-cash payment emerges from the 1981 handling figures of one of the major London clearing banks (Lloyds):

cheques processed	600 million
credits processed	82 million
standing order payments	48 million
direct debits/other automated payments, e.g. salaries	99 million

All non-cash payments have been rising steadily in volume as the number of people with bank accounts has grown. The number of cheques passed is growing in the United Kingdom, as in most western countries, at about 4 per cent per year. It has been forecast that this rate of growth will be sustained throughout the 1980s even if the number of cash dispensers in operation is multiplied several times over.

In 1968, a Post Office giro system was introduced into the UK as an alternative, quick, cheap and convenient money transmission service. The Post Office system has a number of advantages over traditional bank alternatives: all accounts are maintained and updated at one central location; the system is accessible for simple cash payments at any one of over 20,000 post offices; and it can be used by people without current accounts. It provides a facility for people to make payments to any organisation that has a Girobank account, including local authorities, power utilities, building societies and tv rental companies. As an alternative money transmission system it has been less successful than its proponents hoped, certainly less popular than equivalent systems in the rest of Europe. It does collect more than 45 million rents a year for over 180 local authorities and housing associations, and is used by non-bank current account holders using the Transcash facility to make a variety of comparable payments. It is also used for its convenience by account holders with other banks. However, its failure to establish itself as the definitive alternative to conventional payment authorisation by cheque and other means is reflected in the steady transformation of the National Girobank into a look-alike clearing bank complete with cheque books, personal loans, travellers' cheques, limited overdraft facilities and, most recently, direct debits.

The traditional banks operate a similar system called bank giro credits (they were actually nine years ahead of the Post Office). These too are available to non-current account holders for bill payment and other purposes, though in practice they are not extensively used in this way because the unbanked tend not to go into banks. The only real operational difference between the Post Office giro system and commercial bank giro credits is that the former uses a simpler and quicker system for making its internal transfers, an option which is open to individual banks but which they have chosen not to pursue, preferring to stay with conventional clearing arrangements. Most bank giro credit users are current account holders who use the facility to pay bills by attaching cheques.

By any industrial standards, the cost of maintaining conventional bank transmission services, cash and non-cash taken together, is enormous. In their evidence to the Wilson Committee, the Committee of London Clearing Bankers (CLCB) estimated that approximately 60 per cent of the banks' total UK staffs were involved, some 120,000 employees. As long ago as 1976 the value of capital resources employed approached £1,000 million and the total operating cost was about £800 million per annum (2). More recently, most major clearers have estimated the cost of providing transmission services as being equivalent to an effective interest rate of around 10 per cent on current account balances.

Access to cash

Getting hold of cash easily is important to private individuals, employers, retailers, building societies, the Post Office and others. All depend on cash distribution networks operated by the banks.

The banks in England and Wales get bank notes directly from the Bank of England. The Bank of England supplies notes either from its head office in London or from one of its seven provincial branches in major commercial cities. The four big banks then distribute the notes to their own branches via independent networks of cash centres. The total number of cash centres is about a hundred. (Smaller distribution networks are operated by Williams and Glyn's, the Co-operative Bank and the Trustee Savings Banks.) The distribution system for coins minted by the Royal Mint is broadly similar although there are differences of operational detail.

Individual banks are responsible for sorting soiled bank notes from those which are fit for re-issue; bank notes which are surplus to requirements may be returned to the Bank of England. Coins, however, may not be returned to the Royal Mint.

Note issue in Scotland and Northern Ireland is different and is separately discussed in section 10.

People are not accustomed to thinking in terms of 'the costs of cash' although these are considerable. The Price Commission, which looked at the subject in 1978, identified three major types of cost in maintaining cash distribution centres: the capital costs of establishing and equipping them; the costs (including heavy security costs) of storing and distributing cash throughout the country; and the costs of financing large cash holdings in terms of interest foregone (3) (recently put by the chairman of Barclays Bank at £125 million per year to the UK clearing banks as a whole).

The net effect of current arrangements is that the banks (directly) and their customers (indirectly) bear the costs of maintaining £750 million-worth (1978) of note and coin stocks in the banks; and conversely that the Treasury enjoys the benefit of what is effectively an interest-free loan of equivalent value. Clearly the service has to be paid for. Banks do not charge their personal customers on a use basis for supplying currency; it is difficult to imagine how they could. On the other hand, they do exact cash-handling charges from employers, retailers and other large users. These may or may not be passed on, perhaps in the form of higher prices. These arrangements give rise to patterns of cross-subsidisation of unfathomable complexity in which those personal customers who pay bank charges would appear to be subsidising those who do not and, possibly, non-bank customers too. The Price Commission thought the cross-subsidy on these arrangements was unfair and concluded that it should be terminated, arguing that 'the provision of notes to the public at large should be a national expense' (4). Since 1978 arrangements for the distribution of bank notes have been modified somewhat through the introduction of 'hold to order' facilities at distribution centres. These have the effect of diminishing the loss of interest penalty identified by the Price Commission, though by a relatively small sum.

The Price Commission also questioned whether it was sensible, granted the high costs involved, for the banks to maintain totally separate systems for distributing the nation's cash. In a speech in May 1980, Mr Vander Weyer of Barclays implied that existing systems of cash distribution are less cost-effective than they should be (5).

There are two points here. First, it can be argued that since the distribution of cash is a necessary public service, used by bank customers and non-customers alike, the responsibility for running it should not rest with commercial bodies at all but with the government which should finance the service out of general taxation. At present, bank customers, including personal customers, are subsidising the government. Whether this matters or not depends of course on the sums of money involved. The CLCB were unable to give us up-to-date figures; we have therefore been unable to make any judgment about the significance of the issue or to make any recommendation. We are concerned, however, that bank customers may be subsidising the general body of taxpayers.

Nor are we able to judge whether it would be more effective and less costly for the banks to abandon their individual cash distribution networks and set up a single co-ordinated network. When the banks last studied the matter in the early 1970s they concluded that a unified network might have achieved a small cost saving but at the expense of a loss of operational flexibility. We simply note, in passing, that the operational problems involved in providing collective mechanisms for the transmission of non-cash payments have been overcome.

Cheques and credit transfers

After cash, cheques are by far the most common method of making payments in Britain. In 1981, UK account holders wrote about two and a half billion of them.

In order for a payment to be made by cheque, the cheque has to be cleared – that is, the bank of the person who wrote the cheque has to accept it from the bank of the person who received it. The system used for clearing cheques has evolved under the auspices of the Bankers' Clearing House. There are two main cheque clearings: the *town clearing* and the *general clearing*.

Town clearing mainly applies to commercial business involving cheques of a high value. Such cheques are exchanged and settled on the day they are paid in. Compared with the total number of items (mainly personal) transmitted in general clearing, town clearance business is small. In 1982, only 6 million items were handled in town clearing as opposed to 2,106 million in the general clearing. In value terms, however, the balance is reversed. Town clearing handles over 90 per cent of the total value of items cleared. Town clearing is in the process of being automated under the auspices of the Clearing House Automated Payment System (CHAPS).

Private customers' cheques are normally dealt with in general clearing. There are two types. First, there are cheques which are drawn on, and paid in at, separate branches of the same bank. These inter-branch items do not pass through the clearing house but are handled by the clearing departments of the individual banks. Secondly, there are cheques which are drawn on, and paid into, branches of different banks. These are categorised as inter-bank items. They pass through the clearing house operated by the Committee of London Clearing Bankers, a process which normally takes two working days. However, the branch into which the cheque is paid will not normally know whether it has been honoured by the recipient bank until the fourth working day, that is, three working days after it has been paid in.

Smaller banks, like the Yorkshire Bank, which are not either full or functional members of the clearing system must appoint one of the clearing banks to act as

Table 3.3   Cheques handled by London clearing banks (millions)

	General debit clearing		Town clearing	
	inter-bank	inter-branch	inter-bank	inter-branch
1970	723	280	4	1
1971	726	306	3	1
1972	785	343	4	1
1973	841	372	4	1
1974	880	390	4	1
1975	959	425	4	1
1976	1044	424	4	1
1977	1111	444	4	1
1978	1212	460	5	1
1979	1311	463	5	1
1980	1454	494	5	1
1981	1501	524	5	1

Source: CLCB Statistical Unit

its agent in order to get its cheques cleared (6). An indication of the relative dimensions of town and general clearings, and inter-bank and inter-branch clearings, is given in Table 3.3.

The complete process of transmitting cheques from the point of entry into the presenting bank to the point of balance adjustment in the accepting bank is both time-consuming and expensive. It is estimated that it costs between 30 and 55 pence per cheque, depending on the banks involved and the accounting methods used, to perform the sequence of tasks involved in satisfactorily completing this transaction. Since the late 1950s mounting paper volumes and rising costs have obliged the clearing banks to look for various ways of automating this process and thus controlling overheads. The banks' computers can now read and sort cheques at an astonishing speed. However, there are serious constraints on the extent to which these developments can be pursued, short of doing away with cheques written on paper altogether – currently a dubious option for the banks since cheques have a legal status (see below) and act as the bank's ultimate guarantee that a payment has been properly authorised.

Within these limits, computerised cheque handling has reached a high point of technical sophistication. (This explains the variety of figures that appear on cheques in addition to that of the customer's account number.) The time taken to clear cheques in the UK compares favourably with the speed of clearing operations in most other countries; though Canada, which has developed 24-hour coast-to-coast clearance, has an exceptionally advanced system.

The best prospect for improving the efficiency of the cheque clearance system, and for reducing costs, lies in a move towards cheque truncation. Truncation may be defined as a reduction in the physical movement of the cheque after it has first been presented by the payee to the bank. This can be done by capturing the information on the cheque and transmitting it onwards in electronic form. Data can be captured, and thus the movement of the cheque stopped, at a number of points in the system. The impact of truncation upon the economics of cheque transmission will vary depending on where precisely in the system it is decided to stop the voucher movement. This could be done either at the original branch of presentation, or at a regional or central location in the presenting bank, or at some point within the procedures of the receiving bank. To maximise savings in system costs it is necessary to 'truncate' cheque movement at the earliest possible opportunity.

It was estimated in 1981 that approximately 35 per cent of all cheques presented in the UK are personal account payments to third parties, 15 per cent are personal cheques cashed at branches and most of the remainder are transactions effected between businesses (7). (These figures almost certainly now underestimate the importance of personal cheques.) The attraction of cheque truncation lies in the contribution it could make in cutting costs in the first category. However, there are other ways of proceeding in this direction; from the banks' point of view the most promising is an accelerated trend towards the use of pre-authorised payments (particularly variable amount direct debits) as an alternative to cheques (8). The use of personal cheques as a means of obtaining cash is declining due to increased public acceptance of plastic debit cards and the expansion of the banks' cash dispenser networks.

A number of European countries appear to have conquered at least some of the problems associated with cheque truncation. Truncation was introduced in Denmark, for example, at the beginning of 1980 and by mid-1982 accounted for 92 per cent of all cheques.

From the customer's point of view, truncation might have a number of effects, some of which have important legal implications. These derive from the law of cheques which is well developed. A cheque is a type of bill of exchange which in turn is a 'negotiable instrument', that is, it may be written out in favour of one person who may in turn pass it on to someone else by endorsing it with his or her signature. In the classic definition, a cheque may be said to be an unconditional order in writing addressed by one person to another, who must be a banker, signed by the person giving it, requiring the banker to pay on demand a certain sum in money to or to the order of a specified person, or to the bearer. Specific legislation governs the use of bills of exchange and cheques: the principal relevant statutes are the Stamp Act 1853, the Bills of Exchange Act 1882, and the Cheques Act 1957.

Among other issues these Acts have addressed the crucial question of which party (bankers, customers, or others) shall bear the financial loss in cases of cheque forgery and theft. The law has also developed to reduce unnecessary work on the part of banks, particularly in relation to endorsements. The Cheques Act 1957, amongst other things, removed the need for banks to examine most endorsements, except on cheques negotiated to third parties and for cash drawn over the counter. More generally, the common law and specific legislation between them provide for what amounts to a comprehensive code on cheques. The law is well developed in relation to the issuing of cheques, their crossing, determining the 'holder' of a cheque, claims by third parties and so on.

It is not entirely clear how the truncation of cheques sits within this legal framework. We believe that there may be four aspects of truncation which raise legal issues:

* verification of signatures;
* reduced scope for customers to stop cheques;
* the disposal of cheques;
* the effects of the Bills of Exchange Act 1882.

VERIFICATION OF SIGNATURES

It is not possible for the customer's branch bank to verify the signature of a cheque which is not physically presented at the drawer's bank. Under current cheque law, however, a bank is required to obey the precise instructions of the customer as evidenced by his or her signature alone. An excellent forgery is no defence. Truncation could mean that a cheque which has been improperly completed or forged is more likely to escape detection at the outset. There is, therefore, a greater risk of loss through truncation, although the consequences may be kept within reasonable bounds if truncation is restricted to cheques below a certain value. We are clear, however, that those banks which wish to truncate cheques must bear the risks involved. The established principle – strict adherence to the customer's precise instructions – must be retained in this context.

REDUCED SCOPE FOR CUSTOMERS TO STOP CHEQUES

If a cheque is processed by truncation, this will be a much faster process than conventional methods. In consequence, there will be a much shorter time for a customer to stop a cheque, for whatever reason. We do not believe that this is a major problem. No undue difficulties appear to have been caused by the inability to stop a cheque guaranteed by a cheque card. Strictly speaking, a customer remains liable 'on the cheque' after it has been stopped. We do not defend the right of consumers to stop a cheque because they have changed their mind about a payment. It is certainly true that where there is a dispute about goods or services, stopping a cheque may be a practical step on occasions; but this is not strictly a legal remedy. We would prefer to see disputes between bank customers and third parties resolved fairly and legally rather than by an unseemly rush to stop a cheque.

THE DISPOSAL OF CHEQUES

Of more widespread concern is the prospect that the truncation of cheques would involve their early disposal by the receiving bank. According to CLCB, it would be impracticable to hold cheques for any length of time at branches where they are paid. To hold them elsewhere would, according to CLCB, create transport and storage costs which could seriously erode any advantages of truncation. The early disposal of cheques may involve the destruction of evidence that a payment has been made to a third party. We believe that this problem could be avoided by using the techniques of electronic facsimile reproduction to 'represent' cheques. If necessary, it would appear that such copies could be produced in evidence in legal proceedings. More seriously, early disposal of cheques could increase the scope for disputes between customers and banks as to the nature of the 'instructions' which were set out on cheques.

CLCB suggested in their submission to us that this latter problem might be resolved by the introduction of a 'settled account procedure' which sets a limit on the amount of time bankers must store their customers' cheques. Under this procedure, a bank would be obliged to forward a customer's statement of account at stated intervals and the customer in return would be obliged to examine the statement and raise any queries within a specified period of time. After this period has expired, the account would be 'settled', that is, assumed to be correct, and further queries could not be raised. 'In this way', says CLCB, 'storage periods for vast quantities of paper could be reduced to a matter of months rather than years.'

The courts have decided that a customer is under no obligation to examine bank statements (presumably unless such a condition is specified in any written contract). The introduction of a 'settled account' procedure would therefore increase customers' liabilities for any errors and possible frauds not discovered within the time period. The banks, on the other hand, argue that soon they will not be able to cope with the flood of paper they have to handle and store, and that the current cost of storing the millions of cheques involved is 'not insignificant'. Any reduction in banks' costs should mean cheaper banking for all.

From a consumer point of view the argument can be stated as follows: would bank customers be willing to take on an additional legal responsibility in return for an efficient and – one may hope – cheaper service? In our view, a settled account procedure should be introduced only if the potential benefits to consumers can be clearly stated. We would oppose any attempt by the banks to introduce unilaterally such a procedure, for example by incorporating it into a contract with their customers. At the very least, customers should be given an informed choice. A lower scale of charges might, for example, be offered to those willing to accept a settled account procedure.

THE EFFECTS OF THE BILLS OF EXCHANGE ACT 1882

The CLCB told us that the Bills of Exchange Act 1882 may present legal obstacles to truncation. The processing of cheques must conform with the requirements of that Act. It seems that the main problem is that section 45 states that:

> '. . . a bill must be duly presented for payment. If it be not so presented the drawer and indorsers shall be discharged.'

The section goes on to say that presentment must be 'at the proper place', defined by sub-section 4. In the case of cheques this will usually be the address of the paying bank.

Under any process of truncation, where the physical cheque is not sent to the drawer's bank, there would appear, therefore, to be no presentment. It is true that section 46(2)(e) goes on to provide that presentment can be dispensed with by express or implied waiver, but this is hardly a satisfactory basis on which to proceed. The problem goes deeper with the historical classification of cheques as a form of bill of exchange, the law for which places considerable importance on the piece of paper as a source of rights and duties. We return to this issue in the wider context of electronic banking in section 5.

On the non-legal side, truncation might be expected to speed up the whole process of clearing, and therefore reduce the 'float' effect that the process of paper clearing gives now. People obviously take advantage of this – perhaps most notably by writing cheques a day or two in advance of pay day. We do not think it would be desirable to resist quicker and cheaper clearing methods, if they could be developed, on such grounds. Already, clearing can be virtually instantaneous if a cheque is written to someone who banks at the same bank branch as the payee, that is, if the cheque is paid in at the payer's branch. Many cheques – and this is not widely understood – are supported by a cheque guarantee card and cannot be stopped in any event. It should also be noted that ATM withdrawals can involve loss of float, but have grown rapidly none-theless.

Cheque cards

Possession of a cheque guarantee card has become a general requirement of cheque use. The present £50 cheque card limit was set in August 1977, since when retail prices have almost doubled. The inconvenience caused to consumers by this decline in value was a complaint picked up strongly in our MORI research; indeed, an increase in the guaranteed limit above £50 was recorded as the fourth most desired change in banking facilities. At the time of writing, the future of cheque guarantee card limits was under discussion by the banks. One option being canvassed was a change in conditions of use to allow customers to use two cheques up to a total value of £100 to cover a single purchase. (Barclaycard, both a credit card and a cheque guarantee card, currently allows one cheque to be cashed at Barclays branches for up to £100.)

The reluctance of the banks to raise the £50 limit is the consequence of weak security and rising fraud losses (9). The Committee of London Clearing Bankers is considering ways of improving the security of cheque guarantee cards (plans include the introduction of mechanical signature verification devices). An earlier scheme to introduce photographs on cards was dropped apparently because of fears of consumer resistance and the opposition of National Westminster; the scheme may, though, be revived.

Losses involving the fraudulent use of cheque guarantee cards have been particularly marked where cards have been used abroad, so much so that on 1 May 1983 all standard cheque cards were withdrawn from use outside the UK. There are now two quite different schemes available for guaranteeing cheques abroad. Most UK banks opted to issue special Eurocheque encashment cards; these cards can be used with conventional domestic cheques written out in pounds sterling up to a maximum of £50 per cheque but are not valid for use in the UK. The Midland and Midland-owned banks (Clydesdale and Northern), plus the Allied Irish Banks and the Bank of Ireland, have opted for a different system that involves an entirely separate cheque book. Uniform Eurocheques are issued free in books of fifteen, but a charge of £3.50 is made for the accompanying Eurocheque guarantee card. These cheques are widely accepted in shops in Europe; customers can also use their Eurocheques at home to a maximum value of £75 per cheque thus circumventing the current £50 limit on the use of conventional cheque guarantee cards within the UK. However, Eurocheques do incur a one-and-a-quarter per cent handling charge when written in a foreign currency. It is too early to say whether either or both of these schemes will be successful in reducing fraud.

Pre-authorised payments

Cheques are most suitable for irregular payments of differing amounts. Payments which follow some kind of regular pattern – household bills are the largest broad category – can be transacted more cheaply using a variety of what are known as pre-authorised payments.

The standing order (or banker's order) is the oldest and best known of these instruments. Since the 1930s banks have arranged the payment of standing orders by using what was generally known as a 'credit advice'. These existed in a variety of forms and became increasingly popular as a mechanism for meeting regular commitments. By 1960 credit transfers had grown in volume to such an extent that a more systematic method of inter-bank exchange was needed. In that year, therefore, a formalised credit clearing was inaugurated. The credit clearing, which is similar to cheque clearing in procedures, transmission time and settlement time, handled more than one and a half million paper items each working day in 1981, a large proportion of them being bank giro credit slips. Credit clearing is done by a combination of manual and automated techniques; as with the cheque clearing, the banks which are not members of the clearing house must arrange to have their business transacted on an agency basis.

A number of different standing order or credit transfer procedures are now in use. It became apparent during the 1960s that the conventional standing order facility was suitable for computerisation using magnetic tapes. This development offered the promise of slowing down the rate of growth (and ultimately reducing) the volume of paper items handled in inter-bank credit clearing. The switch to computers, which led in 1968 to the creation by the clearing banks of the Inter-Bank Computer Bureau, was of the greatest importance. It was possible only because bank customers in the UK were already accustomed to the idea of pre-authorised payment. This was not true in, for example, the United States which is one reason why UK banks were able to develop their automated clearing house much earlier than their US counterparts. In 1971 the corporate structure of the Inter-Bank Computer Bureau was reorganised, and a separate, bank-owned company called Bankers' Automated Clearing Services Ltd (BACS) created. BACS now handles some 600 million automated (i.e. non-paper) transactions a year.

The volume of automated items handled by BACS, of which direct debits are the largest category, continues to grow rapidly. But the total number of paper items handled through the inter-branch credit clearing is also mounting sharply. Table 3.4 shows the trend in the growth of the banks' handling of both paper (non-cheque) and automated items.

So far we have only described the most common form of pre-authorised payment, the standing order. Standing orders as traditionally understood are credit transfers; they require the bank to originate payment in the form of the transfer of credit. This arrangement is convenient for the customer, less so for the bank, and less convenient still for the payee. The recipient's problem is that standing order payments have to be reconciled in his offices ('he' may be a building society, life assurance company or finance company to take three common examples) by means of a procedure which tends to delay confirmation of payment (or non-payment). What appears to be most important in practice is the payee's accounting policy. Amongst building societies, at least, there are several in use: some credit the customer's account as on the day the payment was initiated; some on the day payment was received; and some on the day the payment was entered into the books.

The banks devised the direct debit scheme, amongst other reasons, to overcome this problem of reconciliation. This system transfers the burden of triggering payment from the bank to the payee, using the mechanism of debit transfer. In this way the payee can get information on non-payment of commitments more quickly. The greatest benefit to the banks of direct debits,

Table 3.4 Payment items other than cheques handled by London clearing banks (millions)

	Credit clearing (paper items)		Automated items (on magnetic tape)			
	inter-bank	inter-branch	direct debits	standing orders (inter-bank)	other credits (inter-bank)	standing orders (inter-branch)
1970	108	118	21	79*	9	?
1971	112	122	43	86*	13	?
1972	117	133	55	98*	13	8
1973	122	144	69	111*	19	9
1974	128	154	80	109*	28	16
1975	138	160	93	110*	37	26
1976	159	171	100	114	48	34
1977	167	179	113	125	59	37
1978	180	185	131	137	70	41
1979	196	195	152	153	82	43
1980	214	208	173	169	96	47
1981	202	212	193	181	115	48
1982	181	231	220	190	139	48

* Contains an unknown number of inter-branch items handled by BACS.

Source: Banking Information Service

however, is that the set-up and amendment costs are much lower than for standing orders.

There are two types of direct debit. The simple version deals only in fixed sums; the amount involved cannot be adjusted without the payer's consent. Fresh consent must be obtained every time the sum is changed. The variable amount direct debit, on the other hand, enables the payee to adjust the amount concerned provided reasonable advance notice is given and the customer has previously authorised such an arrangement.

Whatever method of pre-authorised payment is used, whether of a credit or of a debit nature, the bank must have proper authority from the customer in the form of a signed mandate before setting up the requested procedure. The consent of the payer must also be given before a standing order is substituted by a direct debit. Clearly, such arrangements are heavily dependent for their acceptability upon the integrity of participating organisations. The banks have a heavy stake in ensuring that the correct procedures are honestly and accurately observed because they underwrite the indemnity of all automated transactions. This responsibility appears to be exercised conscientiously. As a further precaution, the operation of direct debiting arrangements has been monitored by the Office of Fair Trading.

Bank customers are making increasing use of pre-authorised payments. They save time and effort; in many circumstances it is no longer necessary to write monthly cheques or to make personal calls with cash. Most banks pass on to their customers the lower relative cost of administering direct debits (compared with standing orders and cheques) in the form of lower charges.

The trend towards the greater use of pre-authorised payments has so far largely been at the expense of cash. The banks are optimistic that future take-up will make greater inroads into cheque volumes and so cut down costs. Already, however, standing orders and direct debits taken together constitute the major payment medium for the settling of regular commitments by current account holders. Figure III gives a breakdown of regular commitment payments in 1981.

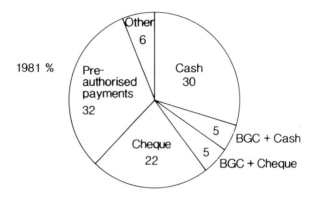

BGC means Bank Giro Credit

Figure III *How regular commitments are paid by current account holders* (1981)

Source: Inter-Bank Research Organisation

Since 1976 the share of regular commitments attributable to pre-authorised payments has increased from around one-quarter to one-third by volume.

It is interesting to note in passing that the increased use of pre-authorised payments is putting a greater and greater distance between the payment behaviour of account holders and that of the 'unbanked'. The unbanked tend to settle their regular commitments far more frequently than the banked. Our group discussions indicate that many people who do not have current accounts regard this as a plus (greater budgetary control), preferring to disregard the advantages of cost and convenience enjoyed by account holders using standing orders and direct debits (see section 2). In 1981, weekly-paid commitments by the unbanked still constituted fifty per cent of the volume of their regular payments, according to the Inter-Bank Research Organisation.

Two questions are raised by pre-arranged payment procedures. The first is that standing orders appear to produce more errors than other forms of current account business. There seems little that individual customers can do about this except check their statements.

The second is that many people are still nervous about direct debits and particularly about variable direct debits. They are unhappy with the idea of giving institutions *carte blanche* to take money out of their accounts. While we can see few problems with simple direct debits, we do believe that before consumers enter into a variable direct debit arrangement they should make certain that they know what procedures the organisation to whom they are paying money will adopt to inform them before payments are increased. The quality of relevant bank literature could be improved.

We received a handful of complaints about some commercial organisations who would accept business only if payments were made by direct debit. This gives customers who do not wish to make payments by direct debit no choice but to take their business elsewhere.

Credit cards

The first UK bank credit card was launched by Barclaycard in 1966. At that time the other clearing banks were sceptical of the commercial future of credit cards: the British were thought financially unadventurous and many US banks had lost money on credit cards. The other clearers therefore invented the cheque guarantee card – the first was introduced by the old National Provincial Group in 1965. This was a compromise of sorts, but the resemblance to credit cards went no further than the plastic form.

By 1970 Barclays' competitors had begun to realise that they might have been wrong. Although Barclaycard was not then particularly profitable, it had proved to be a successful marketing tool – the name 'Barclaycard' was helping to promote other areas of Barclays' business; and customers liked it. The three other major clearers therefore got together (they were later joined by Williams and Glyn's and the Royal Bank of Scotland) and created a competing card called Access, launched in 1972. Barclaycard has subsequently joined forces with the US international payment system giant, Visa. Subsequent entrants into the UK market, including the Co-operative Bank, the Allied Irish Banks and, notably, the Trustee Savings Banks with their Trustcard, have also joined up with Visa. Access, meanwhile, which is owned and run by a holding company called The Joint Credit Card Company Limited, itself owned by its participating banks, has linked up with Visa's principal world-wide competitor in the credit card market, MasterCard.

With the relaxation of credit controls in the early 1970s, the scene was set for substantial expansion in the take-up of credit cards in the United Kingdom. No other country apart from the USA and Canada has adopted them with such enthusiasm. By early 1980 nearly ten million cards were in use in the UK. Access and Barclaycard were competing hard with 4.9 million and 4.2 million cards respectively, followed at some distance by Trustcard with 0.65 million. By 1981, expressed as a percentage of bank/current account holders, Barclaycard were in front with 20 per cent of the market; Access had 19 per cent and Trustcard 5 per cent. Other credit cards made up a further 4 per cent. In addition, a small percentage (about 1 per cent) of non-current account holders had a Barclaycard or an Access card (10). Credit card use grew between 1971 and 1981 in volume terms at an average annual rate of 32 per cent, twice as rapidly as direct debits and three-and-a-half times as rapidly as cheques. About two-fifths of all account holders are now reckoned to hold an Access card or a Barclaycard.

Credit card business has proved to be an unexpectedly profitable area of bank activity and now constitutes an important feature of bank services.

The popularity of credit cards with consumers is not difficult to explain. The use of a single piece of plastic can provide a number of different services:

* a way of reducing the number of cheques that consumers have to write;
* a source of up to six weeks' interest-free credit (large numbers of credit card holders use the cards in this way) provided accounts are settled in full each month;
* a simple way of borrowing to buy goods or services, without the arrangements having to be individually negotiated each time;
* a simple way of providing revolving credit at consumers' own discretion.

In addition, the cost of credit, though higher than for most bank lending to consumers, is often lower than for the types of credit normally available through retailers. On the other hand, credit card transactions do generate a large quantity of paperwork – dealing with the vouchers they create is a highly labour-intensive operation (11). Barclaycard receives over 30,000 telephone calls and 20,000 letters daily.

A great deal of the cost of bank credit cards is met by the commission that retailers pay on sales made using the cards. Since payment by credit cards imposes different costs on a retailer than payment by other means there is a strong argument for saying that the retailer should be allowed to make a different charge to the customer. The customer could then choose what payment method to use, taking cost into account. The Monopolies and Mergers Commission recommended that credit card companies should not be able to enforce the clause in their contracts with retailers which prevents retailers from making a differential charge. However the government did not accept this recommendation and we see little point in re-opening this issue now.

In the United States, rising fraud volumes and handling costs have led US credit card companies to be much more selective in issuing cards and, more seriously, have brought about annual charges for card holders which are unrelated to use. (American Express, Diners Card and other 'travel and entertainment' and 'premium' cards have always carried charges but are not in the strict sense credit cards.) These and other problems have given rise in the US to the emergence of Bank Card Holders of America, the fastest-growing consumer organisation in the United States in 1980/81, with over 100,000 members. It is possible that any proposal to charge consumers for a bank credit card – particularly for one which is also used as a cheque guarantee card – might lead to the emergence of a similar organisation among credit card holders here.

One particular problem has been brought to our attention regarding credit card transactions by telephone. A number of commercial organisations, ranging from travel agents to record and cassette distributors, encourage credit card holders to make purchases by telephone, the effective point of authorisation being the disclosure of customers' card numbers. Some transactions of this kind leave little room for ambiguity; others – holiday bookings appear to be an example – are open to misinterpretation if the customer is not extremely careful (or the travel agent not scrupulously fair). Provisional bookings can be turned into irrevocable dealings; the card holder's account is debited and it may not be possible to have the money returned. We are reluctant to recommend that card holders' accounts should only be debited following receipt of written authorisation – which would be one solution – because of the reduction in service this would bring. Nevertheless, this particular form of telephone transaction should be kept under review. Clearly, prospective customers are under some obligation to exercise care when disclosing their credit card account numbers.

Other bank methods of making payments, including international transfers

Two other methods of payment are available to customers, the banker's draft and the telephonic transfer system. Both are generally used for settling large value transactions and neither is widely used by personal customers. The banker's draft is a cheque made out by a bank on its own head office, an arrangement which strengthens the payment. Telephonic transfers are used for urgent transactions and ensure same day transference of funds from payer's bank to that of payee.

Various methods of making international payments are used by both corporate and personal customers. The development since 1977 of SWIFT (Society for Worldwide Interbank Financial Telecommunication), a private data communication system involving nearly one thousand banks in forty countries, has revolutionised the speed and efficiency with which international payments can be made. But this is largely a business facility. More relevant to personal customers are travellers' cheques. All major UK banks offer this facility – a safe and convenient means of carrying money abroad, making payments and obtaining local currency. Travellers' cheques can be purchased in a wide range of currencies and are available from most banks to customers and non-customers alike. Most UK banks have links with corresponding financial institutions abroad, either to other banks or to payment system organisations like Visa and American Express. Several building societies provide travellers' cheques – a service which their current constitution makes rather cumbersome.

Another method of international payment is available to National Girobank account holders who possess cheque guarantee cards. Post-cheques can be obtained in books of five which may be cashed at more than 80,000 post offices in 28 countries. This service is gradually being extended to other countries, including the USA where post-cheques can now be cashed at some 200 Western Union offices. Other international payment facilities are available – to both Girobank customers and non-account holders using international Giro links.

Bank charges

The money transmission services the banks provide are of a number of different kinds and cost different amounts of money. As we have seen in section 2, our market research demonstrates that many bank customers do not understand bank charges properly and that there is an appreciable amount of dissatisfaction about this.

Interestingly, the group discussions held among bank customers revealed that the customers who were most likely to accept bank charges were those, comparatively few, who had made a reasoned choice to have a bank account because they felt that bank payment systems would be more convenient for them than going on without a bank account. The majority, who had a bank account because their family had always had one or their employers paid by cheque, were more likely to resent having to pay bank charges.

It is certainly true that many bank customers would rather not get involved in worrying about bank charges – those banks that offer 'free' banking (no charges so long as the account is in credit) said to us that the offer was an essential part of their strategy to attract new customers. It will certainly be the case that customers who manage to work whatever system their bank uses to fix charges so as to avoid charges altogether will be less unhappy than those who pay. There are large numbers of such customers. Barclays told us that in 1982, 63 per cent of their customers had paid no charges; Williams and Glyn's (which, unlike Barclays, offers 'free banking') told us that for them the figure was almost three-quarters. More recently, however, bank charges have risen sharply; the number of customers paying no charges is therefore likely to have fallen.

It is important to note that there is no such thing as 'free banking'. Any system which ends up with a charge to the customer of nil, balances income from the customer on the one hand against costs the customer generates on the other. With banking the balance is between the interest the bank earns on the credit balance of the current account and the costs involved in making payments by cheque and other means on the customer's behalf.

The notion of balancing one against the other goes back to the earliest traditions of banking: the customer entrusted his or her money to the banker, the banker used it to invest but at the same time made payments, on the client's behalf. It was not until quite recently – 1972 – that banks accepted the notion that they ought to let their customers know in advance the system they proposed to use to calculate the charges they would impose.

Competition between the banks and the rising cost of money transmission services has led to greater clarity in the explanation of charges. The most common system for charging for current accounts is now

(i) if the account is always kept in credit (or if the credit balance never falls below £50 or £100) no charge is made;

(ii) if this condition is not met, then a charge is fixed by calculating all the payments made (28p for a cheque, 16p for a direct debit for instance) and setting against this an allowance for interest on the account while it is in credit at a notional interest rate rather lower than that being offered by the bank for savings.

Provided that customers can keep their account in credit to the amount their bank lays down for 'free banking', the system has the great merit of simplicity. This is attractive to many people. But there are a number of problems. Some are to do with the way accounts work in practice; the others to do with the different effects such charging systems have on different types of bank customer. Let us deal with the practical problems first.

If a customer does allow his or her account to fall below the specified minimum credit balance, then –

  (i) the amount of whatever charges the bank calculates are due is taken out of the account without prior notice – the first the customer knows about it is when he or she gets a bank statement, on which charges will appear alongside all the other debits;

 (ii) the customer will have been charged for all the transactions in the period in question (usually three months) even though the balance may only have fallen below the specified minimum for a few days;

(iii) it will be extremely difficult for the customer to understand the basis on which charges are made or to check them, because the statement will give no details of how the charges are calculated. Customers may well have had some separate communication from the bank about how charges are calculated (12), but it will be very difficult to apply it and, as our market research has shown, bank customers often cannot remember ever having had charging systems explained to them.

It is not surprising that such a system does not make customers happy. More importantly, if customers understand the basis on which they are being charged, they will run their accounts in the most cost-effective way. This is not only good for them but it also makes it easier for the banks to give customers incentives to use payment methods which are less costly to operate.

The fact that charges may be payable on three months' transactions if an account slips below the specified minimum balance for three days can cause great dissatisfaction among bank customers. We considered whether to recommend that all banks should levy charges only on transactions which occurred while the balance was below this minimum, as is the practice of the National Girobank. If this was done, the banks would doubtless want to recoup the income they lost by putting up their charges in some other way. This could be by increasing the charges for each transaction, by putting up the amount of the minimum balance or reducing or abolishing the notional allowance for the interest gained on the customers' credit balance. It is not clear to us that bank customers would prefer any of these alternatives. In any case, bank customers who want to avoid the system can make the choice of joining the National Girobank.

We therefore recommend to the banks a number of changes in the way they operate charging systems:

(i) banks should not subtract charges from customers' accounts without telling them first. The simplest way to achieve this would be for one bank statement to carry a statement that charges would be deducted on a future date. This deduction would then appear on the next statement. There is a practical problem about this: some bank customers get statements only at relatively infrequent intervals. They should pay charges at the same intervals, or else receive more frequent statements;

(ii) bank charges should be much more clearly presented to customers.

The other problem is the effect that 'free banking' charging systems have on different types of consumer. 'Free banking', broadly speaking, results from the interest the bank gains on the credit balance in the account (this is called the 'endowment effect') being set against the charges the bank makes for transactions made on the customer's behalf. The result of this, again broadly speaking, is that customers with high balances and relatively few transactions subsidise customers with low balances who make large numbers of transactions.

This effect was recognised by the Price Commission, which drew attention to the balance of advantage and disadvantage of existing charging policy – simplicity on one side of the scale, lack of clarity and cross-subsidisation on the other. The Commission felt that the aim of any charging system

'should be to allow the customer to identify and ultimately relate to costs the charges for services that a bank is rendering to him (money transmission) and to be rewarded for the service he is rendering the bank (depositing money).' (13)

It suggested that one way to achieve this would be to pay interest on current account credit balances directly and to charge for transactions as they occurred. The result would be either a payment to or a charge on the customer's bank account. A number of bank accounts which follow this principle have been introduced – by the Co-operative Bank and by the major clearers. Some of these accounts, however, are based on compulsory monthly transfers and incorporate a revolving credit facility; they are therefore not strictly analogous to current accounts.

On the other hand, there is no doubt of the attractions of the simplicity of 'free banking'. These were expressed to us by the Yorkshire Bank:

'The system has the great virtue of simplicity and though extremely abhorrent to sections of the media and consumer protection bodies, it is a fact that for one reason or another the generality of bank customers, who are quite capable of taking action to minimise the endowment effect individually, do not express the same strength of feeling on the matter.'

Bank account holders who use this system also enjoy an income tax advantage. The tax position on payment of tax on interest on current accounts is complex. In a very simplified definition, we can say that if an account creates a sum of interest to which the customer is entitled, then tax will be payable; if notional interest earned is used to abate charges, then no tax will be payable.

Our natural inclination is to support charging systems which make it clear to consumers what they are paying for. So we very much welcome the recent development of interest-bearing current accounts which credit customers with the interest their money has earned and debit them with the charges for the work that has been done on their behalf. On the other hand, we do not believe it would be right for us to suggest that banks should stop offering 'free banking' accounts. Many customers like their convenience and apparent simplicity and these advantages may well be worth more to some people than very small amounts of income earned on credit balances.

We hope that the development of more clearly presented charging systems for current accounts can be left to competition. Customers who maintain credit balances and have relatively few or relatively simple financial transactions are clearly attractive to banks and to other deposit-taking institutions. There is every sign that the trend, already under way, of offering such customers interest-bearing current accounts which will be attractive to them, will continue. This underlines the importance of all deposit-taking institutions being able to compete for money transmission business on equal terms; we discuss this issue in section 9.

It is also the case that with generally lower interest rates the offer of 'free banking' becomes less attractive to the banks, because the amount of interest they can earn on current account balances goes down. A number of banks told us that the unrecovered cost to them of providing a money transmission service was in excess of 9 per cent per annum of cheque account balances. This gives some indication of the level of interest rates at which the offer of 'free banking' is likely to become unattractive, though it is of course open to the banks to increase the minimum credit balance requirement.

This leaves the problem of the tax position of current accounts. The Building Societies Association has argued that the fact that current account charges can be set against notional interest is an anomaly which favours the banks. They have suggested that the total tax which might be payable could be of the order of £100 million a year. We have carefully considered whether there is any way in which this tax position could be changed without detriment to the users of banking services. We have not found a proposal which we believe would work, without giving the tax authorities detailed control over the way current account charges are levied.

We therefore make no recommendation that the tax position on current accounts should be changed. If we are right in our belief that interest-bearing current accounts will continue to grow, the anomaly caused by the tax position should get smaller. In any case, there is some rather crude justice in tax advantages to current account holders since, as we have seen earlier, it may be argued that bank customers subsidise the distribution of cash into the economy, a cost which might be considered appropriate for government to bear.

References to section 3

1. These figures are not strictly comparable owing to the use of a 50p lower value limit in 1976 against a £1 lower value limit in 1981 – an approximate adjustment for inflation. The trend is clear however.
2. *Evidence by the Committee of London Clearing Bankers to the Committee to Review the Functioning of Financial Institutions*, the London Clearing Banks, November 1977, Longman, para. 3.4.
3. *Banks: Charges for Money Transmission Services*, HC 337, HMSO, 1978, para. 8.3.
4. *Ibid.*, para. 8.9.
5. Published as D. Vander Weyer, 'The threats and opportunities facing British banks – a 10-year view', *Journal of the Institute of Bankers*, June 1980, p. 74 (the text of a presidential address to the Institute of Bankers given on 21 May 1980).
6. See p. 136.
7. P. G. Hirsch, *Truncation: the opportunities and the implications*, IBRO report no. 434, June 1981, p. 9, cited in Vander Weyer *op. cit.*
8. But see also p. 43.
9. See also p. 135.
10. Inter-Bank Research Organisation, *Research Brief*, October 1982.
11. Barclaycard employs approximately 4,200 people, of whom nearly 600 are required solely to process vouchers.
12. In fairness it should be acknowledged that the banks are producing better literature of this kind than previously. The Lloyds Bank leaflet, *Bank Charges: How to Avoid Them*, enclosed as a 'stuffer' with bank statements, is an excellent example.
13. HC 337, *op. cit.*, para. 11.7.

Section 4 / Access to banking services

Our research (outlined in section 2) suggests that so far as access to banking services is concerned, the three most important factors for the individual consumer are:

* *place:* are the banking services convenient for me?
* *time:* are they available when I need them?
* *friendliness and helpfulness:* are they run in a way which seems friendly and helpful to people like me?

We deal with each of these factors below. We also look briefly at the special problems of the disabled.

Place: are the banking services convenient for me?

In mid-1982, the major London clearing banks operated a total of about 11,200 branches. The Scottish clearing banks had more than 1,500 branches and the four banks in Northern Ireland another 400 branches or sub-branches. The TSBs had about 1,640 branches in the United Kingdom as a whole. By contrast, there were some 6,500 building society branches and over 20,700 post offices providing outlets for the National Girobank and National Savings Bank.

These 'snapshot' figures do not reveal the significant changes that have been taking place in the numbers of outlets of the different types of institution. The figure of 11,200 branches for the major London clearing banks has come down from a peak of 12,315 in 1968, despite increases in the numbers of customers and transactions. One of the reasons for this fall has been the rationalisation of branch structures following the series of bank mergers in the late 1960s. For example, between 1969 and 1976 National Westminster reduced their branches by a net total of 400 (though this net figure needs explanation: 750 branches were closed and 350 new ones opened). Barclays reduced its coverage by about 150 branches over the same period. More recently, branch closures seem to have been inspired by banks taking a closer look at the economics of branch banking, which we examine more closely in Appendix IV.

The branch networks operated by the Scottish banks seem to be rather more stable, while a number of smaller institutions including ethnic banks and North American-owned 'money-shops' have recently increased their branch networks. Their total numbers, however, remain relatively small when measured against either the major London clearers or the Post Office network, though the latter is also declining slightly. A comparative picture of changes in UK branch networks for 1980–81 is given in Table 4.1.

The most dramatic change in numbers has been in the network of building society branches. A running series of mergers between building societies, a process which continues, has been accompanied not by a reduction in branches, but by a significant increase. In 1960, there were 985 building society branches. By 1973, the figure had risen to 2,808 and in 1982 it was over 6,300. This is still some way short of the number of clearing bank branches but nevertheless represents a major increase in the number of places at which consumers have access to some financial services. A clear indication of relative trends as between the London clearing banks and the building societies is given in Table 4.2.

The simple listing of aggregate networks is in some ways misleading, of course. In financial circles the word 'branch' conceals a wide variety of shapes,

Table 4.1 Outlets of the major UK financial institutions, 1980 and 1981

	Calendar year 1980			Calendar year 1981		
	opened	closed	end/80	opened	closed	end/81
English banks						
National Westminster Group	16	40	3209	29	26	3212
Barclays	12	33	2991	3	14	2980
Midland Group	14	16	2461	13	22	2452
Lloyds	4	17	2298	11	16	2293
Trustee Savings Banks (including Scotland and Northern Ireland)	0	13	1648	3	14	1637
National Girobank/National Savings Bank/Post Office crown	19	7	1582	2	11	1573
sub	0	164	20 892	179	239	20 832
Co-operative Bank	n/a	n/a	1004	32	42	994
(plus cash-a-cheque facilities)	n/a	n/a	3613	23	42	3594
Williams & Glyn's	3	9	314	7	4	317
Yorkshire Bank	4	0	198	5	0	203
Scottish banks						
Royal Bank of Scotland	6	10	602	3	10	595
Bank of Scotland	6	4	569	7	9	567
Clydesdale Bank	1	1	376	5	3	378
Irish banks						
Allied Irish Banks	7	1	115	3	0	118
Bank of Ireland	3	0	61	2	0	64

Table 4.1 (cont.)

	Calendar year 1980			Calendar year 1981		
	opened	closed	end/80	opened	closed	end/81
Ulster Bank	1	1	124	1	6	119
Northern Bank	0	7	171	0	11	160
Domestic finance houses (parents in brackets)						
Lombard North Central (Nat West)	1	1	122	0	0	122
Mercantile Credit (Barclays)	2	0	108	2	0	110
Chartered Trust (Standard Chartered)	2	0	92	0	7	85
Lloyds and Scottish (Lloyds)	0	0	96	0	0	96
Forward Trust (Midland)	0	0	92	0	4	88
United Dominions Trust (TSB)	3	1	87	0	0	87
North West Securities (Bank of Scotland)	1	8	68	0	0	68
FC Finance (Co-op Bank)	1	1	24	2	0	26
Yorkshire Bank Finance	0	0	11	0	0	11
Building societies	n/a	n/a	5684	n/a	n/a	6162
North American-owned institutions						
Bank owned:						
Citibank Trust	2	0	40	1	0	41
Boston Trust (First National Bank of Boston)	2	0	20	6	0	26
Western Trust & Savings (Royal Bank of Canada)	1	0	18	6	0	24
Security Pacific	0	2	10	2	2	10
Non-bank owned:						
Bowmaker	1	0	92	0	0	92
HFC Trust	25	0	107	20	0	127
Avco Trust	7	2	81	2	2	81
Beneficial Trust	9	0	63	7	0	70
Associated Capital Corporation	5	0	50	9	1	58
Commercial Credit	0	0	16	1	1	16
Ethnic banking institutions						
Bank of Credit and Commerce International	0	0	45	0	0	45
United Bank	0	0	28	1	3	26
Muslim Commercial	1	0	25	0	0	25
Habib Bank	1	0	23	0	1	22
Bank of Baroda	0	0	15	0	0	15
National Bank of Pakistan	0	0	14	0	0	14
Bank of India	0	0	13	0	0	13

Source: Noel Alexander Associates

sizes and functions. For example, a large, traditional city bank branch might be twenty times as large as a small provincial TSB branch in terms of transaction values, running costs and staff complement. All statistical measures across financial institutions are crude and, as with Table 4.1, must be treated with care.

From the individual consumer's point of view, changes in the total number of branches may or may not matter. What is most important is whether there is somewhere convenient that provides banking services. The distribution of branches matters, as well as their total number. So far as the major clearing banks are concerned, one aspect of branch distribution is self-evident and requires no research to substantiate it. In general, the distribution of bank branches follows closely the pattern of commercial development rather than where individual consumers live or work.

Table 4.2   London clearing bank and building society branch numbers

	Bank*	Building society
1973	11 788	2808
1974	11 807	3099
1975	11 728	3375
1976	11 659	3696
1977	11 628	4130
1978	11 438	4595
1979	11 364	5147
1980	11 289	5716
1981	11 271	6203

* Full members of Committee of London Clearing Bankers only.

Source: Financial Times

There are obvious historical reasons for this. The clearing banks developed primarily to meet the needs of the business community in the broad sense. They needed to be sited in the commercial centres in which that community worked. What was true in the eighteenth and nineteenth centuries is only marginally less true today. Corporate banking (that is, making profits by meeting the needs of the business community) still dominates the clearing banks though perhaps decreasingly so. We do not say that it is in any sense wrong for the banks to emphasise the importance of this aspect of their work. What it does mean, though, is that certain aspects of the clearing banks' operations are not geared to meeting the needs of individual consumers. One of the most important of these aspects is the distribution of bank branches. Banks historically have tended not to open branches where consumers live or work because there would not be enough profitable commercial business to make it worth their while. Branch locations in high street shopping areas are convenient for business customers and the non-employed, but less so for those who need to shop (and bank) outside normal working hours.

Within the general pattern of branch distribution it is possible to identify some points of banking service 'deprivation'. In general, consumers who live in the country are worse placed than those who live in towns. Even those rural communities which have had branch, sub-branch or agency banking facilities are seeing them withdrawn or cut back. Council estates, new housing developments and the inner nineteenth-century ring of the major industrial cities are also all relatively deprived areas in terms of branch banking facilities.

One possible solution is the use of mobile banks, defining these as travelling banking services housed in purpose-built vehicles operating on a set route (that is, excluding travelling 'temporary facilities' of the kind used by most major banks on an irregular basis for visitors to shows, conferences and exhibitions). Mobile banks are unevenly distributed, with over thirty in Scotland – the Royal Bank of Scotland has the largest fleet. There are only eight in England and, surprisingly, none in Wales. The Irish banks operate a number of mobiles in the Republic (1).

Mobile banks are undoubtedly expensive to equip and operate. The Scottish banks suggested to us that they are provided much as a public service. But perhaps this is not the most important reason for the English banks' evident lack of commitment. National Westminster told us that

'. . . mobility – the most obvious benefit – is at the same time the mobile bank's greatest weakness. Whereas a traditional branch is open at the busiest times, the mobile bank has a planned route resulting in opening at some locations at a time which may not be convenient for all our customers. Thus the route and timetable chosen is of necessity a compromise between reaching areas where the maximum number of potential customers are situated and minimising the wasted travelling time between stopping points.'

On the basis of similar reasoning, it appears that none of the London clearing banks has plans for any significant extension of mobile services.

This is disappointing and reflects an excessively cautious approach. It is unlikely that the disparity between provision in Scotland and the rest of the UK can be explained solely in terms of social conscience; we think it improbable that the Scottish mobiles would be sustained if they were proving to be a significant financial liability. Nor is there any reason to suppose that the remoter parts of Cornwall, the Fens, Cumbria or north and central Wales would be less likely to support mobile services than the Highlands of Scotland, quite apart from housing estates and other residential areas. One problem appears to be the banks' unwillingness to pool resources with other organisations, commercial or non-commercial. Multi-purpose mobiles including, perhaps, banking, nursing, library and generalist advice services might meet a ready response from isolated communities. Although we do not underestimate the problems which would be encountered in putting together such packages, we believe there to be sufficient collective opportunity to justify a more imaginative approach by the banks.

The distribution of building society branches, with heavy concentrations in shopping areas, follows much the same pattern as that of clearing banks, though the historical background is very different. The recent rapid expansion in building society networks has been influenced by a desire to get more personal sector deposits. In this context, time matters more than place. Building society branches are open on Saturdays when shopping centres are being used most intensively by consumers. The building society network is also considerably extended by the use of solicitors, estate agents and others, acting as agents.

The post office network is the one which most closely reflects the pattern of where people live (though not where they work). The National Girobank and National Savings Bank are therefore able to provide the most conveniently situated access to basic banking services for many consumers, though personal service is at a minimum in traditional banking terms. In its country banking campaign, National Girobank is building on the fact that many villages have post offices but do not have bank or building society branches. However, the post office network itself is under pressure. The reduction in the number of sub-post offices has already been the subject of discussion in previous reports by the NCC and the National Council for Voluntary Organisations (NCVO). Both organisations are opposed to the further general reduction of the post office network (2).

We note that there is some evidence that rural consumers are reluctant to use National Girobank services provided through sub-post offices, on the grounds that personal banking transactions conducted in semi-public places by part-time post office personnel may, in small communities, become talked about. We believe these fears to be largely groundless, although National Girobank could do more to dispel them. More generally, we feel that National Girobank should work harder to promote their services and make their counter facilities more attractive to banking customers.

There is no reason why the provision of many of the more straightforward banking services for consumers needs to be tied to the bricks-and-mortar of the bank or building society branch. We have already mentioned the use of mobile banks. Other innovations include operating limited banking services in shops during normal shopping hours – already a well-established practice of the Co-operative Bank, within Co-operative stores. On a much smaller scale, Boston Trust and Savings operate five 'money shops' in branches of Debenhams. Examples of current experiments are the facilities provided by the TSB at Debenhams in Sheffield and by Lloyds at Woolworth's in Victoria, London.

A number of the banks have opened workplace branches, often following agreements between companies and employees about arrangements for cashless pay. These are still few and far between; we would like to see more. Other specialist sites include airports, hospitals, universities and colleges. On almost any estimate of the likely expansion of bank branches in such specialised locations, however, the familiar high-street-type branches will continue to make up much the largest part of total networks. Substantial closures would be bound to reduce the degree of access that bank customers have to banking services. The director of the Inter-Bank Research Organisation has suggested that a more imaginative approach may be needed to the possibility of sharing what are often

prime site premises with other organisations, particularly advice and information agencies. He has suggested that 'the branch network represents an
opportunity as well as a problem . . .' (3).

Current and prospective developments in technology are likely to have
extensive consequences in terms of accessibility for consumers. (These developments are reviewed in more detail in section 5.) Automated teller machines
(ATMs) have so far had very little effect on the geographical distribution and
availability of banking services, as the great majority have been sited either
inside or outside existing bank premises. Security and other practical problems
have limited their spread to non-banking sites. Another limitation is that most
banks' ATMs can only be used by account holders of that particular bank,
though two major sharing arrangements – bringing together respectively
Midland and National Westminster, and Lloyds, Barclays, Williams and
Glyn's, the Bank of Scotland and the Royal Bank of Scotland – have been
announced. At the time of writing, a more radical development was in prospect.
Sainsbury's were about to become the first grocery store chain to install cash
dispensers. An experimental scheme at Sainsbury's Crystal Palace supermarket
in London is being backed by the big four London clearing banks (4). We hope
that such initiatives will lead to further diversification of access to banking
services in shopping areas.

Two building societies, Halifax and Leicester, have already installed ATMs.
A Building Societies' Association study group has concluded that a shared ATM
system for building societies is both desirable and practicable. We understand
that a number of schemes are now being reviewed. If plans along these lines go
ahead, ATMs are likely to offer the individual building society account holder
greatly improved accessibility.

The nature and extent of possible electronic funds transfer at point of sale
(EFTPOS) developments have been a subject of continuing speculation for
some five years or so. If and when EFT/POS develops, consumers will find
themselves able to carry out a small range of banking transactions at a wide
variety of retail outlets. This subject is discussed more fully in section 5.

The most revolutionary change of all is likely to be the introduction of home
banking, via Prestel and/or cable. In principle, there is no reason why home
banking should not provide virtually a full range of consumer banking services,
with the single (but important) exception of putting cash into the consumer's
hand. The combination of home banking and an extended network of ATMs
seems likely to provide consumers with greatly enhanced access to banking
services (5).

Time: are the banking services available when I need them?

We noted in section 2 that the most popular improvement that banks could
make in their services would be to make it easier for consumers to withdraw their
money. Over half (51 per cent) of the respondents in the MORI survey would
like to see their bank open on Saturdays, and for 41 per cent this would be the

most welcome change that the bank could introduce. Twenty-eight per cent of respondents wanted longer opening hours on weekdays and 27 per cent would like to see more tills open at lunchtime.

In all, two-thirds of respondents mentioned at least one of these changes – Saturday opening, longer opening hours on weekdays or more tills at lunchtime. This is a measure of the extent to which banks are not meeting the needs of their customers when it comes to access. What is interesting is that, with one exception amongst the big banks, opening hours have tended to shorten since the early 1970s.

When, in November 1967, the clearing banks announced that they intended to close their branches on Saturdays, it was said that this would be compensated for by longer opening hours during the working week. Weekday hours did indeed improve – 9.30 to 3.30 instead of 10–3. Late opening of selected branches from 4.30 to 6 one night per week was introduced for a short time, but was progressively discontinued in the early 1970s. The two stumbling-blocks appear to have been not enough business during extra hours, and staff opposition. As a result, the number of Lloyds bank branches, for example, with evening opening was reduced from 560 (38 per cent) in January 1971 to 459 (30 per cent) in June 1974. By July 1977 monitoring of business levels had resulted in the cancellation of evening opening at 201 branches and a cut-back of hours at the remaining 258 branches. By mid-1982, only 124 Lloyds branches were offering this service on one day a week, comprising

4.30–6.00pm	27 branches
4.30–5.30pm	97 branches
	124

This pattern was broadly followed by all the major clearing banks.

The one exception amongst the large clearing banks to this trend towards shorter and less convenient bank opening hours has been the Saturday opening scheme launched by Barclays. In May 1982, Barclays announced that 400 of their branches would open on Saturday mornings, beginning in September of that year. No other major competitor has yet followed this step. However, those banks which have not followed Barclays do in some cases recognise that general opening hours arrangements are less than satisfactory. One London clearer, in its submission to us, said that:

'We acknowledge that some of our customers are inconvenienced by the present bank opening hours and we are convinced that if we are to protect the long-term interests of the Bank and of its staff we must improve this aspect of our service. It would be uneconomic to make available at all our branches the full range of banking services during any extended hours of opening that may be agreed. Any extension of opening hours is, therefore, likely to be limited to those locations where there is sufficient demand to justify the considerable additional costs involved and only a limited number of services would be offered.'

We have been unable to evaluate the success or failure of the Barclays initiative, about which there are conflicting reports.

When it comes to opening hours, building societies (along with the National Girobank, Co-operative Bank facilities in Co-operative stores and money shops) clearly have an advantage over banks. They are normally open for longer on weekdays, and on Saturday mornings as well. This advantage is well known to consumers. Our research into consumers' comparisons of banks and building societies shows that the more convenient opening hours of building societies are recognised as an advantage among all groups of consumers who have both a bank current account and a building society account (see page 224).

We have already mentioned the importance of developments in technology in making it easier for consumers to get access to banking services. This applies particularly to constraints of time. Already, many ATMs are available for 24 hours a day, seven days a week. The ATM network is likely to expand considerably, especially if building societies' current plans are fulfilled. Home banking will also make it easier for consumers to carry out banking transactions at times which suit them, rather than obliging them to fit in with the opening times of the banks and other institutions.

Many of these changes will clearly benefit consumers. But the impact of new technology may not be uniformly benign, particularly to those customers who value a high standard of personal service. The increasing use of computerised records and payments systems tends towards the concentration of routine activity in centralised locations. Some payment methods, like bank giro credits and direct debits, bypass the branch completely. Similarly, credit card systems are independent of branch networks. ATMs have further diminished the link between the customer and his or her branch.

The implications of such changes for the future of branch networks have been highlighted by Frazer and Vittas in their study of *The Retail Banking Revolution*:

'There seems to be little reason why banks should not completely eliminate the concept of consumers' accounts being held at individual branches. The concept is largely a fiction and one that seems increasingly out of touch with reality . . . Those banks which have on-line branch terminals can, and often do, provide an identical service at all their branches, whether or not it is the branch at which the bank customer's account is held. *Such a trend in banks would clearly further undermine the importance of branches.*' [emphasis added] (6)

It is not easy to predict the consequences of these trends which, from the point of view of consumer access, may point simultaneously in both negative and positive directions – fewer, smaller and less personalised branches supplemented by round-the-clock automated payment and information systems. This brings us to our third access criterion.

Friendliness and helpfulness of banking services

Our research shows that there is still a substantial minority of people who think that the major clearing banks are not really for 'ordinary people'. This feeling is especially prevalent in the lower socio-economic groups, among those who do not have bank accounts, and also within the ethnic minorities. The image of the bank as an institution geared to the needs of the business community and the middle class still persists.

This is not true of building societies and other institutions like the TSB, the Co-operative Bank and National Girobank, some of which have their roots in thrift institutions, used by generations of workers as safe homes for their savings. Building societies also have a better reputation for friendlier staff among all groups of the population (see page 224).

It is difficult for us to judge to what extent this minority feeling that banks are 'not for people like me' has retarded growth in the number of bank accounts. Other factors have almost certainly been at work: we have already noted that bank branches are not sited where most people live or work and that their opening hours are not very convenient. Certainly, many people either do not want a bank account or find they can manage their lives without one. We are in no position to say that they are wrong, though the NCC has consistently argued the advantages of the possession of bank current accounts (7).

There is, however, one aspect of the image which banks present to consumers on which we would like to comment. The vast majority of bank branches, even when modernised, conform to the traditional pattern: a single counter with necessarily protected staff behind bandit screens on one side and customers on the other. For the most part no distinction is made between corporate and personal business. If the banks perceive their business to be differently based in 1983 from what it was in, say, 1923, there is very little evidence to demonstrate it in the layout of the average branch.

This is now beginning to change. The North American-owned licensed deposit-takers, 'money shops', can take some of the credit for this. Concerns like Western Trust and Savings, Avco and Boston Trust and Savings offer a friendlier atmosphere than most branch banks, together with longer opening hours. Some consumers' reactions to them, though, are contradictory; fears are occasionally voiced that branches that are too friendly and relaxed may be insufficiently secure as a place to leave your money. (There is no objective evidence to support this anxiety.)

The big banks are now embarking on modernisation programmes. Greater efforts are being made to separate personal business from corporate or commercial business, either by reorganising regional and local branch networks on a functional basis or, within branches, of providing separate counters. At some branches Barclays have introduced American-style 'personal bankers' who sit at desks in front of the counter to answer customers' queries and give informal advice. Other banks are experimenting on these and other lines where planning restrictions allow. The Midland Bank's innovative new branch at Leamington

Spa makes full use of new technology to increase security while abandoning the traditional counter and bandit screens. We are disappointed to learn that this scheme is unlikely to be copied by the Midland elsewhere.

Access for the disabled

We concentrate here on those people with mobility problems. We contacted several organisations representing the interests of disabled people. Their shared concern is that the disabled person should be able to lead, as far as possible, a self-managed and independent life. This means that disabled people should be able to carry out business and financial transactions in person and in private.

We were particularly interested, therefore, to identify the specific banking needs of the disabled and to find out to what extent they are being met. We did not commission detailed research on this subject, but invited comments from those with expertise and familiarity with the problems of the disabled. We also received the results of two local surveys on access for the disabled.

Under the provisions of the 1970 Chronically Sick and Disabled Persons Act and the 1981 Disabled Persons Act, anyone providing premises which are to be open to the public is required to make 'appropriate provision' for the needs of disabled people. The following is an indication of those requirements:

* car parking facilities near to an accessible entrance;
* flat or ramped access to the bank;
* some part of the counter lowered to permit communication between a person in a wheelchair and the cashier;
* hand-rails and seating for ambulant, disabled people;
* the siting of ATMs so that they can be reached and operated with ease;
* a sympathetic staff, trained in the requirements of the disabled;
* interview rooms and manager's office which is accessible.

It seems, from the information we received, that the disabled person is still prevented from using banking facilities easily. The Disabled Living Foundation stated that 'many high street banks are completely inaccessible'. In their publication, *Access in the High Street*, the Centre on Environment for the Handicapped write that '. . . too high counters and complex glass screens inhibit privacy and communication and when combined with intricate details for the passing of money etc can make the whole transaction very difficult'. One of the interviewees, with spina bifida, comments in the same publication that 'the banks missed a golden opportunity when they installed cashpoints. This would have been an ideal way of enabling disabled people at least to withdraw cash themselves, but the cashpoints were all installed far too high up on the walls to be useable from a wheelchair' (8). His wife, confined permanently to a wheelchair, complained that she had never seen over the counter in a bank or a post office. Criticisms of cash dispensers outside the bank reveal that some of them at least are too high from pavement level, and if the ground level of the building is stepped or raised, it can be difficult for wheelchairs to draw alongside. If the machines are deeply recessed, it is awkward for the person in a wheelchair to reach up and back. The button control panel and the display unit, unless sufficiently angled, can be difficult to read and operate.

The banks face considerable physical restrictions. Many branch premises are old; some feature the architectural trappings of opulence – stepped entrances, heavy doors and ornate external detail, sometimes subject to protection orders. Flat access is not always possible. Moreover, banks must ensure that their premises are secure. So far as ATMs are concerned, there may be difficulties in siting machines so that they are convenient both for the able-bodied and for the disabled.

Creating the appropriate environment for disabled people often requires no more than good communication and planning, preferably at an early stage in the design process. Simple but careful modification to existing premises may often make bank premises more accessible to the disabled. Detailed guidelines for access for disabled people to buildings are available from the appropriate organisations. In their submissions, the banks indicate that ease of access for the disabled is one of the many points considered in the design of new premises and alternatives to existing ones.

We are not qualified to lay down or discuss individual specifications but we urge the banks, both in design of new facilities and in modification of the existing ones, to have regard for the specific needs of the disabled. Leicester City Council have gone somewhat further and their Disabled Persons Access Officer has suggested to us that a full survey should be undertaken by a mixed group of disabled people to assess banking facilities, particularly the location of ATMs. This suggestion also has the support of the Spinal Injuries Association. It would be helpful if the banks were to take an active part in such a study.

SENSORY DISABILITY

In recent years considerable progress has been made towards providing blind and visually handicapped people with information about bank services. Much of this information is now available on audio cassettes, in braille and in large print braille and large print statements, together with templates for writing cheques and instructions in braille for operating ATMs. The Royal National Institute for the Blind expressed total satisfaction with the degree of consultation and co-operation between themselves and the banks.

Deafness is a form of disability which is often not apparent and many banks now participate in the Sympathetic Hearing Scheme which enables the deaf and hard of hearing to produce a card identifying themselves. Deaf people are also much aided by illuminated signs, indicating that a cashier is ready to attend to the next customer.

References to section 4

1. Mobile banks of various kinds are discussed in greater detail in an interim report on mobile services in rural areas, a research project being conducted by Dr Malcolm Moseley and Mr John Packman for the School of Environmental Sciences at the University of East Anglia.
2. See for example, National Consumer Council, *Post Office: Special Agent*, NCC, 1979, pp. 34–40.
3. J. M. Williamson, 'The branch of the future: information supermarket', *The Bankers' Magazine*, February 1983, p. 8. Mr Williamson's ideas were developed at greater length in an address to a Retail Banker International conference held in November 1982.
4. *The Times*, 22 June 1983.
5. See also pp. 65–76.
6. Patrick Frazer and Dimitri Vittas, *The Retail Banking Revolution*, Michael Lafferty Publications, 1982, p. 101.
7. National Consumer Council, *Consumers and Credit*, NCC, 1980, pp. 58–60; see also Appendix VI.
8. Centre on Environment for the Handicapped, *Access in the High Street*, p. 3.

Section 5 / New technology

Many of the changes in banking technology that have taken place over the last twenty years or so have consisted of accounting and mechanical handling innovations of a 'back office' nature. Most of these have been of little direct interest to the consumer. More recently, automation has moved to the front of the counter – and increasingly outside the branch building altogether – in a way which has a more significant direct impact on banking services for consumers. 'Back office' and 'front office' forms of automation are closely interlinked, but we are mainly concerned in this section with the implications of developments in technology that affect consumers directly.

The banks began to quicken the pace of automation in the late 1950s and 1960s in response to a number of pressures. These included larger numbers of customers, more transactions and a rise in the relative cost of clerical staff. In the early days of automation, the banks proceeded on a largely independent basis; automation was seen as a way of acquiring a competitive edge over rivals. The other major characteristic of this phase of 'modernisation' was that little account seems to have been taken of customer needs and responses. Lacking the aid of market research techniques (now a familiar tool of head offices), the banks forged ahead in a way which prompted one banking journalist to write of 'the arrogance with which the banks had approached automation, believing blindly that they knew best what was best for their customers' (1).

The banks began to rethink their approach in the mid-1970s. Teething problems with certain key components of mechanisation had given rise to customer dissatisfaction. Computers were demonstrating an apparently progressive tendency towards obsolescence (a problem not confined to the banks, of course). Recession influenced the banks to make more rigorous calculations of the opportunity costs of further automation. This process of re-evaluation has had the important consequence that the banks have become less inclined to press ahead with rapid technological change in the absence of some evidence that customers are ready to accept it; the technical expertise of the major banks is now ahead of its practical application. This is particularly true of personal banking services.

Personal account holders do not necessarily long for automated branches and cashierless lobbies, a point which emerges very clearly from our group discussions with consumers. Customer acceptability limits the pace at which the banks and their competitors can move, a point recognised in a number of major bankers' speeches in the early 1980s. Thus the chairman of Barclays Bank has acknowledged that 'to a degree, technology has outstripped its acceptance by consumers, at least in the UK' (2). One problem for the banks is that bank customers do not constitute a homogeneous category: young people are far more enthusiastic about new delivery systems than their parents and grandparents.

The three technological advances that are most likely to affect consumers directly in the 1980s are the continued development of automated teller machines (ATMs), electronic funds transfer at point of sale (EFTPOS), and home banking. The first of these is already familiar, particularly its cash-dispensing function; the second and third are into the experimental stage.

More generally, the medium- to long-term effect of these changes, which will ultimately revolutionise the basis upon which customers are able to gain access to and transfer their funds, should be to intensify competition in the market for all personal financial services. New technology has the capacity to sever the link between branch networks and the supply of basic banking services by raising the multi-purpose computer terminal to new levels of functional competence. These developments will have far-reaching implications for future market structure, consumer choice and a range of other issues which we discuss below.

Automated teller machines (ATMs)

To use an ATM, the customer inserts a specially provided debit card into a terminal, punches his or her own Personal Identity Number (PIN) into a keypad on the terminal, and can then withdraw cash up to a fixed limit. The latest ATMs can also be used in a number of other ways, such as finding out your current bank balance, and asking for a statement of account, cheque book or information leaflet to be sent, though not all models of ATM provide all these services (see Table 5.1). Some allow the customer to deposit cash. Unlike many machines in the USA and Japan, for example, ATMs currently in use in the UK do not allow the customer to make transfer payments between accounts.

The number of ATMs in use in Britain is increasing rapidly (3). By 30 June 1982 it had reached 3,466 (see Table 5.1), an increase of 54 per cent over the previous twelve months. The banks expect to have 5,382 ATMs installed by 31 December 1983. Seventy per cent of ATMs are through-the-wall machines which can be used in the street and most of them are sited in bank branches. Many of the most recent generation of machines are usable 24 hours a day for seven days a week, though earlier machines still in use offer much more limited hours of service. Over eight million ATM debit cards had been issued by the banks by mid-1982; Access and Barclaycard holders can also draw cash from newer ATMs. Reciprocal arrangements between banks, announced during the course of our enquiry, will greatly enhance the overall usefulness of the ATM facility, enabling Midland customers, for example, to use National Westminster

Table 5.1 Automated teller machines in service in banks, 30 June 1982 (as given in *The Bankers' Magazine*)

Bank	Supplier	Model	ATMs in service 30 June 1982					Brand name	Cards issued (000)
			Total	Through wall	Special lobby	Customer area	Stand alone		
NatWest	NCR	770 1780 1770	628	590	1	11	26	Servicetill	1800
Barclays	NCR	770 1780	358	346	—	—	12	Barclay-bank	1765
		1770	2	—	—	2	—		
	IBM	3624	3	3	—	—	—		
Midland	NCR	1780	427	423	—	2	2	AutoBank	883**
Lloyds	IBM	2984 3614 3624	1312	391	55	784	82	Cashpoint	2271
	Chubb		3			3			
Will/Glyn	IBM	3624	82	78	2	1	1	Cashline	80
Roy Scot	IBM	3614 3624	241	230	6	2	3	Cashline	580
Bank Scot	IBM	3624	168	164	—	—	4	Autoteller	340
Clydesdale	Chubb	MD 6250	128	114	4	1	9	AutoBank	220**
TSB (Engl)	Chubb	MD 6000	10	4	—	6	—	Speedbank	25
TSB (Scot)	Philips	PTS 6690	46	43	—	3	—	Speedbank	45
Yorkshire	NCR	1780	58	57	—	—	1	Minibank	167
All banks			3466	2443	68	815	140		8176

* Includes transactions by Barclaycard holders.
** Can be used in Midland and Clydesdale terminals.
† Mini-statement produced by Cashline machine in response to a balance enquiry request.
‡ Applicable to AutoCash Account holders only.
§ For use by over 5m Barclaycard holders.
§§ 120 Burroughs machines now being installed.

machines; similarly, Barclays, Lloyds, the Bank of Scotland, Williams and Glyn's, and the Royal Bank of Scotland have committed themselves to shared provision.

The building societies are not going to be left behind in the ATM explosion. As we noted in our discussion of consumer access, a Building Societies Association study group has concluded that some form of shared ATM network could be successful, and has discussed a range of commercial possibilities (4). It is also likely that a few large retailers will extend ATM facilities during the next two years.

The advantages of ATMs to the customer are considerable. They go some way to overthrowing the twin tyrannies of place and (more especially) time. The customer no longer needs to present himself or herself at a bank some time between 9.30am and 3.30pm on a weekday to get hold of some of his or her own money. This makes life much easier for the person working in a factory at Trafford Park in Manchester or on a Black Country trading estate, for whom the existence of banks has often seemed irrelevant. ATMs also appeal to those customers who prefer to keep their contacts with bank staff to a minimum. It is not unknown for a queue to form at an ATM while the cashiers inside the bank have empty counters.

The advantages to the customer assume that most ATMs work for most of the time. Their reliability has improved over the last three or four years. One major London clearing bank told us their failure rate in 1982 was down to an average 5 per cent of the available service time over a four-week period. A Scottish clearer said that their failure rate averaged little more than an hour a month. Nevertheless, failures are still common enough to feature in many customers' personal catalogue of bank 'problems'. People still experience the 'swallowing' of their cards; inner-city ATMs still run out of money at weekends; and occasionally there are more serious episodes involving the erroneous debiting of accounts in apparently inexplicable circumstances.

We are particularly concerned with the third of these problems. On 19 January 1981 the *Daily Mirror*'s city editor, Mr Robert Head, published a selection of letters from readers who claimed to have been victim to some form of 'robotic theft'. (An unpublished file of letters was also kindly made available to us by Mr Head.) Total sums of between £5 and £1,300 had been debited from correspondents' accounts following alleged withdrawals from cash dispensers by cash card. In each case the withdrawal (or series of withdrawals) was disputed; some writers claimed – often with great indignation – that their cards could not have been used at a particular time or place to make the withdrawal because no one else had the PIN number, they were many miles away from the machine concerned, and so on. Other letters described incidents in which cash dispensers had paid out money to children who had been 'playing around' or, in one dramatic case, paid out spontaneously to no one at all! The response of the banks had generally been to deny that such things could happen, and to refer complainants to the police.

Many older machines have been replaced since early 1981 but it appears that

Weekly average cash trans per machine	Average value of trans (£)	Additional functions offered				Planned ATMs by 31 Dec 1983	Total no. of branches
		Balance	Statement request	Cheque bk request	Other		
933	24	YES	YES	YES	Reciprocity with Midland planned, plus Access	1000	3226
1248*	29*	YES	YES	—	Cash Advance§ Credit availability§ Pay in notes and cheques at 105 MCs	650 min	2981
662	25	YES	YES	YES	Some credit input. Access cards. Reciprocity with NatWest planned, plus Access	750	2454
718	26	YES	—	—		1600	2343
375	30	YES	—	—	WGB Cashline cards can now be used in RBS Cashline terminals	170	315
1350	32	YES	†	—	RBS Cashline cards usable in WGB terminals	320	588
1000	25	YES	YES	YES		200	565
910	25	YES‡	YES	YES		220	380
470	29	YES	YES	YES	Leaflet request	300§§	1181
300	27	YES	YES	YES	Cash and cheque deposit Leaflet request	80	295
1310	30	YES	—	—	Deposit	92	204
843	27					5382	14 532

Source: The Bankers' Magazine, November 1982

problems remain. An initiative taken by a Portsmouth firm of solicitors, who had raised the issue in a letter to the *Law Society Gazette* (of 15 June 1983), has prompted a few other solicitors to give details of cases about which they had been consulted. We have generously been allowed to see the relevant correspondence; we find the cases outlined disturbing, both as regards the facts described and the bank attitudes revealed. We return to these issues below.

More generally, ATMs bring with them four kinds of disadvantage to the customer. First, a customer drawing cash from an ATM usually has his or her account debited instantaneously. This eliminates the small advantage to the consumer of 'float' when cashing a cheque, an advantage which has varying usefulness depending where the cheque is cashed, and how long, therefore, it takes to clear. However, the 'float' facility involved in using a cheque is a matter of custom not of right, and is self-evidently discounted by hundreds of thousands of bank customers using ATMs every day of the week.

Secondly, under existing law debit cards used in ATMs provide inferior protection to the customer against dishonest use (theft) and mechanical error, compared with the terms and conditions of cheque use. In practice, the banks claim they give the customer the benefit of the doubt in cases of dispute but, as we have indicated, this does not always happen. Legally, the UK customer is less well protected in such circumstances than his or her US counterpart. The growing determination of the banks to clamp down on fraud, though wholly admirable in intention, could have damaging consequences for innocent but careless bank customers.

Thirdly, a large number of the first generation of ATMs still in use (by Lloyds Bank in particular) do not provide printed records of debit transactions. Granted the fears that many people still have that budgetary errors can get them into financial difficulties, and on the wider grounds that printed information should always be given when financial transactions are made, this is regrettable. We urge the replacement or modification of such machines as soon as possible.

Fourthly, many customers are worried about personal security. PIN procedures work satisfactorily providing the customer can keep the number in his or her head. Clearly, the customer carries some responsibility for behaving sensibly, but many users find that they are unable to commit their PIN number to memory and therefore carry with them a written record. If the bank's original written notification of the PIN is retained, or the PIN is written down somewhere else, there is always a risk that an unauthorised user will in some circumstances be able to marry the ATM card with its PIN. Even cardholders who take reasonable precautions are vulnerable in this way.

It might also seem that ATMs make their users vulnerable to robbery or mugging. We have uncovered no evidence, however, that this is so in practice. Lloyds Bank is leading the trend in siting ATMs in special lobbies, to minimise security risks. A lobby of this kind usually forms an ante-room to a bank. Out of opening hours, the customer gets into the lobby by wiping his or her ATM card through an electronic lock. ATMs in lobbies are still fairly scarce in the UK (there were 68 in mid-1982) though increasingly common in North America.

In the early years of their introduction in the UK, it seemed as though the technical problems and unreliability of ATMs would prevent them from becoming extensively used. The situation has changed in the last two or three years. There is now no doubt that, in spite of the minor disadvantages we have mentioned, they have made it easier for consumers to withdraw money and have become very popular. What future developments in ATMs would benefit consumers?

First, consumers would find it very helpful if ATM sites were less confined to bank branches. In June 1982 there were 140 ATMs sited elsewhere – a very small number for the whole of the UK. We would like to see more ATMs in factories, hospitals, colleges, railway and bus stations, shops and shopping centres and post offices. We appreciate the problems associated with security and with making sure that the machines don't run out of money, but these should not be insuperable. A more important problem is whether an ATM sited away from bank premises will be used enough to make it an economic proposition. We were told that an ATM currently costs approximately £25,000 to buy and £2,500 per year to run.

We are unable to measure what these figures mean in terms of minimum use requirements, but one way of solving this problem would be if many or all ATMs sited away from bank premises accepted the complete range of different ATM cards, perhaps including building society cards. This would make them more economically viable. The present situation with non-bank sites is that the banks compete for the franchise of, say, a particular hospital and the successful bidder instals an ATM for its own customers. It is difficult to argue that this is an objectionable procedure on competitive grounds, but in practical terms it is worth examining the possibility of more widespread sharing arrangements.

The banks point out that there are a number of practical difficulties, such as the allocation of responsibility for maintenance and repairs, and keeping the shared ATM supplied with cash. Also, it is said that ATM sharing reduces the speed of technological change to that of the least innovative partner. However, these arguments would appear to be undermined by the sharing agreements already concluded; we see no reason in principle why they should not be extended, even if only on a negotiated agency basis.

From the consumer's point of view, ATM sharing brings great benefits in terms of increasing the number of locations at which he or she has access to the banking system. In Japan, the banks have developed a network of over two hundred shared ATMs in public places to which all customers have access. The evidence is that such a development in the UK would be welcomed by consumers. In particular, shared ATMs provide some hope for rural and less densely populated areas where bank branches are few and far between and single bank ATMs are unviable.

Secondly, consumers would benefit if more ATMs were to carry out a wider range of functions, like accepting deposits of cash and cheques and enabling funds to be transferred between accounts. These improvements are more important than mechanical gimmicks like 'talking ATMs' (5).

Thirdly, consumers would benefit if institutions other than banks installed ATMs. At the time of writing, a number of further developments by building societies were under discussion, including at least two schemes for shared networks.

Electronic funds transfer at point of sale (EFTPOS)

Potentially, EFTPOS has far-reaching implications for shoppers and bank customers. One EFTPOS scheme, called Counterplus, was introduced in 1982 by Clydesdale Bank and BP at a filling station in Aberdeen. It is available to customers with Autobank cards issued by the Clydesdale, Midland and Northern Banks, all part of the Midland group, and to Midland group Access cardholders. When paying for petrol, the customer hands his or her Autobank card to the cashier. The cashier 'wipes' it through the terminal, which is on-line to the Clydesdale Bank's computer, and the customer keys in his or her PIN on a keypad. There are two parts to the process – authorisation and debiting. Authorisation involves verifying card and PIN details, and checking that the card limit (which in this case varies between customers) has not been exceeded. If the transaction is authorised, ACCEPTED appears on both the cashier's and the customer's screens. If the transaction is not authorised, REJECTED appears on the customer's screen. The cashier's screen indicates: wrong PIN used; or card out of date; or not authorised (no further details). In the last two instances, the customer is asked to pay by some other means.

The customer may use Counterplus to draw out cash. For example, a customer buying £5 of petrol may have his or her account debited by £15, taking away £10 cash. This combination of funds transfer and cash-dispensing facilities has proved popular with customers. As a consequence, Clydesdale and BP have announced that Counterplus is to be extended to 17 petrol stations in the west of Scotland and four further sites in Aberdeen (6).

There have been other experimental EFTPOS schemes in the UK. Barclays Bank has carried out a trial, called Counterspeed, at a number of filling stations in the Norwich area, in conjunction with several oil companies. There have been many experiments in other countries, notably France and the United States.

EFTPOS is best considered in the context of changes in retailing technology, some of which are already in use. Of particular importance has been the development of a standardised system for printing bar codes on packaging of goods, and the introduction of technology linking cash registers with computers so that automatic checkout operations are now possible. A laser scanner 'reads' the information contained in the bar codes and prints the appropriate price on the till slip. Evidence presented to the Office of Fair Trading suggests that during 1983 most of the major supermarket chains will introduce bar-code scanning of prices at checkout in some of their stores, and that by 1985 ten to twenty per cent of their stores will be using laser scanners.

Simultaneously, stimulated partly by the rapid growth in plastic card and other forms of fraud world-wide, the credit and travel and entertainment card companies and others have developed credit authorisation technology which allows retailers to make almost instant checks on the credit-worthiness of their customers at the point at which goods are being bought. For example, the nine department stores in the Army and Navy group are now able to verify the credit-worthiness of customers using American Express cards by keying into the American Express computer in Phoenix, Arizona, via satellite link, directly from retail terminals. The whole operation is done in seconds, less time than it takes to get out a card from a wallet or a handbag.

EFTPOS has the capacity to link innovations in retailing technology, payment authorisation and direct debiting of customers' bank accounts – although there is a variety of different ways of achieving this. The banks' interest is that a comprehensive, national EFTPOS network would reduce the proportion of payments made by cash and cheque which, particularly in the case of cheques, are relatively expensive to service, and increase the proportion of cheaper automated payments.

However, the numerous EFTPOS experiments in the UK and other countries have yet to be integrated anywhere into successful payment systems. Indeed, the former Director of the Inter-Bank Research Organisation has remarked that '. . . the world is littered with unsuccessful POS systems . . .' (7). Most schemes have failed to get off the ground for one or both of two reasons. First, the volume of transactions going through any one system has not been high enough to justify the installation and running costs of the computer-linked retail terminals connected. This has been generally true of EFTPOS experiments involving only the customers of one bank, leaving people with accounts at other banks to continue paying by cash or cheque. Secondly, and this applies even to some multi-bank schemes, the direct benefits to retailers and consumers have not seemed big enough to make them enthusiastic. The Counterplus scheme in Aberdeen appears to have been exceptional in this respect.

What are the potential benefits of EFTPOS to consumers? It could reduce queues and congestion at store checkouts. Secondly, some consumers might prefer using this payment method to paying with cash or a cheque. Also, the possibility of drawing cash over and above the amount of the bill being paid, as in the Aberdeen scheme, could improve consumers' access to a key banking service, though this is not a feature of all EFTPOS experiments.

There are several possible disadvantages to consumers or, at least, some questions that have still to be answered. First, and most importantly, how will the costs and benefits be shared out between banks, retailers and consumers? The new computer-linked terminals in shops and garages are likely to be expensive, and whether the capital costs are paid by the banks or the retailers, consumers will want to be assured that they will not be asked to foot the bill. Indeed, in the longer term, consumers would expect EFTPOS to reduce either bank charges or prices. The financial aspects of EFTPOS are not at all clear: or at least, no attempt has yet been made to spell them out to consumers.

Secondly, consumers are not likely to be enthusiastic about a situation in which they go into a shop or a filling station to find that the EFTPOS system is available to the customers of only one or perhaps two banks, and not others. Retailers are also unlikely to find this form of discrimination acceptable. Aspects of this problem, and of the desirability and practicality of a shared EFTPOS system on something approaching a national grid, have been the subject of prolonged and confidential discussions among the UK banks under the auspices of the Committee of London Clearing Bankers, with little involvement of retailers and even less of consumers. These discussions have been taking place on and off for five years, and have led to the rejection of at least two major schemes.

Thirdly, if EFTPOS is introduced widely, it should be as an additional way in which consumers can pay for goods or services. Consumers should not be forced, either directly or indirectly (by punitive charging), away from the use of cash, cheques or credit cards. In respect of cash, this is unlikely. Many customers will not qualify for a POS card. Others will simply prefer not to use one. The possible longer-term displacement of cheques and of credit cards is more problematic. We would oppose the use by retailers of the introduction of POS technology as an excuse for excluding cheques or, more likely, the imposition by any bank of charges for the use of cheques which went beyond cost recovery to the point of over-charging. We endorse the OFT's cautionary observations on this point (8). We also believe that those customers who, over the last decade or so, have been persuaded by the banks that credit cards are useful should not, following the introduction of EFTPOS, find their freedom to use credit cards restricted or penalised. In current market circumstances this seems improbable, but banks are not necessarily devoted to the idea that customers have the right to choose how they pay. For example, a 'senior' British banker who writes pseudonymously for the *Retail Banker International* under the name of 'Walter Cornelis', referring to the OFT report, wrote in October 1982:

'The Office of Fair Trading seems to believe that customers have a historic right to choose which method they use to make retail payments. This is nonsense. Customers have never had any right to choose how they pay. It is retailers who have the right to choose how they are paid. . . .' (9)

In formal terms, this may be correct. From the viewpoint of consumer choice and convenience, it is a quite unacceptable attitude.

Fourthly, EFTPOS must match traditional UK banking standards in the privacy that the consumer can expect. This is as true for the apparently trivial matter of the design of visual display units (VDUs) in shops and filling stations as for the setting of encryption (coding) standards in electronic transmission of financial data. Electronic transmission opens up the possibility of the unauthorised capture, storage and use of financial data, for example by retailers building up mailing lists by getting access to the names and addresses of EFTPOS customers. The principle that the customer, and only the customer, has the right to authorise disclosure of his or her personal financial information must remain paramount.

Fifthly, consumers should be given a printed record of every EFTPOS transaction. A printed record enables consumers to check their bank statements and gives them the start of an 'audit trail' if there is any error or discrepancy.

Sixthly, EFTPOS introduces new possibilities for fraud or error. A consumer should not be penalised unless his or her responsibility is established. This appears to be the normal practice of the banks when fraud or alleged fraud takes place, though the situation is less clear when there are errors. However, we know of one instance in which a customer of one of the major UK credit card companies was persistently and wrongly accused of fraud, causing great distress to the family concerned. The development of EFTPOS raises important questions of customer liability which are discussed below.

Seventhly, EFTPOS should not affect the consumer's rights in respect of defective goods.

Eighthly, on-line EFTPOS systems enable the customer's account to be debited instantaneously. A customer who would otherwise have paid by cheque loses the benefit of the time it takes for a cheque to be cleared. It is interesting that in the Counterplus scheme the Clydesdale Bank has deliberately delayed the timing of debits, so that the consumer is no better nor worse off than if he or she had paid by cheque. However, in any future EFTPOS developments it is quite open to banks to plan for customers' accounts to be debited instantaneously. We cannot object to this, but we do consider that customers should be clearly informed about the timing of debits.

Finally, the number of consumers able to use EFTPOS would be greatly increased if accounts in financial institutions other than banks could be debited. Building society accounts are the most obvious example.

There is still a great deal of uncertainty about how EFTPOS will emerge in practice. A working document leaked to *Retail Banker International* in March 1983 indicated that EFTPOS is seen by the banks as 'a vehicle for improving profitability' which promises a rapid and substantial rate of return on investment (10). This expectation differs considerably from the views of some bankers and commentators who take a sceptical view of the financial viability of EFTPOS (11). At the time of writing, the banks had not publicly gone beyond a reaffirmation of support for the development of a national EFTPOS system in general terms, and notification that new trials 'could start in 1986' (12).

Home banking

Verbraucherbank is a small, relatively new bank in Hamburg, West Germany. Using a telephone and a modified tv set, its customers may check their bank balances, call up a statement of their recent bank transactions on the tv screen, and move money from one account to another. They can't deposit or withdraw cash at home, though they can order money to be sent to them by post.

The Chemical Bank of New York began a small-scale home banking service in

1983, using a system which links customers' own personal computers with the bank's computer. Using a combination of telephone, PIN and account numbers, the customer can link his or her own computer with the bank's to carry out a similar range of operations.

These are two overseas examples of advanced developments in home banking. In the UK, the Nottingham Building Society has announced home banking plans which involve Prestel (British Telecom's videotext system) and the Bank of Scotland. Customers will be offered a current account that pays interest on credit balances, and bill payment and information facilities similar to those already described, plus a full range of the usual building society facilities and a Visa card. The first stage of the development involves corporate bodies (not individual consumers) who are willing to deposit £10,000 in the Nottingham Building Society in return for a free Prestel adaptor and keyboard. The second stage will take in any of the Society's 150,000 customers who are prepared to keep a minimum sum of (probably) £3,000 in an ordinary society account – perhaps ten thousand investors would currently qualify. The third stage will see the extension of the facility to other less wealthy customers who are prepared to pay a rental for the adaptor. 'Free' banking will be offered in certain circumstances; charges otherwise look like being competitive.

Some UK banks are also planning home banking experiments. Midland Bank, Clydesdale Bank (part of the Midland Group) and British Linen Bank (a subsidiary of the Bank of Scotland) all have home banking plans in preparation.

The technology for home banking takes various forms. Some involve the use of a home computer as well as a telephone and a visual display unit or tv set. Others require a specially adapted tv set and a telephone. The possible development of fully fledged interactive cable services in the UK provides another framework within which home banking may develop. Different hybrids of these various forms are also possible. We can assert with some confidence that home banking is a realistic prospect for consumers in the second half of the 1980s, although it is not yet possible to say which particular technology will be best or cheapest.

What advantages does home banking promise for consumers? Above all, it means that consumers will be able to carry out a wide range of banking operations without having to go to a branch. The substantial benefits for housebound and isolated consumers are self-evident, but most consumers will also have vastly improved access to banking services.

In the long term, home banking is likely to be of more significance to consumers than the EFTPOS developments we described above. However, some of the points we have raised in relation to EFTPOS also apply to home banking. The most important of these is security. Stories about computer freaks who can use computers either to commit fraud or to gain access to information are commonplace. Intrusions don't have to be fraudulent. In April 1980, a group of students at a private school in New York used a portable keyboard and a pay phone to lock into the computer system of GTE Telenet Communications Corporation in Virginia. This is linked to Bell Canada's Datapac and allowed the students to get access to the databases of 21 Canadian companies and universities on 42 occasions. The list of companies affected included Canada Cement which lost twenty per cent of its database as a consequence of the tampering (13).

Many computer experts say that it is not possible to devise totally secure computer systems. The banks tend to play down this point, for obvious reasons, but consumers will want some explicit assurances that developments in home banking and other forms of electronic funds transfer will not allow unauthorised people to get access to their bank accounts and that the bank (or building society) will accept responsibility for the consequences of any unauthorised access. It will be wholly unacceptable to consumers if they have to stand the loss for security failures which are not their responsibility.

One obvious limitation of home banking is that consumers cannot withdraw cash. From the consumer viewpoint, the development of home banking needs to be accompanied by continuing improvements in ways of withdrawing cash, of which, as we have seen, an expanded system of shared ATMs offers the best prospects.

Electronic banking and the law

A number of legal issues are raised by the introduction of computerisation and other forms of new technology by the banks and their competitors. Legislation has already been passed to deal with some of the evidential problems (14); the legal problems associated with the truncation of cheques were discussed in section 3.

In this section we deal with the legal issues arising from the electronic transfer of funds – principally the use of debit cards in automated teller machines and in point-of-sale transactions (EFTPOS).

The existing law of banking evolved to deal with nineteenth-century paper-based methods of banking. Electronic banking is simply outside the scope of legislation covering specific transactions. But the law has developed an extensive code to cope with paper-based systems of conducting business, and it is necessary to say a little more about that by way of background.

We have touched elsewhere upon the law of cheques in relation to bankers' obligations to honour cheques and to obey the precise instructions of customers. 'Cheques' evolved from the practice of merchants, in the mid-seventeenth century, of drawing bills or notes on their accounts with goldsmiths, and handing these instruments to their creditors in the settlement of debts.

A cheque is a type of bill of exchange which in turn is a 'negotiable instrument', that is, it may be written out in favour of one person who may in turn (by merely handing it over and normally also endorsing it with his or her signature) transfer to someone else the entitlement to be paid on the cheque.

Specific legislation governing the use of bills of exchange and cheques was made necessary by a growth in their use. We have already referred to the importance of such statutes as the Bills of Exchange Act 1882 which deals, for example, with the allocation of financial loss between banker, customer and third parties when cheques are lost or stolen and subsequent statutes like the Cheques Act 1957 which, among other things, eliminates the need for banks to examine most endorsements on cheques.

Between them, the common law and parliamentary legislation therefore provide a comprehensive code on cheques. The law is well developed in relation to the issuing of cheques, their crossing, determining the 'holder' of a cheque, liability for fraud and theft claims by third parties and so on. By contrast, most of this law does not relate to electronic banking. The banks are therefore free to write their own terms and conditions which vary from institution to institution.

THE LEGAL ISSUES

The main legal questions of direct concern to consumers which arise from the use of debit cards in ATMs and (prospectively) in any EFTPOS system are:

* what is the legal status of a debit card under existing law?
* are safeguards needed against unsolicited cards?
* should there be documentary evidence of an electronic transaction?
* what are the consequences of misuse after loss or theft?
* how are mistakes and incorrect records to be resolved?
* should card issuers be liable for the default of suppliers?
* how is the customer's privacy to be protected?

THE LEGAL STATUS OF DEBIT CARDS

As mentioned, no legislation explicitly covers the electronic transfer of funds by debit cards. Such cards perform many of the functions of a cheque but they are not caught by the definition of the Bills of Exchange Act 1882: they are certainly not an order 'in writing' addressed by one person to a banker and signed by the person giving it. More significantly, a payment by debit card is not negotiable, as a cheque may be, and cannot be stopped where the transfer of funds is instantaneous.

In some respects, particularly in an EFTPOS system, debit cards resemble cash, and they may indeed be thought of, in part, as a new form of currency. But a card is considerably more sophisticated than a bank note or coin of the realm. In an ATM machine, it is relaying instructions or requests (directly or indirectly) to the customer's bank. More complicated commands, all with legal consequences, are set off by the use of a card in an EFTPOS system.

In other respects, a debit card resembles the familiar credit card. It is different in that it can be used without a signature which (for credit cards as for cheques) can later be used to authenticate a transaction. But it is certainly similar in physical appearance to a credit card and may perform some similar functions. Both can give access to cash and can be used to acquire goods or services. A 'debit' card can in fact be used to obtain credit where overdraft facilities have been provided. And some credit cards can already be used in ATMs to obtain cash which is debited to the credit card holder's account. The blurring of the distinction between credit and debit cards would, in fact, become hazier still if (as is possible) a single card were to be issued by a bank to perform all these combined functions.

The law at present does not fit neatly with these developments. A credit card holder is protected by the Consumer Credit Act 1974 which, among other things, imposes a limit on the customer's liability in the case of fraud and theft; requires card issuers to provide information about interest rates; and imposes liabilities on the card issuer where the retailer has defaulted on his obligations to the customer.

There is some doubt about the extent to which the Consumer Credit Act currently covers debit cards. Where such a card can be used to obtain credit (for example by creating or enlarging an overdraft) then it would appear to be within the definition of 'credit token' set out in section 14 of the Act (15). This also seems to be the case where the card may be used in a machine owned by another bank. In such cases, the Act may then provide some safeguards and may have an effect on some of the transactions involving the use of the card. On the other hand, it seems that the Act has no application at all to a card which cannot be used to obtain any form of credit or to obtain cash from another bank's ATM.

Current arrangements can only lead to confusion and inconsistency. Let us assume that a person owns a cheque book, a bank credit card, and a debit card, and that all three are stolen and used fraudulently. It is unlikely that the customer would bear any financial loss for the use of the cheque book. For the use of the credit card, liability will be limited to the sum of £50 (once section 84 of the Consumer Credit Act 1974 is in force) until the card issuer is informed, after which the card holder will normally be under no further liability. On the other hand, the customer's liability for the fraudulent use of the debit card is not restricted by statute – unless, of course, the card is one which is caught by the 1974 Act. We believe that these uncertainties and inconsistencies can only be resolved by legislation.

ARE SAFEGUARDS NEEDED AGAINST UNSOLICITED DEBIT CARDS?

In the USA, federal and state laws have been concerned to ensure that plastic cards giving access to EFT devices will not be distributed indiscriminately to consumers who have not properly requested them. There is a parallel in the Consumer Credit Act which prohibits the unsolicited issue of a credit card – the definition of which may, as we have seen, also catch some debit cards.

The security hazards of sending out unsolicited debit cards would clearly be immense, and it is a matter of speculation whether banks would ever want to do so. The legal issues involved need to be reviewed when EFTPOS plans are more advanced.

SHOULD THERE BE DOCUMENTARY EVIDENCE OF AN ELECTRONIC
TRANSACTION?

One of the main disadvantages of a debit card, as compared to a cheque, could be
the absence of any documentary proof that a transaction has taken place or of its
details. The absence of any written record also makes it that much more difficult
to resolve disputes over errors, systems failure or fraud. We have already made
clear our view that a written record should be provided for every transaction
involving a debit card. In the absence of universal adoption of this principle, we
believe that (as in the USA) specific legislation is necessary.

WHAT ARE THE CONSEQUENCES OF MISUSE AFTER LOSS OR THEFT?

Holders of some cards appear to be protected by the Consumer Credit Act if the
card is stolen or lost. A 'pure' debit card – which cannot be used to obtain credit
and cannot be used at other banks – does not have the same protection. Fear of
the consequences of loss or theft are chief amongst consumers' worries. Most of
the terms and conditions for existing cash cards hold the customer liable for all
amounts paid out through the use of the card. This liability generally continues
until proper notice of loss or theft is given. National Westminster's conditions
say, for example:

> 'I/we agree that I/we will remain liable for any disbursements made in respect
> of a SERVICECARD before such notice is received by you as if I/we had used
> such SERVICECARD personally.'

It may be weeks, or even months, before loss or theft is discovered. Under the
conditions used by most banks, the customer remains liable for any use made.
Barclays Bank does, however, place a limit on the customer's liability:

> 'Until the Bank has received such notification the account holder(s) will
> remain liable for any disbursements effected against the lost or stolen card, *but
> provided the account holder has acted in good faith the liability shall not exceed
> £30.*' [emphasis added]

A stolen or lost card should cause any loss only if the PIN number is available
with it. Banks are naturally concerned about their liabilities if the family or
friends of the card holder should (by intent or accidentally) get hold of both card
and number. The same is true if a written record of the number should be lost or
stolen along with the card.

Nevertheless, the dangers of computer and other fraud mean that it remains
possible for an unauthorised person to make use of a stolen or lost card. It is also
entirely possible for someone to obtain possession of both card and number in
circumstances which fall well short of negligence on the part of the card holder.

A card may be stolen by someone who has previously observed its use; a PIN
number may be obtained by false pretences; a card and record of the number
may be stolen from different parts of the owner's home. A card holder's

'unlimited' liability for the unauthorised use of a debit card is of greater concern than with loss or theft of a credit card. The result will be the transfer of funds held on deposit as opposed to an increase in the 'debt' due to the credit card company.

We believe that legislation, modelled on the Consumer Credit Act, should set limits on the liability of customers in the event of unauthorised transfers. There should, in particular, be a financial limit on misuse where the customer has acted in good faith. There should also be a statutory guarantee that no further liability can be incurred after loss of the card has been notified. We would also like to see a provision, as in the Consumer Credit Act, requiring the bank to give the name, address and telephone number of a person to whom notice of loss should be given. Even with the protection of these proposals, the owner of a lost or stolen card would still be worse off than the owner of a lost or stolen cheque book who (in the absence of negligence) cannot be held liable for any misuse of those cheques.

There may also be a need to define in legislation the respective liabilities of banks and retailers where a stolen or lost card has successfully been used in an EFTPOS system.

HOW ARE MISTAKES AND INCORRECT RECORDS TO BE RESOLVED?

Human error, systems failure, malfunctions, fire, flood and computer fraud might, as we have seen, also lead to wrongful deductions from the customer's account which may not be detected (if at all) until some time after the event. An international study conducted for the American Institute of Internal Auditors concluded that the following, in order of frequency, were the potential losses arising from the use of computer systems:

    (i) errors and omissions;
    (ii) improper controls;
   (iii) inadequate system design;
   (iv) fraud and defalcation;
    (v) failure to comply with standards or procedures (16).

The common law principle is, of course, that a bank may make a deduction from a customer's account only if it can establish that it has been so instructed – whether by cheque, or by some other means. Conditions of use for existing cashcards seek to modify this principle with such provisions as:

'You may debit my/our account with all amounts withdrawn through any of your Cashline machines by means of any cards issued to me/us . . .' (Royal Bank of Scotland)

or

'You are irrevocably authorised to debit any account in my name . . . with all amounts disbursed by the use of any Cashpoint cards and personal numbers which are issued to me . . .' (Lloyds Bank)

Such conditions may be caught by the Unfair Contract Terms Act, in which case they would only be valid if the bank could prove that they were reasonable. Whatever the legal position, we do not believe that it is acceptable, as a matter of practice, for a bank to hold the customer automatically liable for each and every transaction which the bank claims has been conducted with the card. We have already dealt with lost and stolen cards. So far as alleged mistakes are concerned, we believe that the banks should be more ready to investigate the claims of their customers.

A real problem for customers is that there is usually little or no concrete evidence and little or no opportunity to challenge what their bank says. A bank holding the customer's account can deduct the disputed amount and the initiative is thrown on to the customer. Determined legal action by an aggrieved customer may lead to a final resolution but the obstacles to conventional court action are likely to inhibit most forms of challenge. In the correspondence mentioned on page 68 above, we were struck by the frustration obviously felt at the lack of a realistic forum for these disputes to be resolved. This was reflected in the correspondence from solicitors:

'. . . my clients are very simple people who are not prepared to face a bank in circumstances such as this, even with my support and help.'

The client of another solicitor claimed that £500 was withdrawn over a period of three weeks. At the time of several of the withdrawals he was able to establish that he was in a different town. The solicitor wrote, however:

'. . . our client may have a cause of action against the Bank, although the position is by no means certain and as the amount involved is only £500 [sic] it may be a Legal Aid Certificate would be difficult to obtain.'

We have considered the case for some form of statutory error correction procedure. Under recent US law, for example, the consumer may notify an error to the bank within 60 days of receipt of a statement. If the bank cannot establish the validity of the transaction within 10 days, the money must be returned to the customer's account. If no error is subsequently found, the customer must return the money to the bank.

Provisions on these lines do shift the initiative to the bank. But they are less necessary where there is no 'settled account procedure'. They are also open to abuse by customers. We would prefer to see the introduction of simpler and more informal means of investigating and resolving disputes. A Banking Ombudsman (as discussed in section 7) would, in our view, eliminate the need for any special legislation to deal with errors.

SHOULD CARD-HOLDERS BE LIABLE FOR THE DEFAULT OF SUPPLIERS?

This is an issue which only arises where a card is used in an EFTPOS system. Section 75 of the Consumer Credit Act provides that (amongst others) credit card issuers are jointly liable if suppliers are in breach of their contract with the card user. Should a similar principle – known as the right of 'charge-back' in North America – be established for debit cards where they are used to pay for goods or services which prove legally unsatisfactory?

The banks believe that it is inappropriate for section 75 to apply to debit cards. Their argument is that such a card, used to take money from a current account, is not within the debtor/creditor/supplier type of agreement at which the section may have been primarily directed.

However, the Director-General of Fair Trading has taken a different view. Sir Gordon Borrie wrote in his introduction to the OFT report on micro-electronics and retailing:

'Section 75 of the Consumer Credit Act implemented the Crowther Committee's recommendation that all kinds of connected lender should be liable for representations relating to goods made by the seller and for defects in title, fitness or purpose. I regard this as a significant safeguard for the consumer and I would view with concern any substantial erosion of it. In relation to EFT, therefore, I consider that in any circumstances parallel to those in which section 75 applies, a debit card company should have a similar liability. It is also for consideration whether liability should attach in all cases to a debit-card issuing company which enters into agreements with retailers to facilitate the use of debit cards. The basis for the Crowther Committee's recommendation which led to Section 75 was that the lender and the retailer were engaged in a "joint venture"; a debit-card company and a retailer might be said to be in a similar relationship.' (17)

Where a bank's computer has been programmed to allow a debit card to be used to create or increase an overdraft, credit is being provided to the customer. The bank has the ability to deny that credit. Parliament has thought it right to provide for joint liability where credit is provided by a 'connected lender'. This has been a valuable benefit for consumers, especially where a supplier has gone out of business. We do not see why debit cards which are, with the bank's 'electronic' approval, used to obtain credit should be treated differently from other forms of credit.

It would clearly make direct debiting systems less attractive to consumers if the existence of this legal duty made banks more restrictive in accepting debits which put accounts into overdraft by electronic means than they are by cheques – refusing to pay a £35 grocery bill because the account goes a few pence into the red, for instance. We can see no reason why banks should not set their charges for such transactions at a level which will cover whatever risk is involved.

On the other hand, we see no reason to make banks jointly liable for what is bought when a debit card is used without any overdraft facility. In that case, the card will be performing the same function as a cheque or cash. (But for a contrary view see *The Canadian Payment System and the Computer: Issues for Law Reform* (18).)

HOW IS THE CONSUMER'S PRIVACY TO BE PROTECTED?

The anxieties about the loss of privacy which is threatened by EFT have already been discussed. In section 6, we describe the general common law duty upon bankers to keep confidential their clients' affairs. Most privacy problems with EFT are likely to arise from the technology itself and the ease with which authorised and unauthorised people may have access to the information which it holds. Consumers may be concerned with the accumulation of information and access to it, and disclosure of it.

Overseas experience suggests that it is impossible to guarantee total security. One commentator has written:

> 'Recent studies have shown that the range of frauds perpetrated by unauthorised access to files is wider than previously imagined. The short truth of the matter is that no existing security system is secure: wires may be tapped, operators bribed, codes broken . . . Security is a problem with no apparent total solution.' (19)

The American National Commission on EFT came to the view that the privacy issue was its most difficult and important problem and similar conclusions have been reached by a number of Canadian reports.

Financial information about an individual can be very valuable. The increasing use of plastic cards will enable bank computers to keep tabs on a customer's travel and spending patterns. For the EFTPOS transaction there will be recorded information on the time, place, amount and the type of goods or services acquired.

Data protection legislation is obviously relevant here. Once an independent Registrar is established, as proposed by the government's current Bill, he or she will have a duty to enforce observance of certain principles relating to personal data held on computers. The eighth principle calls for 'appropriate security measures' for personal data. The Bill goes on to say that:

> 'Regard shall be had –
> a) to the nature of the personal data and the harm that would result from such access, alteration, disclosure, loss or destruction as are mentioned in this principle; and
> b) to the place where the personal data are stored, to security measures programmed into the relevant equipment and to measures taken for ensuring the reliability of staff, having access to the data.' (20)

We are doubtful that general data protection legislation will, by itself, be sufficient unless statutory codes of practice are introduced which, at the time of writing, seems improbable. We would like to see the common law duty of a bank to keep confidential its clients' affairs expressly spelt out in relation to EFT. In other words, banks should be expressly liable to their customers for any breach of this principle. There may also be a need for liability to be imposed where incorrect information is disclosed (21).

A COMPREHENSIVE EFT STATUTE

The need for legislation on some of the specific issues we have identified suggests that a comprehensive statute is needed to provide a legal framework for EFT. Although the Committee of London Clearing Bankers put it to us that 'the rights and benefits as between customer and the Bank can be covered by contract . . .', it went on to accept that:

'. . . the interests of third parties may need to be governed by statute. Examination will have to be made before long of the question whether some new form of statutory protection is desirable in order that the use of such (electronic) forms of money transfer are as recognised in law as bills of exchange have been and in order that the rights of the customer, the banker and third parties are adequately defined and protected.' (22)

America is one of the few countries so far to have enacted specific legislation for electronic payment methods: the Electronic Funds Transfer Act, and Regulation E of the Board of Governors of the Federal Reserve System. The main provisions have been summarised as follows (23):

  (i) Conditions for the issue of access devices (plastic cards) are laid down. Unsolicited debit cards may be issued, but only if they require validation at the customer's request before they can be used.

 (ii) The liability of customers for unauthorised transfers is limited to $50 if notified within two days after discovery of the theft of a card. This limit increases to $500 if notice is given after two days; and becomes unlimited if unauthorised transfers are not reported within 60 days after the mailing of an account statement.

(iii) There must be a full disclosure to the customer of the terms and conditions under which the bank provides EFT services, and changes in the terms must similarly be disclosed.

(iv) Terminals operated by customers must be provided with a means of giving all customers who want them written receipts for transactions;

 (v) Institutions must either inform customers when each direct credit has been received or else inform them when a credit has not been received on time. Conditions are also laid down for customer authorisation of direct debits.

(vi) Institutions are given fixed time limits within which all errors notified less than 60 days after receipt of the statement must be investigated and regulated.

The EFT Act sets up procedures for the notification and resolution of errors, and requires clear language in automated banking rules. The Board of Governors of the Federal Reserve System has itself prepared a very attractive and comprehensive booklet on consumer protection and the Electronic Funds Transfer Act, *Alice in Debitland* (24).

Apart from providing the appropriate legal framework, we believe that a comprehensive EFT statute is needed to act as the vehicle for the specific safeguards which we have proposed and would deal with issues (such as third party rights) beyond the direct scope of this report. To sum up:

* the existence of a solid body of common law and statute law has, on the whole, served the customer well so far as paper-based transactions are concerned. There is, by contrast, a legal vacuum so far as electronic banking is concerned;
* the existing laws developed slowly as problems arose with the leisurely development of paper-based transactions. The pace of technological change and the potential volume of business handled by automated processes mean that such an evolutionary approach to the development of a new legal framework would be inappropriate;
* given the potential exposure of the customer, it is desirable that, as far as possible, the legal safeguards should be as rigorous for debit cards as for cheques and credit cards;
* it is not in the interests of banks, their customers or third parties that the development of electronic banking should be shrouded in uncertainties and inconsistencies in the law. There should be certainty and uniformity as to the respective rights and obligations of banks, customers and third parties;
* statute law is needed to ensure that a written record is provided for each transaction;
* it is needed to place the customer's liabilities for lost or stolen debit cards on a similar basis as for credit cards;
* it may be needed to allocate risks as between banker and retailer for unauthorised use of a card;
* such an Act is likely to be needed to guarantee the customer's right to privacy and to provide specific remedies when that is threatened or broken;
* the same legislation could be used to make such amendments as are needed to the Bills of Exchange Act to facilitate the development of cheque truncation. (See section 3.)

We are not arguing that the further development of electronic banking should be conditional upon the introduction of legislation, but that it would be a mistake to defer legislation until such time that a proliferation of foreseeable problems have undermined public confidence in the new technologies. Legislation along the lines that we have proposed will be very effective in allaying many of the anxieties that consumers have about new banking technology. Moreover, not all those who offer debit cards will be banks; some may not adopt the high standards of commercial practice that characterise the clearing banks.

References to section 5

1. Tim Hindle, 'The customer comes first', *The Banker*, March 1980, p. 89.
2. Deryk Vander Weyer, 'The economics of retail banking in the future', speech to an international summer school for young bankers, St Andrews, June 1982.

3. See p. 143 for Northern Ireland.
4. *Financial Times*, 8 March 1983.
5. *Financial Times*, 4 February 1983.
6. *Financial Times*, 28 April 1983.
7. Charles Read, 'The implications of technological change', speech to an international summer school for young bankers, St Andrews, June 1982.
8. Office of Fair Trading, *Micro-electronics and Retailing*, September 1982. Report of the Working Party, paras. 2.64 and 2.65.
9. *Retail Banker International*, no. 33, 18 October 1982.
10. *Ibid.*, no. 43, 21 March 1983.
11. Mr Trevor Nicholas of Barclays Bank has referred to the 'dubious economics' of 'a nationwide POS system . . .'. *The Banks and Technology in the 1980s*, Institute of Bankers, 1982, p. 28.
12. Banking Information Service, press release, 27 May 1983.
13. Alix Granger, *Don't Bank On It*, Doubleday (Canada), p. 254.
14. The Civil Evidence Act 1968, for example, sets out ways by which a statement contained in a document produced by a computer may be admissible as evidence. And the Banking Act 1979 amended the Bankers' Books Evidence Act 1879 so as to allow evidence in the form of copies of bank records which are kept on microfilm, magnetic tape, or any other form of mechanical electronic data retrieval system. This applies in most proceedings, but not to those in which the bank itself is a party.
15. See Guest and Lloyd, *Encyclopedia of Consumer Credit Law*, 1983, 2-015. It also appears that – even where there is no overdraft – a card will be caught by section 14 where a system is not 'on-line' so as to debit the customer's account immediately.
16. Quoted in Stanley Goldstein, *Changing Times: Banking in the Electronic Age*, Government of Canada, 1979, p. 249.
17. Office of Fair Trading, *op. cit.* Report by the Director-General of Fair Trading, para. 25.
18. *The Canadian Payment System and the Computer: Issues for Law Reform.* Study paper prepared for the Law Reform Commission of Canada, 1974.
19. A. L. Tyree, *Electronic Funds Transfer in New Zealand*, 1978, 8 N.Z.U.L.R. 139; see also Nycman, *Security for Electronic Funds Transfer Systems*, 1974, 37 Pitt. L. Rev. 709.
20. Data Protection Bill (H.L.), Schedule 1, Part II, para 6.
21. See Stanley Goldstein, *op. cit.*, p. 355 et seq. for an elaboration of possible rules to protect privacy.
22. Committee of London Clearing Bankers, 'Personal Banking Services: Legal Issues', Evidence to NCC, July 1982.
23. J. R. Revell, *Banking and Electronic Funds Transfers; A Study of the Implications.* This report was prepared by Professor Revell for the Organisation for Economic Co-operation and Development (OECD). He kindly allowed us to see it in draft.
24. *Alice in Debitland*, Consumer Protection and the Electronic Funds Transfer Act, Board of Governors of the Federal Reserve System, June 1980.

Section 6 / Banking services and the law

This section looks at the law as it relates to banks and their personal customers. We have concentrated upon the law relating to banks in the conventional sense, but a number of the points are relevant, directly or indirectly, to others providing banking services, particularly building societies.

This section concentrates almost exclusively on the banker/customer relationship arising out of the operation of a current or deposit account. The law relating to the electronic transfer of funds and the need for a more effective way to resolve disputes between banks and their customers are separately discussed in sections 5 and 7 respectively.

Much of the law of banking developed during the nineteenth century and ignores two important subsequent developments. First the law was designed to cope with paper-based systems and it cannot, without amendment, be extended to cover new, computerised banking technology. Second, the nature of bank customers has also changed. When the law was being developed, bankers catered for a small minority of the population only, and 'the possession of a bank account was presumed to be the hallmark of financial respectability and wealth' (1). This is no longer the case. By the end of 1980 banks in Britain had some 27.684 million current account customers. The breakdown of these figures was as follows:

21.769 million with London clearing banks
1.806 million with Scottish clearing banks
0.5 million with Co-operative Bank
2.756 million with Trustee Savings Bank
0.853 million with National Girobank

The common law concerning the banker/customer relationship is substantially the same in Scotland as in England and Wales and the two principal statutes – the Bills of Exchange Act 1882 and the Cheques Act 1957 – expressly apply to Scotland.

What is a banker?

The Bills of Exchange Act 1882 defined a banker as someone who carries on the business of banking, which does not advance us very far. The Banking Act 1979 introduced the concepts of 'recognised banks' and 'licensed institutions', and limited the use of the term 'bank' to recognised banks and a number of specified institutions (for example, the Bank of England, a Trustee Savings Bank, and the Post Office in its banking operations). Banks not recognised under this Act, however, may still be recognised as bankers for the purposes of other Acts.

The traditional view of the courts is that no one may be considered a banker unless he pays cheques drawn on himself (2). The three characteristics of banking, usually accepted by the courts, have been described as:

(i) the acceptance of money from, and collection of cheques for, customers and the placing of them to their customers' credit;

(ii) the honouring of cheques or orders drawn on the bank by their customers when presented for payment; and

(iii) the keeping of some form of current or running accounts in their books in which the credits and debits are entered.

The nature of the banker/customer relationship: debtor and creditor

Just as there is no statutory definition of a banker which can be applied in all circumstances, there is no single statute which defines the relationship between bankers and their customers. Instead this relationship has been built up largely as common law, that is by legal arguments and judgments in specific cases.

The basic relationship between banker and customer is contractual. The parties have entered an agreement, or a 'contract' (even if unwritten and unsigned), which is normally that of creditor and debtor. When the customer's account shows a surplus, the bank is his or her debtor, and when the account is overdrawn the roles are reversed.

This debtor/creditor relationship was stated by Lord Cottenham L.C. in 1848, in Foley v. Hill, as follows:

'Money, when paid into a bank, ceases altogether to be the money of the principal; it is then the money of the banker, who is bound to return an equivalent by paying a similar sum to that deposited with him when he is asked for it. The money paid into a banker's is money known by the principal to be placed there for the purpose of being under the control of the banker; it is then the banker's money; he is known to deal with it as his own; he makes what profit of it he can, which profit he retains to himself, paying back only the principal, according to the custom of bankers in some places or the principal and a small sum of interest, according to the custom of bankers in other places. The money placed in the custody of a banker is, to all intents and purposes, the money of the banker, to do with as he pleases, he is guilty of no breach of trust in employing it: he is not answerable to the principal if he puts it in jeopardy, if he engages in a hazardous speculation; he is not bound to keep it or deal with it as the property of his principal; but he is, of course, answerable for the amount because he has contracted, having received the money, to repay to the principal, when demanded, a sum equivalent to that paid into his hands. That has been the subject of discussion in various cases, and that has been established to be the relative situation of banker and customer.' (3)

The banker as agent

The debtor/creditor relationship arises out of the deposit of money with a bank. In other circumstances the relationship might be that of agent (banker) and principal (customer). For example, bankers usually collect the proceeds of cheques as agents for their customers; they act as agents when accepting customers' instructions for the purchase or sale of stocks and shares; and so on.

Lack of a written contract

Although the relationship between banker and customer is contractual, personal customers are rarely asked to sign a written contract specifying the rights and obligations of both parties. Rights and obligations have nevertheless been established at common law. These are said to be 'implied terms' of the contract.

The position has been summarised by Professor J. Milnes Holden:

'A remarkable feature of the creation of the contracts between banker and customer in England is that the terms of the contract are not usually embodied in any written agreement executed by the parties. Thus, there is no formal agreement which provides that a banker must maintain strict secrecy concerning his customers' accounts or that customers must exercise care when drawing cheques so as to prevent the amounts from being fraudulently increased. It is true, of course, that when certain accounts are opened, e.g. joint accounts or the accounts of limited companies, a mandate is executed which gives the bank express instructions concerning the operations on the account, but even in those cases no attempt is made to prepare a comprehensive list of the respective rights and duties of banker and customer.

The contractual relationship which exists between banker and customer is a complex one founded originally upon the customs and usages of bankers. Many of those customs and usages have been recognised by the courts, and, to the extent that they have been so recognised, they must be regarded as implied terms of the contract between banker and customer. It follows, therefore that this is a branch of the law where implied terms are of vital importance. Little does a new customer realise when, with a minimum of formality, he opens a bank account that he is entering into a contract the implied terms of which would, if reduced to writing, run into several pages.' (4)

Duties and obligations of bankers

The principal rights and obligations of bankers in which we are interested concern:

(i) the duty to exercise reasonable care and skill
(ii) receiving money

  (iii) repaying money
  (iv) honouring cheques
   (v) confidentiality
  (vi) the provision of advice
 (vii) the termination of accounts
(viii) charging for services

THE DUTY TO EXERCISE REASONABLE CARE AND SKILL

There is an implied term in the contractual relationship that a bank is under a duty to exercise reasonable care and skill in carrying out all the operations that it undertakes on behalf of its customers, extending over the whole range of banking services. The Committee of London Clearing Bankers pointed out, in evidence to us, that 'what is reasonable care and skill has been held to be an objective standard applicable to banks, and whether or not it has been attained in any particular case has to be decided in the light of all the relevant facts.'

Certain Acts covering specific banking transactions require bankers to have acted 'in good faith' and 'in the ordinary course of business'. These are discussed later in this section.

The common law duty to exercise care and skill has (in England and Wales, but not Scotland) been restated in the recent Supply of Goods and Services Act 1982. Part II of this Act covers services, and came into force in July 1983. This stipulates among other things that in a contract for the supply of a service, the provider (i.e. in this context the bank or financial institution) will 'carry out the service with reasonable care and skill'.

The duty to take reasonable care extends to advice given to customers. In many situations the same standard of care is owed to non-customers, such as those seeking references. These points are discussed below. It also now appears that equivalent duties may be owed to customers in their capacity as guarantors of loans made by the bank. The case of Lloyds Bank Ltd v. Bundy (1974) illustrates the importance which the courts are prepared to attach to the relationship of trust and confidence between banker and customer. In that case:

'The defendant was an old farmer living on the farm which was his only asset. The farmer had given a guarantee to the bank to secure an overdraft which the bank had extended to the farmer's son in his business affairs. He had charged his house to the bank to secure the overdraft. The farmer, his son, and his son's company all had accounts at the same branch of the bank. The overdraft and the farmer's guarantee were raised several times to the point at which the entire farm was mortgaged to the bank. By 1970, a receiving order was made against the son's company, which ceased to trade, and proceedings were later brought to evict the farmer and his family from the farm. The farmer claimed that he had been induced to sign the guarantee and the charge under the undue influence of the banker, and the transaction should therefore be declared void. The bank had failed to discharge their fiduciary duty. This defence was upheld because of the banker's responsibilities of trust and confidence of handling its customer's affairs. The father, in coming to his decision, was liable to be influenced by the bank's proposals. As the bank was seeking to obtain a benefit from the farmer there arose a conflict of interest, and the bank should have ensured the defendant had independent legal advice before signing the documents.' (5)

THE DUTY TO RECEIVE MONEY

In the case of Joachimson v. Swiss Bank Corporation (1921) it was laid down that the bank undertakes to receive money and to collect bills for its customers' accounts (6).

THE DUTY TO REPAY

The money received from a customer becomes the property of the banker, who is indebted to his customer for an equivalent sum (plus interest where specified). The ordinary rule that a debtor must seek out his creditors does not apply. Instead, the bank is under a duty to repay the debt only when he receives instructions from the creditor/customer who may instruct repayment either to himself or to some third person. In the Joachimson case, Atkin, L. J., who gave the leading judgment, declared that 'the bank borrows the proceeds and undertakes to repay them. The promise to repay is to repay at the branch of the bank where the account is kept, and during banking hours. It includes a promise to repay any part of the amount due, against the written order of the customer addressed to the bank at the branch . . .'

Requests for repayment will normally be made in writing, but no legal judgment states categorically that they must be.

THE DUTY TO HONOUR CHEQUES

The banker must pay cheques drawn on him by the customer in legal form (for example, cheques that are not post-dated; cheques on which words and figures agree) on presentation during banking hours – or within a reasonable margin after the bank's advertised time of closing – at the branch of the bank where the account is kept. This obligation to honour cheques applies only if the customer's account is in credit (or below any agreed overdraft limit) and there are no legal bars to payment. This has been described as the most important of the banker's duties. If the bank fails in this duty, the customer whose cheque has been wrongfully dishonoured can sue for breach of contract. However, in Gibbons v. Westminster Bank Ltd it was held that a private customer, as opposed to a trade customer, is not entitled to recover substantial damages unless it can be established as a definite loss (7). The case was heard in 1939 and the principle has not been re-tested. Given more recent developments in the law of contract, where courts have been more ready to award damages for annoyance or vexation, that principle may no longer be applicable. The bank's wrongful dishonour of a cheque presented by a third party may also in some cases constitute defamation for which higher damages may now be awarded.

The duty to honour cheques is, of course, part of the broader duty to obey its customer's instructions, and not those of anyone else. It is established beyond all doubt that the bank is not entitled to pay out money on a cheque where the customer's signature has been forged. If it does so, the loss is that of the bank, not the customer. It does not matter that forgery was very difficult to detect or that the circumstances were entirely plausible. This principle is qualified only by the customer's obligations to notify the bank of any known forgery and to draw cheques with sufficient care so that they cannot be easily altered.

CONFIDENTIALITY

Bankers have a clearly established duty to keep their customers' affairs confidential. In Tournier v. National Provincial & Union Bank of England Ltd (1924), the defendant bank was worried about a customer's overdraft and told his employers that he appeared to be gambling. The customer, who was fired from his employment, succeeded in an action against the bank for breach of contract. Lord Justice Atkin laid down the rule as follows: the obligation of secrecy

> 'clearly goes beyond the state of the account . . . It must extend at least to all the transactions that go through the account, and to the securities, if any, given in respect of the account; and in respect of such matters it must, I think, extend beyond the period when the account is closed, or ceases to be an active account . . . I further think that the obligation extends to information obtained from other sources than the customer's actual account if the occasion upon which the information was obtained arose out of the banking relations of the bank and its customers – for example, with a view to assisting the bank in conducting the customer's business, or in coming to decisions as to its treatment of its customers.' (8)

The banker's duty of confidentiality is not an absolute one. In the case mentioned above, Bankes L.J. laid down that this duty was qualified by the following four exceptions:

(i) where disclosure is under compulsion by law;
(ii) where there is a duty to the public to disclose;
(iii) where the interests of the bank require disclosure;
(iv) where the disclosure is made by the express or implied consent of the customer.

Bankes L.J. went on to give examples of these four categories, as follows:

(i) the duty to obey an order under the Bankers' Books Evidence Act;
(ii) cases where a higher duty than the private duty is involved, as where

danger to the state or public duty may supersede the duty of the agent to his principal;

(iii) the case of a bank issuing a writ claiming payment of an overdraft, stating on the face of it the amount of the overdraft;

(iv) the familiar case where the customer authorises the banker to give a reference.

When a customer gives express consent to the provision of a banker's reference, few problems should arise. However, as we have seen, disclosure of a customer's affairs may be made by the latter's 'implied consent'. Banks generally have no special procedure for informing customers when requests for references are made, though some may provide references only to other bankers or certain bodies such as deposit-taking institutions or trade enquiry houses.

It appears that the question whether or not a banker is justified in law in giving to another banker an opinion concerning a customer's credit-worthiness without the customer's express authority is an open one, and has not been fully tested by the courts. We return to this later on page 101 when we look at possible changes to the current terms and conditions of banking.

THE BANK AS ADVISER

There is no duty on a bank to volunteer advice to a customer that a particular borrowing, say, is or may be imprudent from the customer's point of view. However, once a bank agrees to give advice it must do so with reasonable care and skill. This principle was demonstrated in Woods v. Martin's Bank (1959) (9). The plaintiff had asked a branch manager for financial advice. The manager had recommended investment in a company which was a customer of the bank. However, unknown to the plaintiff, this company had a considerable overdraft at the time; the bank's district head office had been pressing for the overdraft to be reduced. Eventually the plaintiff – described by the court as 'the very prototype of the lamb waiting to be shorn' – lost his entire investment of £14,800 which he proceeded to claim as damages from both the bank and branch manager, claiming that there were no reasonable grounds on which the manager could have advised that the company enjoyed a strong or sound financial position, or that the investment was a wise one. The bank and the branch manager were judged to be responsible for the full extent of the plaintiff's loss:

'. . . the bank had provided advice within the ordinary course of its business, and the defendants had failed to act with the ordinary care and skill which they should possess.'

The duty of care extends beyond the contractual duty owed directly to customers. The case of Hedley Byrne and Co. Ltd v. Heller and Partners Ltd (1964) established that a bank could be held liable for a negligent statement – given as a reference – which resulted in financial loss (10). This case concerned the response of a bank to a question as to the status of one of its customers.

The questioners eventually sued the bank which had, it was subsequently agreed, negligently produced a favourable reply to the question. The House of Lords ruled that, in cases such as this where reliance is to be placed upon the information, a duty of care is imposed when an answer is prepared. The bank would have been liable in this case for its admitted negligence, but for the fact that they had tendered their response with a disclaimer of liability: 'a man cannot be said voluntarily to be undertaking a responsibility if at the very moment when he is said to be accepting it he declares that in fact he is not'. This case was heard before the passing of the Unfair Contract Terms Act 1977, and the final outcome might have been different if that Act had been in force.

TERMINATION OF ACCOUNTS

The relationship between banker and customer may be terminated by mutual consent, or unilaterally, by either party. In Joachimson v. Swiss Bank Corporation (1921) it was said that an implied term of the contract was that 'the bank will not cease to do business with the customer except upon reasonable notice'. Precisely how long is 'reasonable notice' will vary with the circumstances of particular cases. In Prosperity Ltd v. Lloyds Bank Ltd (1923) one month's notice was considered insufficient (11). It would seem that at the very least the period must be long enough to cover any cheques drawn before the notice of termination was given. Customers may at present terminate their accounts whenever they choose, and for whatever reason.

CHARGING FOR SERVICES

The banker has the right to charge customers a reasonable sum for services rendered, except in such rare cases in which agreement exists to provide services free. The Supply of Goods and Services Act 1982 section 15 (1) has effectively confirmed that in the absence of agreement between banker and customers as to charges, the customer is not obliged to pay more than a reasonable charge.

The duties of customers

The terms implied into the contract between bank and customer impose obligations on the latter as well as the former. Failure to observe these obligations can prove costly. The two chief duties of customers are:

(i) the duty to draw cheques carefully; and
(ii) the duty to disclose forgeries.

THE DUTY TO DRAW CHEQUES CAREFULLY

The duty to draw cheques carefully was established in the leading case of London Joint Stock Bank Co. v. Macmillan (1918) (12). The details of the case were as follows:

An employee, whose duty it was to prepare cheques for his employers, wrote out a cheque payable to the firm or bearer. He filled in the amount in figures as '£2' but left a space between the '£' and the '2'. The amount in words was not filled in at all. After obtaining a signature from one of the partners he altered the amount in figures to £120 by placing '1' before and an '0' after the '2', filled in the corresponding amount in words, cashed the cheque and absconded. The employers maintained that the cheque ought not to have been cashed and that the bank was liable for the loss.

The House of Lords decided the case in the bank's favour. Lord Finlay L.C. observed:

'It is beyond dispute that the customer is bound to exercise reasonable care in drawing the cheque to prevent the banker being misled. If he draws the cheque in a manner which facilitates fraud, he is guilty of a breach of duty as between himself and the banker, and he will be responsible to the banker for any loss sustained by the banker as a natural and direct consequence of this breach of duty. On the facts of the case, the employers had "neglected all precautions" and so the bank was entirely justified in paying on the instrument.'

It should be noted that there was nothing on the face of the cheque to alert the bank's suspicion that it had been altered fraudulently. Had any alteration been apparent, the bank would have had to suffer the loss because it would have acted negligently in 'honouring' the cheque.

There will always be room for doubt as to whether or not a customer had exercised 'reasonable care'. This will often be determined by current practice. In the case of Slingsby v. District Bank (1932) the bank argued that the drawer of a cheque had been negligent in not drawing a line after the payee's name and so enabling a fraud to be committed (13). The Court of Appeal rejected the bank's argument since it was not – at the time when this case arose – a 'usual precaution' to draw lines either before or after the name of the payee. It was added, however, that if this type of case became more frequent, it might become a usual precaution.

THE DUTY TO DISCLOSE FORGERIES

Customers must inform their banks as soon as they discover that cheques supposedly signed by themselves have, in fact, been forged. This was established in Greenwood v. Martin's Bank (1932) (14). The case was as follows:

The plaintiff had an account with Martin's Bank, for which his wife looked after the pass-book and cheque book. One day when he requested a cheque she confessed that the account was empty as she had been drawing money to help her sister by forging his signature. He agreed to his wife's plea that the bank should not be informed of what she had done, and no more forgeries were committed. Some time later he discovered that the reason given by his wife for the forgeries was false. He told her that he would inform the bank about the forgeries, but, before he had done so, she shot herself. A few months later he brought an action against the bank for a declaration that he was entitled to be credited with the amount 'lost' through the forgeries.

The bank's defence was that the plaintiff was under a duty to disclose the forgeries as soon as he became aware of them. Had he done so, the bank could have sued his wife directly in tort (and – at the same time – the husband would have been responsible for his wife's tort). The bank maintained that the plaintiff's silence until after his wife's death amounted to a representation that the cheques were not forgeries, and so deprived the bank of its remedy of suing the wife. The House of Lords finally held that the husband's failure to inform the bank deprived him of a remedy.

As we have stated earlier, if the forgery had been obvious the bank itself will be under a clear duty not to accept the instrument for payment.

NO DUTY TO EXAMINE STATEMENTS

Although passbooks and bank statements would help customers detect possible frauds, they are under no obligation to check statement entries, either at all or within a specified period after receiving it. (See Kepitigalla Rubber Estates v. National Bank of India Ltd (1909) (15).)

It is open to banker and customer to agree that the customer must check the entries in his passbook or statement within a stated number of days and point out any errors. After that period the agreement could provide that it is to be conclusively presumed that the entries are correct. Although such a course of business is not followed in this country, we understand that it is quite common in other parts of the Commonwealth.

National Girobank Handbook

Alone among the banks we have studied, National Girobank sets out its terms and conditions in a *Handbook*. As they explained to us in their submission:

'When National Giro was being planned in the late 1960s, it was considered that its methods of operation were so different from traditional banks that it would be better to have a written contract. This is set out in the National Giro Handbook. Initially personal account customers were supplied with a copy when their account was opened, but this policy attracted a fair amount of criticism from customers who did not want to be troubled with the Handbook so we changed to a policy of only supplying it if requested. Our account opening leaflets say that the conditions are available on request. This method enables conditions to be changed more speedily and economically as services develop and change. Those customers who wish to have a personal copy of the full conditions can obtain one from us. We adopted a similar policy of having conditions available on request when we introduced deposit accounts and budget accounts. On the other hand customers who apply for personal loans have always been given a copy of the personal loan conditions.'

The handbook is concerned mainly with providing information about how to use the giro system. It gives useful details about, for example, the frequency with which statements are sent and is accompanied by a list of personal account or business account charges. It is less useful on rights and obligations. It does not, for example, specifically cover liability in cases of theft or fraud, though it notes (in para. 93), that 'if as a result of a careless or incorrect completion by you of a Giro form, we carry out a transaction which you did not intend us to make, we do not undertake to put the matter right'. It also appears that National Girobank will not accept liability for the fraudulent use of a giro draft (which, like a banker's draft, can be used as cash, for example for a house or car purchase. The payee's name is written by National Girobank on the draft, which is crossed 'account payee only – not negotiable'). The handbook states: 'If a Giro draft is lost or stolen notify the National Giro Centre immediately. . . . We may, at our discretion, issue a duplicate draft if you agree to indemnify us against any claim made in respect of the original draft' (16).

In certain cases, the handbook is more stringent in its terms and conditions than the courts have been for banks generally. For example, National Girobank reserves the right to close a Giro account 'at any time without notice'. It also expressly sets out the circumstances for which it will accept no liability, including 'the consequence of any omission, error or delay arising from any failure by you to notify us of any change in your account details'.

When the handbook was first published in 1973, National Giro (as it was then still known) undertook to give three months' advance warning of any changes to the terms and conditions by publishing in the London, Edinburgh and Belfast *Gazettes* and 'exhibiting in most post offices'. This clause was itself changed in 1978: changes and additions may be made 'by giving by such means as we may select not less than one week's advance notice of the change or alteration . . .'

Are changes required to the banker/customer relationship?

This first issue can be dealt with quickly. Our survey of the duties imposed on a bank leads us to conclude that no major changes are required to the basic legal relationship. It is true that there are one or two uncertainties. For example, it is not entirely clear whether a customer's demands for repayment must be in writing; nor whether banks are under an obligation to provide customers with a statement of their accounts (though they invariably do so on request). There may be some slight uncertainties, too, as to the extent of the customer's duties to take care in drawing cheques and to safeguard cheque books and cheque guarantee cards.

We have also suggested that the principle which apparently states that personal customers may seek only nominal damages when banks wrongfully dishonour their cheques may be out of date. We would like to see this principle changed but recognise that – in the absence of legislation – a modern case might be sufficient to test whether the courts would continue to adopt this rigid approach.

These uncertainties and reservations are not, however, important enough for us to seek legislative changes. Nor do we see any immediate advantages in a comprehensive banking statute. Although it may be surprising that there is no single statute which regulates the banker/customer relationship, we do not feel that this has caused any particular detriment to consumers. We could press for such legislation only if there was a need for important new provisions.

Our broad conclusion, therefore, is that, so far as the law is concerned, the customer is well protected in his or her dealings with a bank. The various duties which we have described impose high standards on banks. We believe therefore that the basic law covering the conventional current and deposit account is satisfactory. As Borrie and Diamond say in *The Consumer, Society and the Law*:

> '. . . a bank customer cannot complain that the law is loaded against him . . . it would seem that the customer's interests are fairly protected by the law. The law seems to lean over backwards in looking after his interests.' (17)

Improving customers' knowledge of their rights and duties

The law may be broadly acceptable, but it is important that customers should know and understand the nature of their relationship with their bank. There is less room for satisfaction here. Customers need to know the main rights and obligations of both parties, as well as other matters such as how charges are calculated, procedures for correcting errors and handling complaints, and so on. We consider three options:

* written contracts
* statement of terms and conditions
* explanatory leaflets

WRITTEN CONTRACTS

It may be surprising that there is usually no written contract between banker and customer. Although written agreements are provided for specific bank services such as credit cards and cash dispenser cards, they are not provided for current or deposit accounts. Customers are therefore entering into a contract with a number of implied terms of which they may be completely unaware.

As a general principle, both parties to an agreement ought to know what they have agreed. A written contract might well be thought of as a useful means of informing customers. It is surely in the interests of banks themselves that their customers enter into agreements with open eyes, so that they do not later feel aggrieved if banks refer to implied conditions of which customers knew nothing.

When a customer opens a new account, he or she might be asked to sign a legally binding contract or written agreement specifying the terms and conditions of business. This could be made a statutory requirement. Legislation could require the use of written contracts, or could specify the matters to be included or indeed prescribe actual terms and conditions.

The advantage of such a written contract would be to set out, in one place, all the terms and conditions. It should remove any ambiguities in the banker/customer relationship, and the signing of contracts is an accepted way of conducting business. If it were a legal requirement, it could ensure that customers were informed of matters such as bank charges.

Against this, the proposal has a number of disadvantages. First, it is likely that such a contract would be relatively complex and expressed in formal language. One might partly overcome this by prescribing the language to be used, but this might involve loss of flexibility and an over-elaborate system. Secondly, many people do not read the small print of contracts. Thirdly, the experience of National Girobank suggests that bank customers positively do not want a detailed statement of the terms and conditions of business.

Fourthly – and perhaps most seriously – banks might draft such contracts too much in their own favour. Following the Unfair Contract Terms Act 1977, they would not be able unfairly to exclude liability for the consequences of any negligent acts (and we do not suggest they would attempt this). Nevertheless such contracts might seek to restrict consumers' rights or place unduly restrictive burdens on consumers. This has happened already in the contracts some banks have prepared for cash dispenser cards. A customer's liability for the fraudulent use of such cards may, in certain cases, be more than the legal limit set in respect of credit cards by the Consumer Credit Act 1974. Stating our argument baldly, we prefer the present system under which the courts ultimately decide the main rights and responsibilities, bearing in mind the interests of banks and their customers, to one in which the banks may, in practice, determine most of the rules. If written bank contracts were required by law, at the very least there would have to be some means of vetting them to ensure they were not weighted too heavily in favour of banks.

This leads to the fifth disadvantage; that such contracts might restrict the ability of banks to respond flexibly to their customers' needs, particularly if the list of terms and conditions were to be imposed by statute. One would be erecting a new system of regulation, with all the bureaucracy which that entails, to govern a 'problem' (customers' ignorance of the terms of the agreement) which might not be solved by that new system.

The primary purpose of a written contract in this context would be to inform, rather than to define. The disadvantages which we have outlined are substantial. Accordingly, we conclude that the case for written contracts is not proven.

TERMS AND CONDITIONS OF BUSINESS

As an alternative means of improving information, banks could prepare a written statement detailing all their terms and conditions. This statement would be available for inspection at bank offices, and notices displayed in banks to this effect. Alternatively, it could be provided on request, like the National Girobank *Handbook*.

There are a number of disadvantages in this proposal:

- (i) if such a statement is to cover all possible eventualities, it will probably be complex and certainly long – the National Girobank *Handbook* runs to 113 paragraphs and does not fully cover issues such as privacy;
- (ii) more seriously, it is likely that few customers will take the initiative and ask to see such a statement; and
- (iii) the statement might conceivably change – and perhaps erode – consumers' rights without positively informing them that this is the case.

It would seem that a statement of terms and conditions would suffer most of the disadvantages of a written contract and would probably be no more effective in informing customers. A displayed statement could run the risk of remaining unread by the customer until a dispute arises and may then be used against him or her.

On balance, this is also not a proposal we could support.

AN EXPLANATORY BOOKLET

Our lack of enthusiasm for a declaratory statute, for written contracts, or for displayed terms and conditions leaves unresolved the customer's need for information. We believe that the most effective solution would be simple, explanatory literature designed for the specific purpose of informing customers where they stand legally in relation to their banks.

When new customers open accounts, they would be given a booklet outlining the main rights and obligations of bankers and their customers. This would cover the kind of broad points we have discussed above and, most importantly, would inform customers of their own duties, such as the need to draw cheques carefully and to disclose any forgeries. As these rights and obligations have been established at law, the same terms and conditions apply to all banks; at least part of this leaflet might therefore be drafted co-operatively. We think it could go further and include individual banks' procedures for correcting errors and resolving complaints. The basis for charging should also be outlined. This leaflet should be written in plain English and attractively designed so that it is actually read by customers. The leaflet could be supplemented by punchy summaries interleaved in cheque books.

Of all the various options, this is the simplest and, we believe, the most attractive. The disadvantage in such a proposal is the cost to the banks of preparing and distributing such leaflets, a cost that would ultimately be borne by customers. We consider that the benefits would outweigh these costs. Many banks, of course, already go some way towards meeting our proposal. The Midland Bank's *How to Use a Bank Account*, which won a Plain English Award in 1982, contains some of the information which we have in mind. Williams & Glyn's publish a leaflet on *Current Accounts for Personal Customers* which lists charges for overdrawn accounts; other banks have produced similar literature.

The status of such a booklet would need to be considered. We have proposed it should cover the *main* rights and obligations of both parties. It would not be a comprehensive statement to cover every possible situation that might arise. We are not proposing that it should become a form of written contract between banker and customer. Although it might carry some evidential weight, we envisage that the booklet itself would clearly state that it is not intended to have any legal effect between the parties. We recommend therefore that banks should give all new customers opening current or deposit accounts a simple, attractively designed statement outlining the rights and obligations of their customers. It should also cover bank procedures for correcting errors and resolving disputes, and the basis on which charges are calculated.

The 'success' of this booklet in communicating information should be monitored, by the banks and perhaps by the Office of Fair Trading or the National Consumer Council.

Does the law of banking need further development?

Our survey of banking law has led us to conclude that there are two specific areas where we consider changes do need to be made. These concern:

* bankers' references; and
* access to personal files.

BANKERS' REFERENCES

We have already suggested that the customer's 'implied consent' to the provision of information by bankers to third parties about his or her affairs has not been fully tested at law. There is no doubt, however, that this is common banking practice.

We asked the clearing bankers whether they had procedures for informing customers when bank references were requested by third parties, and whether references were given 'with the prior knowledge and consent' of the customer. The Committee of London Clearing Bankers told us that:

> 'there are no such procedures, and the Banks are unaware of any genuine call on the part of their customers to institute them. They are equally unaware of any desire to incorporate into the general law a requirement that all referees are to be placed under an automatic obligation to inform the subjects of references that a third party has sought a reference on them. References are given on the same basis as other banking services and practices, with the implied consent of the customer.'

The CLCB recalls that the Younger Committee 'received no complaints about banking practices from members of the public', and they note, in response to a supplementary questionnaire from the National Consumer Council, the continued absence of any such complaints. A few individual banks defined the types of requests for references they would grant. The Co-operative Bank, for example, stated that they would not inform customers when references were requested by the bankers of third parties. And the Royal Bank of Scotland said that 'references are only given by this Bank in response to enquiries received from recognised banks, licensed deposit takers and certain respectable trade enquiry houses. No responses are given direct to other bodies excepting Government Departments and Head Postmasters, and in these cases, only after explicit authority has been given by customers.'

A few banks pointed to the practical difficulties which might arise if this practice were changed, for example that if a bank failed to respond to a request for a reference, such failure might be adversely construed by the enquirer.*

In the Report of the Committee on Privacy (the 'Younger Committee') it was recommended that 'banks should make clear to all customers, existing or prospective, the existence and manner of operation of their reference system, and give them the opportunity either to grant a standing authority for the provision of references or to require the bank to seek their consent on every occasion' (18). The Committee made this recommendation because it did not believe that the practice of giving references without the customer's knowledge was as well known and accepted among customers, particularly individuals, as the banks had asserted in their evidence. As far as we know, this recommendation has not been implemented by the banks. We support this recommendation of the Younger Committee that banks should take steps to inform all customers about the operation of their reference system. Customers should be given the option to insist on individual consent whenever a reference is sought from their banker. Banks might feel obliged to charge for such a service, and any such charges should be made clear to the customer. The booklet on rights and obligations we have proposed would provide an obvious means of informing customers of the bank's practice in relation to references and of any choices available.

A point of detail relating to references concerns the Statute of Frauds Amendment Act 1828, which applies to England and Wales, but not to Scotland. Section 6 of that Act states that a party who gives information about the credit, or financial, position of another is not liable for any loss arising from the falsity of the information, unless the information was provided in writing and signed by the party to be charged. The House of Lords, in Banbury v. Bank of Montreal (1918), held that this section applied only to fraudulent representations (19). The operation of section 6 is illustrated by reference to the case of Hirst v. West Riding Banking Co. Ltd (1910) (20). In that case, the plaintiff claimed damages from the bank for a misrepresentation made in writing and

---

* One bank drew to our attention *Bankers' References* by A. W. Wright which sets out reasons why a bank should *not* disclose to a customer that an enquiry has been received. One of the reasons given is that this would breach the confidentiality that ought to exist between the banker and the person seeking an opinion.

signed by the bank manager. The bank used section 6 to avoid liability, on the grounds that the signature of the bank manager was insufficient to impose liability on the bank. (An action against the manager personally might, however, have succeeded, as it had done in the earlier case of Swift v. Jewsbury and Goddard (1874) (21).) This Act has led to the modern practice in banking whereby, in many cases, the reply to a status enquiry, although in writing, is not signed, and is sent on stationery which often does not disclose the name of the replying bank. We see no justification for banks enjoying such protection from the consequences of an alleged fraud. We recommend that section 6 of the Statute of Frauds Amendment Act should be repealed.

ACCESS TO FILES

In principle we believe that bank customers should be able to get access to factual records about themselves and see that they are changed if they are wrong. Banks already have a duty to maintain any files accurately by exercising reasonable care and skill. In certain circumstances a customer may be able to sue a bank that releases inaccurate information to third parties of a nature which damages the customer. Such an action would of course be possible only after any alleged damage has occurred.

The information contained in a bank's files, including judgmental comment where a bank employee has seen fit to insert it, may also affect the terms on which banks are prepared to lend money to particular customers. In its evidence the Committee of London Clearing Bankers said to us:

'The banks certainly approve of the fundamental principle that the customer should be entitled to know just what information is recorded about him and there is only one aspect upon which they have reservations. In the successful management of a lending activity, there must be the accumulation of a certain amount of judgmental experience arising in relation to a particular customer. The banks are firmly of the belief that in providing borrowing facilities, banks or other lenders should be entitled to have regard to the previous record of a particular borrower. If that particular borrower's record is exemplary, then he should be entitled to the provision of a lending at the lowest possible rate. On the other hand, a troublesome borrower should expect to have to pay for the additional administrative burdens and the greater risk of default which he creates and we do not subscribe to the view that there should be an across-the-board rate of charge regardless of the characteristics of the borrower himself. We would not like to see such judgmental information made available to the customer as of right since the end result would be the abandonment of such records and the subsidisation of the doubtful by the good.'

Whether or not CLCB's arguments about 'judgmental' information are convincing, it is clear that both we and they are agreed on the principle that bank customers should have access to factual information about themselves.

We believe that this principle is important enough to enshrine in law, but we hope that the banks would not need to wait on legislation to take action to give their customers access to factual records about themselves (22). We believe that procedures along the lines of those laid down in the Consumer Credit Act for consumers to gain access to records held about them by credit reference agencies would be a suitable model.

References to section 6

1. The Committee of London Clearing Bankers, 'Personal banking services: legal issues', evidence to NCC, July 1982.
2. J. Milnes Holden, *The Law and Practice of Banking: vol 1 Banker and Customer*, Pitman, 1982. We have drawn heavily on this work for a description of the banker/customer relationship. See also F. E. Perry, *Law and Practice Relating to Banking*, Methuen, 4th edn 1983.
3. *Foley v. Hill* (1848)(2) HL Cas. 28.
4. Milnes Holden, *op. cit.*, p.29.
5. *Lloyds Bank v. Bundy* (1974)3 AER 757.
6. *Joachimson v. Swiss Bank Corporation* (1921) 3KB: 110.
7. *Gibbons v. Westminster Bank Ltd* (1939) 2KB 882.
8. *Tournier v. National Provincial and Union Bank of England* (1924) 1KB 461.
9. *Woods v. Martin's Bank Ltd* (1959) IQB 55.
10. *Hedley Byrne and Co. Ltd v. Heller and Partners Ltd* (1964) AC 465.
11. *Prosperity Ltd v. Lloyds Bank Ltd* (1923) 39 TLR 372.
12. *London Joint Stock Bank Co. v. Macmillan* (1918) AC 777.
13. *Slingsby v. District Bank* (1932) 1 KB 544.
14. *Greenwood v. Martin's Bank* (1932) 1 KB 3371.
15. *Kepitigalla Rubber Estates Ltd v. National Bank of India Ltd* (1909) 2 KB 1010.
16. *National Giro Handbook*, Post Office, September 1973.
17. Gordon Borrie and Aubrey L. Diamond, *The Consumer, Society and the Law*, Penguin, fourth edition 1981, pp. 219 and 235.
18. *The Report of the Committee on Privacy*, Cmnd 5012, HMSO, 1972, para 307.
19. *Banbury v. Bank of Montreal* (1918) AC 626.
20. *Hirst v. West Riding Banking Co. Ltd* (1901) 2 KB 560.
21. *Swift v. Jewsbury and Goddard* (1894) L.R. 9 QB 301.
22. At the time of writing, it was too early to judge what precise consequences the enactment of the government's Data Protection Bill might have for bank customers as regards 'subject access'. The Bill's scope does *not* extend to manual files.

Section 7 / The resolution of disputes between bank and customer

In this section, we look at how banker/customer disputes – whether of fact, of law, or of banking standards – are resolved. How, in practice, does the consumer enforce his rights and obtain redress?

The volume of business transacted by banks and other financial institutions inevitably generates customer grievances. Disputes arise over issues of fact (for instance, 'What has happened to an allegedly missing credit transfer?'), of law ('Has the bank's duty of care been broken?') and of banking practice ('Has there been an unacceptable delay in dealing with this matter?'). Most will arise in the context of the banker/customer relationship; but not always so – for example, where a person uses another bank to pay money into his or her account. And, as we make clear in section 11, there is scope for disputes to arise from the work of bank trust corporations.

The great majority of banker/customer disputes are resolved simply and at an early stage. But there are occasions when customers feel that there has been no satisfactory response to their complaint. Even when a complaint is referred to a bank's head office where it may well be reviewed anew, as far as the aggrieved consumer is concerned, no independent judgment has been brought to bear on the issues. It is not unnatural, therefore, that those who remain dissatisfied after making a complaint should feel – rightly or wrongly – that the bank's main concern has been to defend its own interests. The only satisfactory means of resolving intractable and genuine disputes is through an independent third party.

Many disputes between customer and bank could, in principle, be brought before a court. This will be so where issues of law are in dispute and in most – but not all – cases of disputed fact. We do not wish to see any reduced recourse to the courts. It is important that banks should not be seen as being above the law and that the courts should continue to be able to apply the law to them. We have also seen how court judgments have been instrumental in developing the law of banking in a way which is fair to all concerned.

However, very few individuals ever take a dispute with a bank to court. (We have already mentioned the evident reluctance of consumers and their legal advisers to start court action where they strenuously deny that an ATM card has been used.) The various barriers which make it so difficult for an individual to bring a case against a large organisation in the ordinary courts are well known: they include

*   the isolation of the individual in dispute;
*   the lack of access to information, advice and legal services;
*   lack of familiarity with the law and the legal system;
*   the costs of litigation, particularly in relation to the sums in dispute;
*   the delays of litigation.

Facilities such as the legal aid scheme and the small claims procedure in the county courts of England and Wales do remove some of these barriers. But these are by no means universally available and have their own imperfections. The difficulties of using small claims procedures, for example, were fully explored in the National Consumer Council's report, *Simple Justice*, published in 1979.

In general, the private individual in dispute with a business organisation will fare badly in terms of money, time and competence. The consumer's inequality of bargaining power has been widely recognised, as reflected in legislation such as the Unfair Contract Terms Act and the Sale of Goods Act (concerned primarily with the formation of the consumer/business contractual relationship). The same inequality is present when the parties are in dispute. That has, to some extent, been recognised in the public sector where the various nationalised industry consumer councils deal with complaints that have not been handled satisfactorily by the industry. In the private sector, the difficulties of pursuing redress in the ordinary courts have been acknowledged in the promotion of trade association conciliation and arbitration schemes by the Office of Fair Trading and by initiatives such as the Insurance Ombudsman Bureau.

The NCC has consistently argued for simpler forms of justice for individuals, on the grounds that there is no point giving people rights if they cannot enforce them. We have pressed for ways of resolving disputes which are accessible, simple, relatively informal, cheap to use and to operate, quick, effective and fair.

Our principal concern has been, and remains, the official court system. We have concentrated upon the system for resolving small claims – currently those involving not more than £500. But we also recognise the need for the entire processes of civil litigation to be reviewed – a need which has been voiced by bodies such as the Royal Commission on Legal Services, the Law Commission and the Law Society. We recognise the danger that the establishment of alternative or supplementary systems may deflect attention away from the deficiencies of the court system. There are other dangers with such 'private' systems: consumers may be confused and bewildered by a multiplicity of schemes; they cannot have powers of compulsion; and the dependence upon private 'sponsorship' can pose serious problems in terms of their insecurity and the quality of service provided. Most serious of all, such schemes may not be – or may not be seen to be – sufficiently independent of business interests.

Nevertheless, there are positive advantages in privately organised schemes. They obviously avoid the real and imagined psychological obstacles that surround the courts. They provide additional choice to consumers. They offer wide scope for innovation and are more likely than the courts to adopt 'active' styles of fact-finding and informal, simple and flexible means of decision-making. They can also reap the benefits of a 'specialist' approach – a scheme which deals with just one industry will know far more about that industry than the courts. A privately organised scheme can also be set up to deal with more than the strict issues of law and fact, to which the courts are confined. Such a scheme can, for example, be authorised to deal with complaints that there has been maladministration or a failure to observe the proper standard of professional behaviour. Finally – and this is important – a scheme can observe and comment on (for example in an annual report) the wider trends and practices revealed by individual disputes.

Our general conclusion is, therefore, that privately organised schemes can bring positive advantages for both consumers and businesses. But it is vital that any scheme incorporate a number of safeguards; that recourse to the ordinary courts should remain available; and that attention should not be diverted away from overdue reforms in the courts themselves.

A banking ombudsman

It is not difficult to relate these issues to banking services. Indeed, the general problems of pursuing redress may well be exacerbated when the individual's opponent is a bank. To take on the corporate bureaucracy of a bank is a very intimidating prospect for any private consumer who obviously does not have the huge resources of the banks, their access to expert legal assistance or their familiarity with legal processes.

So on a theoretical level, it makes sense to argue the case for the establishment of a mechanism to resolve customers' banking disputes. The sheer inequality of power between the two parties in itself suggests such a need. But we have to ensure that a dispute mechanism would be useful in practice. The evidence in this report suggests that customers' dealings with banks do not give rise to vast numbers of problems that might lead to disputes, particularly if we exclude grievances about matters such as opening hours which clearly would not develop into disputes. At the same time we have uncovered a small number of cases where customers feel – rightly or wrongly – that they have been very badly treated indeed. They have not had a real opportunity to have their grievances independently investigated and resolved. Our market research revealed that about a quarter of bank customers see 'a great need' to establish an independent agency to resolve complaints.

This evidence suggests that there is no real need for a mechanism that can process vast numbers of small complaints and problems (as far as we know, these are handled relatively satisfactorily by banks themselves). What is needed, however, is an independent body which can investigate both sides of an intractable dispute and – if necessary – provide an authoritative means of resolving it.

A properly constituted redress scheme would open up a new and accessible avenue of redress for dissatisfied bank customers. It would have obvious benefits for those who believe that they have been badly treated over a legitimate grievance. We suspect that many grievances may well prove to disclose no reasonable basis – or, perhaps more likely, to be the result of misunderstandings. But the value of such a scheme can lie as much in the independent explanations and reassurances which can be given as in the prospects for a 'successful' outcome. As well as being more approachable, it could also go beyond the courts in its ability to deal with 'non-legal' disputes.

The advantages do not lie only with customers. The banks have much to gain as well. Such a scheme would be an effective means of improving and maintaining public confidence. It could provide banks with valuable information about the causes of dissatisfaction amongst their customers. It could enable them to improve their services. And it could reduce the risks of the bad publicity for a bank which surrounds the occasional case which does get to court.

A system of redress: an outline proposal

It is not for us to make specific proposals about the form of a new scheme at this stage. They should come, in the first place, from the banking institutions. We can, however, set out some of the characteristics of such a scheme which we would expect to see and then speculate about a possible way forward.

In our view, any such scheme should be set up on the following broad lines.

ALL BANKING SERVICES

The scheme should, ideally, be set up and supported by all the principal institutions which provide personal banking services. There should not be a multiplicity of schemes. There is no reason in principle why a single scheme should not cover building societies as well as banks, though there may be difficulties in practice in getting agreement. (We disagree with the Spalding Report which rejects the case for a building societies' Ombudsman on the ground that complaints can be dealt with by the societies' own Association or by arbitration under the rules of an individual society (1).) The scheme should be financed by the institutions in proportion to the volume of personal business which each undertakes. It should be available to all personal customers and others directly affected by personal banking services. It should – as discussed in section 11 – embrace disputes arising from the work of bank trust corporations.

INDEPENDENCE

It is crucial that a suitable constitution should be found to guarantee the independence of the scheme, bearing in mind the financial support from the banks and other financial institutions. We expand on this point below.

TERMS OF REFERENCE

The scheme should be empowered to deal with any legal claim made by a personal customer against a member. It should also have the power to deal with any complaint that a member has failed to observe standards of good banking practice or has been guilty of maladministration. So far as bank trust corporations are concerned, it should have the power to deal with the four types of case set out on page 178.

POWERS

The scheme should have power to investigate any case properly brought within its terms of reference. It should be able to obtain papers and other information from both sides. It should have power to promote an agreed solution, through conciliation or other means, where that is possible. In other cases, we have come to the view that it should have the power to recommend a solution, rather than impose one. We say this because:

* it would make the scheme more acceptable to the businesses concerned;
* it does not deny either party access to the courts, even after the involvement of the scheme;
* it does not oust the jurisdiction of the courts (where, for example, the conduct of a trustee is under question);
* it would be extremely rare for a bank or building society to ignore a recommendation without excellent reason for doing so.

It might be thought that a conciliation and arbitration scheme should be set up under the Fair Trading Act 1973. The Director-General of Fair Trading has the duty, under section 124 of that Act, 'to encourage associations to prepare, and to disseminate to their members, codes of practice for guidance in safeguarding and promoting the interests of consumers in the United Kingdom'. Codes have been prepared for a number of private-sector trades supplying consumer goods and services, and for the Post Office, British Telecom and appliance servicing and repairs by electricity boards. The codes generally allow for independent conciliation by the trade association and arbitration of unresolved disputes by a member of the Institute of Arbitrators.

A similar scheme could be devised for the banking sector. Their trade associations – the Committee of London Clearing Bankers, the Committee of Scottish Clearing Bankers and the Northern Ireland Bankers' Association – could agree, with OFT approval, a code of practice which would allow for conciliation and arbitration of unresolved disputes.

Although this proposal has some merit, it is not one we endorse. When we reviewed the operation of trade association arbitration schemes in the late 1970s, we expressed a number of reservations about the way these schemes operated (2). Deficiencies revealed by our study included ignorance among consumers about their existence; fears that they were not impartial; delays; and dissatisfaction with the outcome of some disputes.

The operation of these schemes has since been reviewed by the OFT, and certain changes introduced. A major stumbling-block remains in consumers' fears (whether justified or not) that because the schemes are run directly by trade associations, they may not be impartial. In short, the major defect of these schemes is that they have not been constituted with a sufficient degree of independence.

We believe that the Insurance Ombudsman scheme offers a sounder and more suitable precedent for a banking scheme. In particular, we believe that its constitution shows how it is possible to reconcile the over-riding need for independence of decision-making with financial dependence on the industry in question.

The Insurance Ombudsman Bureau (IOB) was set up voluntarily in 1981 by a number of insurance companies for the purpose of investigating and resolving disputes arising from claims made upon member companies by their policy holders. In addition, the Bureau advises policy holders who have problems which are not yet either complaints or disputes. The kind of complaints investigated by the Bureau include disputed settlements of insurance claims; delays; allegations of unfair treatment; etc. All complaints have to be referred to the insurance company's chief executive before referral to the Ombudsman. In addition to the Ombudsman, the Bureau has a small staff, and a Council chaired at present by Mrs Joan Macintosh (Vice-chairman of the NCC and formerly the Honorary President of the National Federation of Consumer Groups). In 1982 the seven other members of the Council included four people with a 'consumer background', two from insurance companies and one academic. In the first nine months of operation it dealt with over 1,500 enquiries and in the following year 2,500. In 1982, the cost to the member companies was £105,000. At the end of 1981, 44 companies belonged to the scheme; by March 1983 the number had increased to 109. The member companies provide all the financial resources of the IOB, but the Ombudsman is employed by, and is answerable to, the Council. Information about the scheme is published annually by the Council. The 38 insurance groups now involved cover approximately two-thirds of the UK market for individual policies.

The Ombudsman may make awards up to £100,000, binding on members. Policy holders can reject his decision, and take further legal action if they wish. In this case, their legal rights will not have been changed by the Ombudsman's decision. (This feature corresponds fairly closely with our proposal that a banking scheme would only have powers of recommendation.)

The IOB Council has made a number of observations which suggest how a similar organisation might be of use to the banks and their customers:

(i) by no means all enquiries are complaints. The IOB is often used as an impartial source of advice and information, in this case averting problems rather than resolving them. The difference between an enquiry and a dispute is often a very simple piece of information. 'We go so far as to state that no impartial adjudication procedure is adequate unless it is preceded by an equally impartial and accessible advice service.' (Of the

2,504 enquiries reaching the Ombudsman in 1982, 1,232 related to member companies. Only 179 cases were actually adjudicated by the Ombudsman;)

(ii) the Ombudsman is not the 'consumer's protagonist' – 'It is the Ombudsman's impartiality, guaranteed by the Council, which assures both insured and insurer fair consideration of their dispute.' Of the 179 cases adjudicated, the company decision was confirmed in 141 cases and was revised in 38 cases. In addition, 298 disputes were resolved by companies themselves after referral;

(iii) the existence of the scheme enables the IOB to identify trends in complaints. Specific points can be highlighted in annual reports or, as was the case with evidence on household insurance, submitted to appropriate bodies – 'There is no equivalent central collection of UK personal insurance experience covering a wide range of companies and comprising detailed case histories.' (3)

Conclusion

We conclude that both financial institutions and their customers would benefit from the establishment of a means of resolving complaints and enquiries from bank customers who have not received satisfaction from their banks. We have indicated some of the features which such a scheme should incorporate. It is for the banking community to bring forward specific proposals, but our present view is that the best model for a suitable scheme is the Insurance Ombudsman Bureau. We therefore recommend the establishment of a Banking Ombudsman Bureau, financed by the banks and guided by an independent Council with a majority of members drawn from a broadly defined 'consumer' background.

References to section 7

1. Building Societies Association, *The Future Constitution and Powers of Building Societies*, BSA 1983, paras 2.40–2.44.
2. National and Welsh Consumer Councils, *Simple Justice*, NCC, 1979.
3. The Insurance Ombudsman Bureau, *Annual Report*, IOB, 1982.

Section 8 / Saving and borrowing

The savings services offered to consumers by banks need to be considered in two different ways:

* first, as homes for consumers' savings, in competition with other financial institutions which seek to attract deposits;
* secondly, in relation to bank current accounts, since, as we have seen, the distinction between a savings account and a current account is becoming increasingly blurred by the offer of accounts which both pay interest and give payment facilities.

We have not attempted in this report to provide a guide to all the savings services offered by banks and competing institutions. Our intention is

* to see whether any improvements can be made in the information given to consumers about savings schemes so that they can make better choices on their own behalf;
* to review the competitive structure of the market place.

The market for consumers' savings is a very complex and competitive one.

Table 8.1   Deposits of personal sector savings: end-June 1982

	£ million	% of market
Monetary sector	50 560	38.3
Building societies	60 874	46.2
National Savings	19 874	15.1
Other	551	0.4
Total	131 859	100.0

Source: Financial Statistics, HMSO

Note: The term 'monetary sector' includes all personal deposits held by the clearing banks. Trustee Savings Banks are now part of the monetary sector – previously they were recorded as part of National Savings. The amount involved in this transfer is about £6,000 million.

Many different organisations, including the government itself, compete for consumers' money. However, as Table 8.1 shows, the savings market is dominated by the banks, building societies and National Savings.

Over the last ten years or so the major change has been the increased share of consumer savings going to the building societies. The share held by the banks has held steady while that of National Savings has decreased. Table 8.2 shows how deposits in building societies, banks and National Savings moved between 1970 and 1981.

Table 8.2   The relative growth of personal sector deposits, 1970–81

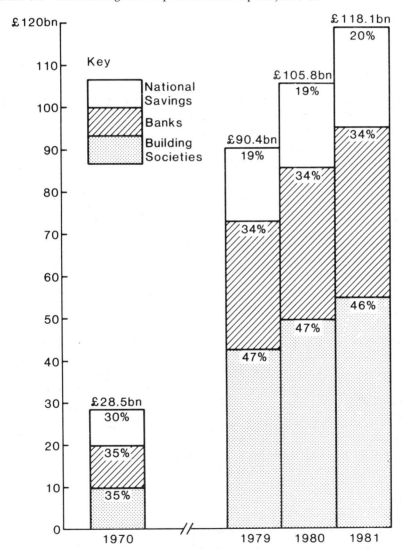

Source: Central Statistical Office

Table 8.3 Savings comparisons (reproduced from *The Guardian*, July 1983)

	Amount of interest %	When interest paid	Tax	£ min	Withdrawal
Banks					
deposit	6	½ yearly	To pay	1	7 days
savings	6¾–8	½ yearly	To pay	10/month	7 days
lump sum 3 months	8½–9¼	yearly	To pay	2–5000	Fixed term
National Savings Bank					
ordinary account	3	yearly	1st £70 free	1	£100 on demand
ordinary account	6	yearly	1st £70 free	500	£100 on demand
investment account	10.5	yearly	To pay	1	1 month
monthly income bond	11	monthly	To pay	2000	6 months
National Savings Certificates (25th issue)					
1–5 year	6.00–7.51	When cashed in	Tax free	25	
Index-linked Savings Certificates	RPI linked +0.2 monthly	When cashed in	Tax free	10	
Saye-indexed (3rd issue)	RPI linked +0.2 monthly	When cashed in	Tax free	4/month	Penalty

	Rate	Interest	Tax	Amount	Term
Building societies					
deposit account	7	½ yearly	Paid	—	Demand
share account	7¼	½ yearly	Paid	1	Demand
subscription account	8¼	½ yearly	Paid	100	1–5 years
Trustee Savings Bank					
savings	4	yearly	To pay	5p	Demand
investment	6	yearly	To pay	1	1–4 weeks
term	7½	¼, ½ or 1 yearly	To pay	1000	1–5 years
Local authorities					
1 year	9¾	½ yearly	To pay	100–1000	Fixed term
2 years	10½	½ yearly	To pay	100–1000	Fixed term
3 years	11	½ yearly	To pay	100–1000	Fixed term
4 years	11	½ yearly	To pay	100–1000	Fixed term
5 years	11	½ yearly	To pay	100–1000	Fixed term
6 years	11	yearly	To pay	100–1000	Fixed term
7–10 years	11	yearly	To pay	100–1000	Fixed term
yearling bonds	10½	½ yearly	To pay	1000	—

Source: The Guardian, July 1983

One of the marked trends of the 1970s was that while personal disposable incomes on average increased, so did the proportion of incomes that people devoted to savings (1). It is not surprising, therefore, that as the amount of consumers' money there is to bid for has grown, so has competition for it. In particular, each of the competing savings institutions has developed and is continuing to develop a range of savings accounts offering different advantages linked to a range of conditions.

Clearly, in principle, we welcome the wide range of offers being made to consumers. People who have money to save can pick the offer that suits their individual needs best. However, the very range on offer creates its own problems for savers who have to take into account differently quoted rates of interest, the effect of different timetables for the payment of interest, and differing conditions about sums invested and conditions of withdrawal. Table 8.3 (produced by kind permission of *The Guardian* (2)) illustrates some of the complexities involved.

There are a number of different ways in which the rate of interest quoted can be affected:

* whether it is net or gross of income tax;
* how often interest is credited/paid. (At any given rate of nominal interest, the more frequently interest is credited/paid the higher the return on the savers' money;)
* the effect of withdrawal conditions which may reduce the interest earned.

The most obvious example of the difficulties caused by quotations net or gross of income tax are building societies' rates. Because building societies pay interest net of basic rate income tax, their rates are not directly comparable to those quoted by banks and other institutions which pay interest in full, leaving tax to be deducted later. As a result, in order to emphasise the attractiveness of their rates they always quote the return that a basic rate taxpayer would get as well – so savers are told, for example, that a rate of 6.25 per cent equals a return of 8.93 per cent if they pay tax at basic rate. A typical building society window may well have four different savings accounts each advertised with two interest rates quoted to two places of decimals.

The confusion that this causes was demonstrated in our market research. In the sample survey MORI carried out for us, the sample was asked whether building societies or banks were the better place for savings, first for people who paid basic rates of tax and then for people who do not pay tax. While 71 per cent correctly identified building societies as being better for basic rate taxpayers, the sample was very confused about the position for non-taxpayers: 43 per cent said building societies were better, 34 per cent banks. Seven per cent said there was no difference and 16 per cent admitted to not knowing. (All the sample had both bank and building society accounts (3).) In fact, at the time, whether a bank or building society would be better for a non-taxpaying investor depended on the type of bank or building society account the saver chose.

The next problem is the difference that the frequency with which interest is calculated/paid makes to the rate of return on savings. We are grateful to Consumers' Association for the calculations in Table 8.4 which demonstrate the point:

Table 8.4   Real interest rates by variable calculation periods

Nominal rate	*True (effective) rate if interest is paid or added –*				
	half yearly	*quarterly*	*monthly*	*weekly*	*daily*
6	6.090	6.136	6.168	6.180	6.183
6.5	6.606	6.660	6.697	6.712	6.715
7	7.123	7.186	7.229	7.246	7.250
7.5	7.641	7.714	7.763	7.783	7.788
8	8.160	8.243	8.300	8.322	8.328
8.5	8.681	8.775	8.839	8.864	8.871
9	9.203	9.308	9.381	9.409	9.416
9.5	9.726	9.844	9.925	9.956	9.965
10	10.250	10.381	10.471	10.506	10.516
10.5	10.776	10.921	11.020	11.059	11.069
11	11.303	11.462	11.572	11.615	11.626
11.5	11.831	12.006	12.126	12.173	12.185
12	12.360	12.551	12.683	12.734	12.747
12.5	12.891	13.098	13.242	13.298	13.312
13	13.423	13.648	13.803	13.864	13.880
13.5	13.956	14.199	14.367	14.434	14.451
14	14.490	14.752	14.934	15.006	15.024
14.5	15.026	15.308	15.504	15.581	15.601
15	15.563	15.865	16.075	16.158	16.180
15.5	16.101	16.424	16.650	16.739	16.762
16	16.640	16.986	17.227	17.322	17.347
16.5	17.181	17.549	17.807	17.909	17.935
17	17.723	18.115	18.389	18.498	18.526
17.5	18.266	18.682	18.974	19.090	19.120
18	18.810	19.252	19.562	19.685	19.716

Source: Consumers' Association

For the individual who invests £1,000 over 10 years at a quoted rate of interest of 10 per cent, the difference at the end of the period is £113 (if interest is calculated monthly rather than yearly), as the example in Table 8.5, again kindly provided by Consumers' Association, illustrates.

It may be argued that the differences are not large, particularly at low rates of interest. However, savers have no way of knowing whether the differences do matter to them or not, without seeing the figures. And certainly at higher rates the differences are quite large enough to mislead savers into choosing one rate of return rather than another. Moreover, while a difference of £113 over 10 years may not be very large, certainly, other things being equal, savers would want to opt for it if they knew about it.

Table 8.5   How £1000 grows if interest at 10 per cent is added

	Yearly	Half-yearly	Quarterly	Monthly
After 1 year	£1100	£1103	£1104	£1105
After 2 years	£1210	£1216	£1218	£1220
After 5 years	£1611	£1629	£1639	£1645
After 10 years	£2594	£2653	£2685	£2707
True return	10%	10.25%	10.38%	10.47%

Source: Consumers' Association

Finally there is the difficulty caused by those institutions, including some building societies, who pay no interest on some accounts during the period of notice of withdrawal. All investors in such accounts must, to a greater or lesser extent, receive less than the advertised rate of return. The only way to get the advertised rate of return is never to withdraw the money.

For all these reasons we believe that it would be useful to have a standard method for quoting rates of return on savings in advertising and promotional material. We asked the banks for their reaction to the idea of a 'truth in savings' calculation, along the lines of the annual percentage rate for consumer credit. The Trustee Savings Banks responded in a way with which we fully agree. They said that they supported the idea in principle provided that

   (i) research indicates that the need exists;
  (ii) it is precise, clear and easily understood by consumers;
 (iii) the cost implications do not result in a reduction in overall benefit to the consumer;
 (iv) it can be easily and fairly complied with by all financial and savings institutions.

We believe that a need does exist. Table 8.6, produced by kind permission from the *Daily Telegraph* (4), shows how the accuracy of consumer choice can be improved by the use of a standard annual percentage rate. We also believe that the TSBs are right to say that all savings should be covered – local authority and government as well as commercial. The evolution of a suitable measure would have to involve consultation with the financial institutions: our own first suggestion would be for an annual percentage rate figure, quoted net of standard rate of tax, leaving institutions free to draw attention to any advantages their mode of savings presented for other categories of taxpayer and non-taxpayers.

It will not be easy to achieve a consensus on a way of quoting rates which all types of financial institutions can agree to. It is tempting to suggest that government should legislate, since that is the most effective way of seeing that the interests of the various institutions involved are fairly balanced. We are reluctant to do this, except as a method of last resort. In part, we say this because we recognise the lack of enthusiasm for detailed legislation that now pervades financial institutions dealing with consumers after the Consumer Credit Act. In part, we say it because we believe that financial institutions ought to be able to recognise their collective self-interest in ensuring that the offers they make to consumers clearly express the relative advantages that are on offer.

We therefore recommend that government should accept the principle that savings rates should be quoted in a standard, comparable way; that it should ask the Director-General of Fair Trading to explore with the relevant financial institutions ways of achieving this; and that it should make clear that, while preferring voluntary action, it is prepared to consider a direct legislative solution. We also recommend that the government should not exempt its own savings schemes from any solution that is reached.

The competition for consumers' savings

First, we deal with the position of government itself. Two points have been made to us:

(i) first, that the offer of £70 of tax-free interest on National Savings Bank ordinary accounts confers an unfair fiscal advantage upon government savings and muddles competition;

(ii) second, that government savings institutions, by virtue of being state-run, can offer interest terms which commercial banks in a competitive market place cannot meet.

So far as the first point is concerned, we agree that it would be better if government did not make the terms of competition for savings more obscure by offering tax-free interest concessions on particular types of saving (subject to the general point about government's duty to small savers which we raise below).

On the other hand, we believe that it is necessary to be realistic about the terms which the government offers to achieve its targets for national savings. The government will decide what amount of money it will want to raise in national savings each year; it will then set the terms it offers in such a way as to be as certain as it can be that this target will be reached. It will want to do this whatever the competitive conditions in the savings market. It does not seem useful to us to challenge this process: what is important is that the government's savings targets should be clearly expressed and subject to challenge in parliament and that the methods it chooses to reach these targets should be efficient.

The National Consumer Council has always believed that government has a special responsibility towards small savers. We believe that people on low incomes have a particular difficulty in saving on a regular basis and that they may need easy access to their money in an emergency at short notice. Equally those who have very little money to save need to be absolutely certain that its value is not eroded through inflation. We have suggested on a number of occasions that government should provide a no-strings-attached savings account which would guarantee a rate of return equivalent to the rate of inflation plus, say, 3 per cent for a relatively small sum – £3,000. Such a savings account would not be difficult to provide at times when the rate of inflation is relatively low compared with

Table 8.6 Some specimen annual percentage rates (APRs) for savings (reproduced from the *Daily Telegraph*, June 1983)

This table shows two rates of interest for each savings scheme. The nominal rate is the rate used by companies in their advertisements: the annual percentage rate (APR) of interest is the effective rate of return you would receive if your money was left invested for a year.

The difference between the nominal and the APR rates is determined by the number of times that interest is paid or credited during the year.

For example, if the current nominal rate of 8 per cent for a clearing bank deposit account remained constant, in practice a £100 investment would be credited with £4 interest at the end of six months and £4.16 after a further six months. In other words, after twelve months a £100 investment would grow to £108.16.

When comparing the rates of interest between different investments, the APR should form the basis of comparison. Sometimes interest is paid only once a year, or alternatively the company already shows the APR return in its advertisements. In these cases, the nominal and APR rates are the same. Investors have to take into account that some of the rates are variable and some are fixed (shown by (v) and (f) in the table.) As soon as the nominal rate changes, so does the APR.

	Nominal rate	Annual percentage rate			Investment limits	
	%	nil tax %	30% tax %	50% tax %	minimum £	maximum £
Clearing banks						
deposit account	6.75	6.86	4.80	3.43		
term deposit					10 000	—
1 month	8.63	8.98	6.29	4.49		
3 months	9.38	9.72	6.80	4.86		
6 months	9.50	9.73	6.81	4.57		
12 months	9.50	9.50	6.65	4.75		
National Girobank	7.75	7.90	5.53	3.95	—	(v)
National Savings Bank investment account	10.50	10.50	7.35	5.25	1	200 000 (v)
Index-linked						
savings certificates	4.0	4.0	4.0	4.0	10	10 000 (v)
save as you earn (3rd issue index-linked)	4.0	4.0	4.0	4.0	4	50 (v)
National Savings certificates (25th issue)						
1 year	6.00	6.00	6.00	6.00	25	5 000 (f)
2 years	6.24	6.24	6.24	6.24		
3 years	6.57	6.57	6.57	6.57		
4 years	6.98	6.98	6.98	6.98		
5 years	7.51	7.51	7.51	7.51		

National Savings income bonds	11.0	11.57	8.10	5.79	2 000	200 000 (v)
Money funds						
Simco 7-day	9.79	10.02	7.01	5.01	1 000	(v)
Tyndall 7-day	10.00	10.38	7.26	5.19	1 000	(v)
Mallinhall (Call)	9.66	10.05	7.04	5.03	1 000	(v)
Save & Prosper (Call)	9.48	9.94	6.96	4.97	2 500	—
Lombard						
14-day account	9.75	9.99	6.99	5.00	2 500	—
Western Trust						
1 month plan	9.38	9.79	6.85	4.90	2 500	50 000 (f)
Trustee Savings Bank						
savings account	4.00	4.00	2.80	2.00	—	(v)
investment account	6.75	6.75	4.73	3.38	1	(v)
term deposit account	6½–9				1 000	(v)
Building societies						
ordinary account	6.25	6.35	6.35	4.54	—	30 000 (v)
extra interest account	7.00	7.12	7.12	5.09	500	30 000 (v)
United Dominions Trust (5/50 scheme)						
6 months	9.75	9.75	6.83	4.88	5 000	50 000
12 months	10.00	10.26	7.18	5.13		
24 months	10.50	10.78	7.55	5.39		
Average rate deposit	9.75	10.12	7.08	5.06	5 000	150 000
Finance for Industry						
3 years	10.50	10.78	7.55	5.39		(f)
Local authority bonds						
1 year Worthing	10.00	10.25	7.18	5.13	500	—
2 year Nottingham	10.50	10.78	7.55	5.39	500	—
3 year Kirklees	11.00	11.30	7.91	5.65		(f)

Return: (f) = fixed; (v) = variable.

Source: *Daily Telegraph*, June 1983

market rates of interest, but in times of high inflation only government could provide such a system. We repeat our recommendation.

The next major competitive imbalance in the savings market is the composite rate provided by the building societies. By agreement with the government, building societies pay interest to their savers net of basic rate tax; the building societies pay a calculation of the tax that is due direct to the Inland Revenue. Since both people who are liable to tax and people whose income is too low to make them liable to tax invest in building societies, the income tax that the building societies pay is less than the total tax that would be paid if all building society investors paid tax at the basic rate. Building societies adjust the interest rate they pay out to take this into account. The result – the composite rate – means that basic rate taxpayers get a higher return from building societies than they would otherwise: the effect, in 1982–83, was as if they were paying tax at 25.5 per cent on their investment rather than 30 per cent.

This arrangement gives two different types of advantage to building societies over other types of savings.

* paying interest net of tax is attractive to many consumers because it means they have no subsequent dealings with the tax authorities about which they feel unsure (this point was made in our group discussions by a number of people, including members of ethnic minorities);
* it gives the building societies unfair advantage over other savings institutions when competing for the savings of taxpayers, since the rate paid to them is effectively subsidised.

The subsidy to taxpayers comes from non-taxpayers. This is effectively a subsidy of the better-off by the worse-off. We believe that such subsidies should be avoided wherever possible.

The banks have objected to us about the operation of the composite rate; the CLCB repeated to us the argument previously made to the Committee to Review the Functioning of the Financial Institutions (the 'Wilson Committee'). The Wilson Committee recommended the abolition of the composite rate (5). We agree that the composite rate is undesirable.

However, there are formidable practical problems. The operation of the arrangement of the composite rate means that the Inland Revenue gets the basic rate tax owing on building society accounts simply and cheaply. Changing the system would involve one of two difficulties:

* if interest was paid without deduction for tax, it would be more expensive for tax to be collected since taxpayers would have to be individually assessed. There would also be a likelihood of greater evasion of tax. In any case, as we have seen, many consumers like to be able to receive their interest with tax already deducted:
* if interest was paid with tax deducted, those with incomes too small to attract tax would have to reclaim the tax payments from the Inland Revenue, a process which is cumbersome and off-putting for the individual

and expensive for the Inland Revenue. Many non-taxpayers will find particular difficulties with this type of paperwork.

The best way forward would seem to be to change the system for all savings institutions. Many consumers see the payment of interest with basic rate tax deducted as an advantage. The Trustee Savings Banks have suggested that all financial institutions should be able to pay interest in this way, at the choice of their customers. If non-taxpayers were able to choose to collect interest without tax deducted, this should solve the problems about reclaiming.

We therefore recommend

(i) the composite rate for building societies should be abolished;
(ii) the Inland Revenue should make arrangements with banks, building societies and other savings institutions for interest payments to be made available net of basic rate tax. Savers should be able to choose whether to receive their interest gross or net; if this is impractical for all savers, provision should certainly be made for non-taxpayers to receive interest without tax deduction, perhaps after the completion of a suitable declaration.

Financial advertising

Advertising standards on commercial radio and television are controlled by the Independent Broadcasting Authority (IBA). Under the Independent Broadcasting Authority Act 1973 the IBA has a statutory obligation to prevent the broadcasting of any misleading advertisement, to draw up a code covering standards and practice in advertising and to secure compliance with the code. The IBA ensures that all tv and radio advertisements are examined prior to broadcasting. Advertising in other media is regulated by the Advertising Standards Authority (ASA), an independent body financed by a surcharge of all display press advertisements. The ASA was set up by the advertising industry to ensure that its system of self-regulation works effectively. The Authority publishes the British Code of Advertising Practice (BCAP) and conducts a continuous programme of monitoring and checking advertisements. Individual complaints relating to the content of advertising are also investigated and the results of these investigations are published regularly. Both the IBA and the ASA codes have separate sections relating to financial advertising. The ASA also now has a Financial Advertising Sub-committee of the Code of Advertising Practice Committee. The Building Societies Association has also issued advice to societies in its guide to *The Advertising of Building Society Shares and Deposits* and various circulars. We considered the codes published by the ASA and IBA and did not feel it necessary to suggest any changes to them.

During 1982, the ASA upheld in whole or in part a total of eight complaints against banks and building societies, all relating to investment and saving opportunities. During a similar period, the IBA informed us that there were no complaints in this area.

The Monitoring Department of the ASA also undertook a four-week scrutiny of financial advertisements offering investment opportunities in September/October 1982, checking adherence to the Code. We are very grateful to the ASA for giving details of this exercise. In total, 147 advertisements were scrutinised. The results were categorised as follows: 82 were judged immediately as complying with the Code; in a further 57 cases a detailed point of interpretation was raised which was resolved satisfactorily. The ASA queried eight advertisements; of these one was judged to comply with the Code in the light of the substantiation received, while seven were amended or withdrawn.

We concluded that:

(i) the volume of complaints about financial advertising is not particularly large in relation to the amount that is published;

(ii) in general terms, the regulatory mechanisms of the ASA and IBA appear to be working satisfactorily;

(iii) however, a small number of advertisements that do not meet the requirements of the British Code of Advertising Practice are occasionally published; the Advertising Standards Authority should continue to monitor this area regularly.

POSSIBLE NEW MEDIA FOR FINANCIAL ADVERTISING

The development of direct broadcasting by satellite (DBS) may mean that television advertising originated outside the United Kingdom will be broadcast to the United Kingdom and received by television viewers here. There is as yet no agreement on how this type of international advertising will be regulated – if, indeed, it is regulated at all. We believe that any financial advertising carried out on an international basis is likely to be one of the more sensitive areas. We recommend that financial advertising direct to the UK should meet the standards set by the IBA and the ASA.

Cable television may also carry financial advertising. Again we recommend that any financial advertising on cable television should meet the standards set by IBA and ASA.

Borrowing

We have already covered consumers' use of credit at length in our 1980 report, *Consumers and Credit*. That report, like this one, was a response to a government remit. We have therefore not felt it necessary to retrace our steps in detail. We have, however, considered three points:

(i) the banks' response to the recommendation in *Consumers and Credit* about the declaration of the cost of overdrafts;

(ii) the way in which comparative rates for house mortgage loans are quoted;

(iii) suggestions that building societies should be given powers to lend more widely.

DECLARING THE COST OF OVERDRAFT

Overdraft lending is currently exempt from the consumer credit regulations which lay down, among other things, that all credit quotations and detailed advertisements must contain a statement of the annual percentage rate (APR), an indication of the comparative cost of credit based upon a standard calculation.

Because the APR calculation takes into account both the length of time for which money is borrowed and the frequency with which parts of it are repaid, it is difficult to produce an APR for any individual overdraft in advance. It is, however, possible to compare in general terms an APR for overdrafts with that for other forms of lending. We are anxious that consumers should be made aware of this figure, since an overdraft can be cheaper than borrowing in most other ways (6).

We are also anxious that consumers should have better information about overdraft costs, since these effectively form part of current account charges, about which, as we have seen in section 2, many are confused and dissatisfied. In *Consumers and Credit*, we said

> 'We recommend that banks should be prepared to give their customers information about overdraft costs, in a form which would let them compare it with the cost of other types of credit. We hope that this can be achieved voluntarily, by a uniform code agreed among the banks.' (7)

In the detailed discussion that led to this recommendation, we made it clear that we were addressing two particular situations:

(i) when an overdraft facility is formally agreed in advance, the customer should be told, in standard comparable terms, what the costs and the rate are;

(ii) when banks write to customers when their accounts become overdrawn without prior arrangement, they should indicate the costs which the customer faces.

We did not suggest that banks should always let customers know what overdraft costs would be on each occasion before allowing an account to go into overdraft; clearly this would involve delays in clearing cheques, extra costs which would doubtless be passed on to the customer and the possibility that banks would be less likely to honour cheques that led to inadvertent overdrafts. We did not believe that this would be helpful to customers.

However, we remain convinced that a standard rate quotation for prearranged overdrafts would be useful and that it would be helpful, when banks write about overdrawn accounts, for some indication of costs to be given. This could be in general terms drawing attention to the rate of interest currently being charged and to the fact that having an account in overdraft means that bank charges are payable on all transactions. We cannot believe that such a procedure would add to banks' costs. It should help both banks and customers by drawing attention to the advantages of an arranged overdraft as a form of credit and by bringing more forcefully to customers' attention the cost penalties of having an unarranged overdraft.

We were therefore disappointed by the lukewarm reception by the banks of what we hoped they would see as a positive suggestion for voluntary action. The CLCB responded:

'Insofar as Recommendation 22 recommends that whenever a customer specifically arranges an overdraft with his bank, the bank should voluntarily provide certain information, the Banks do not oppose the Recommendation.'

So far as we can discover, no individual bank has adopted the procedure we suggested.

We continue to believe that the recommendation in *Consumers and Credit* about the declaration of overdraft costs would be helpful to consumers. We therefore repeat it.

COMPARATIVE COSTS OF MORTGAGES

Mortgages provided by building societies and local authorities are exempt from the advertising and quotations regulations of the Consumer Credit Act and building societies, and therefore do not have to quote an APR. The situation has been reviewed by the Office of Fair Trading, who have re-examined the grounds for exemption, especially as the banks have had to find ways of quoting an APR when advertising mortgages. In July 1982 the Director-General of Fair Trading recommended to the then Minister of State for Consumer Affairs that this exemption should now be removed and that building societies should be required to quote an APR when advertising mortgages. In September 1982, the NCC wrote to the Minister, expressing our agreement with the Director-General's recommendation and suggesting early action to implement it. Our submission to the Minister is at Appendix V. As yet, no action has been taken. We again urge the government to accept and implement the Director-General's recommendation.

LENDING BY BUILDING SOCIETIES

General lending is one of the primary services provided by banks. At the moment building societies are prevented from providing these banking services by the terms of the legislation under which they operate, just as they are prevented from offering certain kinds of money transfer facilities like chequing accounts and credit cards, other than through linking arrangements with banks. Section 1(i) of the Building Societies Act 1962 states:

'The purpose for which a society may be established under this Act is one of raising, by the subscriptions of the members, a stock or fund for making advances to members out of the funds of the society upon security by way of mortgage of freehold or leasehold estate.'

This has the effect that building societies can lend only on the security of a first mortgage on property. Various societies suggested to us – and the Spalding report on the *Future Constitution and Powers of Building Societies* does so more formally – that building societies should be allowed to lend more widely (8). It has been suggested both that building society accounts should be allowed to go into overdraft (at the moment, a society would be breaking the law if it allowed this) and that building societies should be enabled to lend for other purposes besides housing, sometimes described as 'things to do with the home', like furniture and domestic appliances.

In considering this question, we are limited by the terms of our remit. We are directed to examine banking services available to the consumer and not the provision of housing finance. Giving building societies the freedom to lend more widely clearly has major potential consequences for the provision of housing finance, which we cannot consider in this report. Would a move by building societies into more general lending decrease the amount of money available for financing house buying and improvement? Would that be a good or a bad thing? What would be the likely effect on the provision of housing finance by banks and other institutions? Is it right that credit for housing should be given preferential treatment over credit for other consumer purchases?

We look at the issues involved, therefore, from a somewhat narrower viewpoint. Would the competitive position in the market for general consumer credit be improved if building societies were allowed to enter it? And what would be the effects on the prudential regulation of building societies? From the point of view of consumers wanting the widest possible access to and choice of credit, there are clear attractions in the prospect of building societies being able to lend more widely. Building society branches are widespread, and most research suggests that societies are generally regarded as helpful and friendly.

On the other hand, allowing building societies to lend more generally might well be the most profound change it is possible to make in their nature and in the way they are supervised by the Registrar General of Friendly Societies. At the moment the risks involved in building societies' lending are very small, since they are lending only on first mortgages on property. Their bad debts are tiny in comparison with the size of their total business. A change to other types of lending would involve the societies acquiring new skills. It is possible that such changes might make investing in a building society less attractive to depositors. It would certainly narrow the distinction between a savings bank and a building society almost to the point of extinction; there would be a case at that point for suggesting that building societies wishing and able to lend more generally should be subject to the regulatory controls appropriate for banks rather than to the Registrar General of Friendly Societies.

However, it is possible to conceive of halfway houses: lending by an individual building society could be limited to a proportion of the society's total lending, or to a maximum sum, or to both. From the evidence we received from building societies, it is clear that some do not want to lend more generally, but still see themselves as essentially dedicated to financing housing.

Considering both sides of the argument, we can see no reason in principle for not allowing some freedom to those building societies who want to lend other than on the security of a first mortgage, subject to appropriate prudential controls. A limited freedom to give overdrafts would allow building societies to compete more effectively in the market for current accounts (9); a limited freedom to lend on items other than property might prove a useful service to building society members and potential members. Certainly it seems to us preferable that building societies should have these powers directly and be publicly accountable for their use than that they should be allowed to set up 'banks' as subsidiaries, whose public accountability would be diffuse and unclear (10).

We therefore recommend that building societies should be given limited powers to lend without the security of a first mortgage, subject to appropriate prudential safeguards. Such powers should be subject to review after, say, five years, to see whether they should be extended or further limited.

References to section 8

1. The personal savings ratio, as this calculation is called, has subsequently declined; people are now saving less in proportion to incomes.
2. *The Guardian*, 2 July 1983.
3. See Appendix III, table 24.
4. *Daily Telegraph*, 11 June 1983.
5. *Report of the Committee to Review the Functioning of Financial Institutions* (the Wilson Report), Cmnd. 7937, HMSO, para. 698.
6. See *Which?*, July 1983, pp. 322–327.
7. National Consumer Council, *Consumers and Credit*, NCC, 1980, p. 9, recommendation 22.
8. Building Societies Association, *The Future Constitution and Powers of Building Societies*, BSA, January 1983.
9. See also pp. 135–40.
10. This possibility has been floated in the Spalding report, pp. 16–17 (see reference 8 above).

Section 9 / Competition and regulation

The consumer interest in competition between banking services is two-fold:

   (i) competition should provide a wide range of choice of services aimed at meeting consumers' needs;

  (ii) the pressures of competition should ensure that services are provided at prices which are related to the costs of the suppliers who are most efficient.

However, consumers have another and, to a degree, contrary interest in the safety of their money. Again this works at two levels:

   (i) consumers obviously suffer individually if their money is lost;

  (ii) major instability in the banking system can lead to a loss of confidence in the system as a whole.

The traditional role of regulation has been to try to ensure stability and security in the provision of banking services. In this section we deal largely with the sharpening of competition. This does not mean that we are ignoring the importance of effective regulation; costly accidents still do happen worldwide, even in advanced banking systems. In 1982 Penn Square Bank of Oklahoma was one of 33 American banks to be liquidated, and if Mexico had not succeeded in retrieving its national finances from the brink of disaster more than 70 per cent of the common equity of two of the four largest US banks could have been wiped out overnight (1). However, regulation in this country has been strengthened recently by the Banking Act of 1979 which among other things provided for the protection of bank depositors by the formation of a bank protection fund. We have seen no need to go into detail over this ground, though we do consider what effects changes in the competitive situation would have on regulation.

During the last few years, including the time that this report has been in preparation, there have been very great changes in competition in banking services, both between individual banks and between banks and other types of financial institutions, most notably building societies. The National Girobank has extended its range of services; the Trustee Savings Banks have vigorously promoted their ability (since the 1960s) to provide current accounts and have attained clearing bank status; the Co-operative Bank has expanded rapidly; and some differences in practice have emerged between the big four high street clearing banks which would have been unthinkable some years ago. In this section we review the major competitive developments and consider in what ways competition between banks and other financial institutions could be usefully developed.

It is worth recalling that banks are complex institutions, offering a wide range of services, and, of course, that they have other important markets besides those personal customers whose interests we are examining in this report. Indeed for many years the 'retail sector' was regarded as the Cinderella of banking compared with corporate and international business. This is now much less true than it was ten years ago; the onset of an era of mass banking has changed bankers' terms of reference, though old attitudes and prejudices die hard.

Banks developed as deposit-taking institutions which 'looked after their customers' money'. Customers allowed banks to use their money in return for interest or services; banks made their profits by lending, including of course to their depositors. What is new about recent competitive developments is that other deposit-taking institutions, previously thought of primarily as providing a home for personal savings, are finding that, to continue to attract customers, they need to be able to offer services as well as interest on deposits. The building societies are now beginning to follow the Trustee Savings Banks down this road. As we saw in section 2, many building society customers would like their society to offer money transfer services. All the major societies who talked to us made it clear that they were being drawn into seeking to provide money transfer services by a demand from a proportion of their customers. The result is that the building societies, operating from within a wholly different regulatory frame- work and financial tradition from the banks, are being brought into increasingly direct competition with them.

Both the savings market and the credit market (dealt with in detail in our 1980 report *Consumers and Credit*) are highly competitive (2). We discuss them more fully in section 8; we need do no more here than draw attention to the vigorous competition for personal savings between government, the banks, building societies and other deposit-taking institutions. The credit market, too, is highly competitive: nearly 100,000 licences of one sort or another have been granted by the Office of Fair Trading under the Consumer Credit Act. Indeed, the banks' own entry in a major way into mortgages for house purchase in the early 1980s served, at least for a time, to make the credit market even more competitive. It is certainly our belief that this worked strongly to consumers' advantage as regards housing finance in that competition from banks forced building societies to reconsider some of their own practices in a way which has proved valuable. Our major anxiety is that, having entered this market so boldly, the banks should retain some commitment to it. This is now in doubt, as far as new mortgages are concerned, with several banks having apparently all but exhausted their current home loan allocations (3).

At first glance, it may be surprising that money transmission services should be a focus for competition. Dealing with the pieces of paper that making payments involves is expensive: most of the clearing banks emphasised the magnitude of the costs incurred and, they said, their unprofitability (4). Certainly many customers resent paying bank charges – not surprisingly, since writing a cheque or having a standing order implemented is not a benefit in itself but only an intermediary to what consumers regard as the real benefit, the week's groceries or paying off a bit more of the mortgage. Having to pay for making a payment is not popular, which is one reason why the offer of 'free banking' made by the Co-operative Bank, the Yorkshire Bank, Williams and Glyn's and the National Girobank (plus the Clydesdale Bank and the TSBs in Scotland) is attractive.

Perhaps consumers' own behaviour gives some clue to why institutions compete for this business which they claim to regard as expensive and unprofitable. As we have seen in section 2, many bank customers do not make a particularly considered choice of bank; they open an account at their parents' bank or at the first one they come across in the high street. And they have tended to be remarkably loyal to their original choice. It is quite common for bank customers to have their account in a branch originally chosen because it was close at hand long after they have moved hundreds of miles away. There are a number of reasons for this. One must be that, as our research shows, most bank customers are, on the whole, highly satisfied with bank services. But they also want to preserve the value of the credit they believe they get for being a long-term and reliable customer. And, again, as our research shows, once a customer has amassed a collection of standing orders and direct debits, the notion of change seems to involve all sorts of hazards: will the rates payment get lost? Will the mortgage standing order get sent off to pay the *Which?* subscription?

Just as important, from a bank's point of view, customers who come to a bank primarily for money transmission services may also buy other services – personal loans or insurance brokerage – which are profitable (5). So it is perhaps not in the end surprising that banks should seek to capture new customers at the earliest possible age and that building societies should see the offer of money transmission services as a way of winning new depositors and providing existing ones with extra reasons for staying.

It follows that competition in one market for banking services cannot be considered entirely separately from that in other markets. We therefore need to consider more closely whether more vigorous competition in money transfer has implications for saving and lending. In the rest of this section, therefore, we consider separately:

* issues which arise from competition between the existing banks most involved in personal accounts:
* issues which arise from competition between banks and other financial institutions.

Competition between banks

A number of points have emerged from our research among consumers or have been raised with us in discussion. They are:

* special offers to students and school leavers;
* opening hours;
* charges for transactions at a different bank from the one at which the customer banks;
* the £50 limit on cheque guarantee cards.

SPECIAL OFFERS FOR STUDENT ACCOUNTS

The banks are engaged in vigorous competition for new accounts among school leavers and students. Besides various free gifts, typically the new account holder gets free banking, perhaps for his or her whole student career, and invariably on terms which are more generous than that for other customers. The bank's motivation is obvious: as we have seen, there is a tendency for bank customers to stay with their banks for many years and, of course, today's students are likely to be tomorrow's high earners. It can however be objected:

(i) that such inducements involve a cross-subsidy between one type of bank customer and another (established account holders pay higher charges because student account holders pay none);

(ii) that the provision of free banking on preferential terms does not educate students in the sensible use of a bank account.

We see no need to intervene in this question. In so far as there is any cross-subsidy between bank customers, it can be thought of as cross-subsidy between the different periods of the same customer's banking life. And other bank customers besides students enjoy 'free' banking that reduces the pressure on them to operate their accounts in the most cost-effective way. Conversely, we can see some long-term advantage in competitive advertising for student accounts. If students choose a bank on the basis of the specific advantages offered when they become students, they may be more likely to opt for an account that suits them in later life on the basis of similarly rational comparison. This may lead them to make new and different choices.

OPENING HOURS

As we have seen in section 2, better opening hours are at the top of the list of improvements which bank customers would like to see in bank services. Prior to the Barclays initiative on Saturday opening, banking hours among the major high street banks were virtually identical and in some cases a matter for informal collective agreement. On 18 November 1982, for example, the Banking Information Service of the Committee of London Clearing Bankers issued a press release to say 'Branches of the London clearing banks will close at 12 noon on Friday 24 December 1982 . . . Branches will be closed all day on Monday 3rd January 1983' (6).

In September 1982, Barclays started the process of re-opening some of their busiest branches on Saturdays. Of course customers of the Co-operative Bank and the National Girobank already had access to their bank accounts on Saturdays as did customers of a number of much smaller licensed deposit-takers, like Western Trust and Savings, plus all the building societies.

The Trustee Savings Bank told us that it was not in favour of general opening on Saturday mornings, though it does have one experimental branch in a department store which is open on Saturdays during shopping hours. It does find opening late one evening a week a success. However, it was clear from our conversations with the major clearing banks other than Barclays that they did not greet the idea either of Saturday morning or of late evening opening with much enthusiasm. They felt that the most effective way to provide their customers with better access to their accounts was through the provision of automated teller machines (ATMs) which have the advantage of giving service for much longer hours than any bank is ever likely to open (7).

Unions representing bank employees told us that they were opposed to the re-introduction of Saturday opening. They believed that the extension of ATM facilities had substantially diminished public demand for Saturday personal banking which therefore could not be profitable.

As we have said in section 5, we accept that the provision of ATMs is useful: our market research shows that bank customers want more of them. However, banks provide more services than allowing people to cash cheques.

The National Consumer Council has always believed in relation to shop opening hours that shops should be free to choose for themselves when to open, unfettered by legal restriction, as is generally the case in Scotland. In a competitive market place, this should lead to a pattern of opening which comes closest to meeting consumers' needs in the most cost-effective way. Clearly we must apply the same principles to banks. We are pleased that the monolithic pattern of bank opening hours is showing some cracks, since this gives customers the opportunity to demonstrate by their actions how seriously they take the complaints they make about opening hours.

The only formal recommendation which we make is that all agreements on bank opening hours, however arrived at, should cease (8). As we have noted, there are a number of banks and other institutions which provide banking services at hours which do not conform to standard high street clearing banks' opening times. We believe that opening hours should be one major criterion which individual consumers should consider when deciding where to open or keep their account.

CHARGES FOR TRANSACTIONS AT OTHER BANKS

In 1981 Barclays introduced a 50 pence counter charge at most of their branches for encashing cheques drawn on other banks. Previously, the clearing banks had mutually agreed to process each other's cheques without charge. Barclays' action prompted selective retaliation by some of the other banks. It was defended by Barclays on the grounds that improved counter service had led to non-Barclays customers using their facilities in large numbers. This, it was argued, had had two consequences: first, Barclays were cashing twice as many cheques for other banks' customers as other banks were for Barclays' customers, so incurring costs which had to be borne by Barclays' customers; and secondly that some Barclays banking halls were becoming congested at peak hours to the detriment of the service that the bank was able to offer to its own customers. This account of events was strongly disputed by the other banks to whom we spoke; most entered a vigorous defence of earlier reciprocal arrangements and some questioned the figures which had been used by Barclays to justify the charge.

Williams and Glyn's, in their evidence to us, claimed that a continuing 50 pence counter charge would make the unbanked even more reluctant to open accounts. They went on to claim that the imposition of the 50 pence levy may persuade customers of banks with smaller branch networks (like themselves) to switch their accounts to their larger competitors. More broadly, Williams and Glyn's asserted an overall disadvantage to the consumer, claiming that counter charges 'will lead ultimately to a diminution in the degree of competition and flexibility and quality of service and convenience that the customer should be able to expect'.

There is some evidence that the smaller banks have lost a few customers as a consequence of the Barclays initiative, but the total effect in terms of the movement of accounts has not been significant and related administrative costs have been high. The (then) general manager in charge of retail services at Barclays admitted in an interview with *Retail Banker International* in early 1982 that 'in terms of persuading people to transfer their accounts to us it has not gone well at all. We've gained 2,500 new accounts and we lost 1,800 because of this move' (9).

There is some conflict of interest between different groups of consumers here. There seems little doubt that the usefulness of the whole banking system to consumers is to some extent reduced by obstacles to using parts of it. Our market research showed a substantial number of bank customers who wanted the charge to be stopped. Individuals who live in places where there is only a single bank branch may find themselves disadvantaged, if they do not bank there. We heard from a citizens' advice bureau of difficulties caused to an elderly pensioner in this situation.

However, it has to be said that where Barclays offer services – and incur costs – that other banks do not, they are clearly justified in making a charge for making these services available to other banks' customers. Moreover a 50 pence charge (now £1 on Saturdays) does not make the Barclays network unavailable to other banks' customers: they can in most circumstances make a decision whether to use the service and pay the fee or not. They are also free to move their account if they feel that this is justified by the additional convenience.

We do not, therefore, feel justified in making any general recommendation about the 50 pence charge. We do, however, urge that individual bank managers should use their discretion to waive the charge in circumstances where individuals, such as pensioners, are seriously disadvantaged by it.

THE £50 LIMIT ON CHEQUE GUARANTEE CARDS

Suggestions that the £50 limit should be raised came in our market research among bank customers and from retailers. The limit is part of a registered trade agreement which the Office of Fair Trading has decided not to challenge (10).

The value of the cheque guarantee card has been pegged at £50 by all the UK banks since 1977, when the limit was raised from £30. The big four banks' losses through fraudulent use of chequing facilities have risen over this period from £1.85m (1977) to an estimated £17.49m (1982), according to figures supplied by the Banking Information Service. This mounting fraud bill relates more to the greatly increased use of guarantee cards than to the higher limit on their valuation. Nevertheless, we recognise that the banks do have a problem as regards organised plastic card crime (11). The long-term answer is clearly to develop a more fraud-resistant plastic card: the problems this involves have still to be solved.

There is no doubt that the £50 limit will increasingly become an irritation to consumers and retailers, even with relatively modest levels of inflation, and that there is therefore a strong case for increasing it. The existing maximum limits the usefulness of cheques for any shopping where customers want to take the goods home straight away. It also leads consumers and retailers to conspire together to evade the terms of the restriction. However, granted the wider use of guarantee cards and the consequent mounting fraud bill, we do not feel able to make a formal recommendation that banks should put up the limit, though we are unhappy about their agreement. Certainly, if the banks were able to produce a more fraud-resistant cheque guarantee mechanism, as we hope they will, we believe that the Office of Fair Trading should then reconsider whether the amount of the limit is a reasonable subject for such collective agreement. We understand that the banks are in practice unlikely to want to compete with each other in offering different limits to cheque guarantee cards and that differing limits would be a little inconvenient to retailers. However, the restrictive agreement is on a matter of some importance to customers and we believe that agreements which formally limit the ability to compete on matters like this should not continue.

Competition between banks and other institutions

As we have seen in section 2, there is pressure from consumers for some of the money transmission services currently provided by banks – cheque books and standing orders, for instance – to be provided by building societies. Some major building societies are interested in competing for this business, and the Abbey

National, in collaboration with the Co-operative Bank, has already started to provide such services. Other organisations, too, including those licensed deposit-takers known loosely as money shops already provide a range of payment services. We concluded in section 3 that the best hope for developing current account systems that meet the needs of different types of consumer and for promoting bank charging systems that relate charges to cost, is through competition, both between banks and between banks and other deposit-taking institutions. We therefore need to examine whether the current situation places any obstacles in the way of such competition.

At the heart of any money transfer arrangement, whether based on paper vouchers like cheques or electronic messages like many salary payments, lies the payment clearing system. We have briefly described the way the clearing house works for cheques and Bankers' Automated Clearing Services Ltd (BACS) works for automated payments (section 3). What is important is how decisions are made about who can join in the system (or, more accurately, systems) and what the price of entry is.

The clearing house for cheques is jointly owned by Barclays, Lloyds, Midland, National Westminster, Williams and Glyn's and Coutts. These together make up the Committee of London Clearing Bankers (CLCB). The Co-operative Bank, National Girobank and Central Trustee Savings Bank are functional members of the clearing house but do not have any stake in its ownership. The Bank of England is also a member. BACS is jointly owned by the full members of the CLCB, minus Coutts. The Co-operative Bank, National Girobank and Central Trustee Savings Bank are sponsoring or second tier members (this appears to be broadly equivalent to functional membership of the cheque clearing house).

All other banks and financial institutions who wish to offer their customers a cheque book service have to do so by making an agency agreement with one of the clearing banks. So the Yorkshire Bank and the Bank of America have their cheques cleared by Williams and Glyn's and the Abbey National has its Cheque Save Account cheques issued by the Co-operative Bank. It is usual to get competitive tenders for agency arrangements: terms are negotiated individually between the organisation wanting cheques cleared and the clearing bank.

The Co-operative Bank and the Central Trustee Savings Bank became members of the clearing house in 1975 on payment of a fee of £200,000 (12). The National Girobank later became a member at an entrance fee of £400,000, having previously turned down an invitation to join. The Yorkshire Bank was invited to become a member in 1975, but felt that abandoning its existing agency arrangement would not enable it to improve its services to its customers. The Yorkshire Bank is in a unique position being owned by four of the London clearing banks. The Scottish clearers have also turned down the opportunity to gain direct access to the London clearing.

Functional membership of the clearing house is open to any cheque-issuing bank which, among other things, issues one per cent of the total number of cheques processed by the clearing house. This is a somewhat higher fence to climb than it sounds: the Co-operative Bank issues only about this number of cheques. The National Girobank appears not to have qualified at all on this criterion, but has been admitted nonetheless (13).

The Price Commission considered the question of access to clearing in 1977, having discussed the advantages and disadvantages of membership of the clearing house with a variety of the 'newer' banks. It concluded that the clearing banks had attempted to make clearing facilities available to other institutions on what the Commission considered reasonable terms. However, the Commission went on to say:

'. . . we feel that more could be done to avoid the impression that the Clearing House (which is a national resource albeit owned by the CLCB) is being used to restrict competition from new-comers to the retail banking scene.'

The Commission proposed that

'regulation of admission to the Clearing House should lie in the hands of the Authorities (who should also arbitrate on the allocation of costs in the event of dispute) and that those banks which are admitted to membership be offered seats on the Board of the Bankers' Clearing House' (14).

In 1980 the Wilson Committee noted that in many other countries the central clearing infrastructure was publicly owned, with payment services being provided by private sector institutions. The Committee concluded:

'Had we been starting anew, there might have been some attraction in a publicly-owned central clearing system. But the present arrangements appear to be working satisfactorily and we have little reason to believe that bringing them into public ownership could be expected to increase the efficiency with which the system is presently operated. Because of the strength of the public interest in this area, however, we recommend that the Bank of England should become more closely involved than it has been in the past in regulating admission to the Clearing House. The Bank is, however, itself a member of the Clearing House engaging in a significant amount of commercial banking for government departments and therefore has a vested interest of its own in one aspect of membership, that of cost allocation. This potential conflict of interest would best be adjudicated upon by some totally outside body' (15).

Since then, the Office of Fair Trading has investigated the clearing system. They wrote to more than thirty non-clearing banks, none of whom complained about the agency arrangements used and none of whom argued for direct access to clearing. As a result, in 1982, the OFT obtained a direction from the Secretary of State for Trade discharging the Director General from his statutory obligation to refer registered restrictive arrangements, in this case the clearing arrangements, to the Restrictive Practices Court (16).

Our own experience is somewhat different from that of the OFT. Two of the institutions we wrote to, one a bank, the other a major building society, complained vigorously about the nature of the arrangements they were forced into: the Bank of Ireland said that having to use an agency arrangement 'places us at a considerable disadvantage in terms of cost and competitiveness'. The Bank of Cyprus (London) Ltd wrote to us in similar, though more muted, terms. We were also left in no doubt that, among the building societies, the Abbey National had found considerable difficulty in interesting any of the London clearing banks in providing an agency arrangement for its cheque services, before it reached agreement with the Co-operative Bank.

The cheque clearing system (like the clearing system for electronic payments which grew out of it) is a natural monopoly, in much the same way as a telephone network is – everyone who subscribes to the system has an interest in seeing that everyone is connected to the same system. In principle at least, there are very powerful arguments against such a system being jointly owned by a small group of those providing the service.

Applying these arguments of principle to the bank clearing system it is clear that

* joint ownership enables the CLCB member banks to dictate terms of entry to any organisation wishing to join the system directly, for example by determining criteria of acceptability;
* it also enables the members of the clearing house to negotiate from a position of considerable strength when making arrangements for agency agreements with those wanting access to clearing services. To what extent this bargaining strength is mitigated by competition among the clearers for new agency business is unclear to us.

Automated payments are, as we noted in section 3, becoming increasingly widespread. It is therefore important to note that non-members of BACS suffer a competitive disadvantage, when competing for the accounts of hitherto un-banked employees: an employee's pay will generally take at least a day longer to reach his or her account in a building society, via a BACS intermediary, than it will if the account is held with one of the clearing banks. The delay can be much longer. Since people want access to their pay as fast as possible – particularly if they are used to being paid weekly in cash – this competitive disadvantage may prove significant and will perhaps have a detrimental effect on the growth of building society account holding.

With this in mind, we considered whether some other form of organisation would be possible. We considered two options.

First, the banks might be required to sell ownership of the clearing house and of BACS to a group of financial institutions not directly interested in providing money transmission services themselves. Clearing services would then be operated as a commercial service to anyone with the technical and financial expertise to join, but would be institutionally distinct from the ownership and control of the system. The Bank of England might need to have some interest in seeing that terms of entry were appropriate and that the financial supervision of the operation was sound. It would certainly be necessary for the Bank or some other body (17) to exercise a careful eye over the credentials of applicants.

Alternatively, the banks could extend ownership of the clearing system along the lines recently introduced in Canada, where ownership and control has been taken from the exclusive control of the banks and transferred to a new body called the Canadian Payments Association (CPA). Now all institutions offering cheque accounts can apply to become members of the clearing system. As of mid-1982, 119 institutions had become members of the Canadian Payments Association including the Bank of Canada; 69 chartered banks, including 57 foreign bank subsidiaries; 25 central co-operatives, representing over 3,000 individual credit unions and *caisses populaires*; and 25 trust and mortgage loan companies. The CPA is established by statute and the Bank of Canada appoints one of its officials to chair the board. These arrangements appear to work very well.

However, it is clear from our conversations with CLCB that suggestions that their members should lose the ownership or the exclusive ownership of clearing mechanisms will not be welcome. Is there justification for government action to change the ownership of a system which by general agreement is efficient? Let us first remind ourselves of the consumer interest. Throughout this report, we have seen that greater competition in the provision of banking services has led to a wider choice for consumers across a range of services. In a number of instances where we have identified shortcomings in the way the banks organise their business, we have expressed our belief that the further development of vigorous competition is the right way to gain improvements. It is largely in the provision of money transmission services that there appear to be serious obstacles to greater competition.

However, we believe that it is behaviour in the market place and not formal market structure which is important when considering competition. Neither the Price Commission, the Wilson Committee nor the Office of Fair Trading has been able to find significant evidence that the clearing banks have used their ownership of the clearing system to restrict competition. Some specific disadvantage was alleged to us and so was a great deal of more generalised disaffection. However, the evidence we have does not appear to us to justify a recommendation that at this moment the government should remove from the clearing banks ownership of the clearing system.

But the market for personal banking services is currently going through a period of almost revolutionary change. Building societies wish to provide money transmission services – and, as we have seen, many of their customers want them to. Pressures to encourage cashless pay are growing; we believe it to be in the public interest that the widest possible range of deposit-taking organisations are able to compete on equal terms to provide services to currently unbanked employees (18). And the new technology of electronic funds transfer is bringing closer the time that payments can be made in shops (see section 5) directly debiting the customer's account. EFT technology will provide other cheaper methods of transferring money from one account to another and should not be the exclusive preserve of existing clearing banks; nor should it only be available to other institutions on terms which are convenient to the clearing banks.

The behaviour of the clearing banks faced with this competition should determine government's attitude to them. If building societies are unable to gain access to cheque clearing systems on an equitable basis; if deposit-taking institutions at which employees want to deposit their pay cannot compete on equal terms with the clearing banks in terms of access to automated processing of credits; if other financial institutions are excluded from competitive access to nationwide EFT facilities; then we believe the case for a more open clearing system, or systems, will be established.

We therefore recommend that the government should announce its intention now to review the development of money transmission services in two to three years' time. If these criteria have not been met, the government should consider whether the joint ownership of the clearing systems by the full members of the CLCB is still appropriate.

OTHER COMPETITIVE ANOMALIES

It has been represented to us by the banks that there are other statutory provisions besides the composite rate, discussed in section 8, which give anomalous advantages to the building societies over themselves. The first is the exemption from restrictive practices legislation under which the Building Societies Association can recommend mortgage and investment rates to its members. It is true that the greater part of savings in building societies is now in premium accounts to which the recommendations do not apply directly, but basic rates to investors and mortgage rates to borrowers are fixed by most societies in accordance with BSA recommendations. We can see no justification for the continuance of this practice in an increasingly competitive financial environment. We therefore recommend that the Building Societies Association should cease to recommend rates (19). If it does not, we recommend that the exemption it enjoys from restrictive practices legislation should be withdrawn.

It is argued, also, that building societies should lose their preferential status under arrangements for the payment of corporation tax and that their tax liability should be raised to 52 per cent, the same figure that is applied to the banks. Building societies dispute the validity of this criticism. They say that the actual rate of corporation tax paid by the banks in recent years has fallen way below the nominal rate of 52 per cent. It was reported in March 1981 that by getting heavily involved in leasing business the London clearers had successfully deferred corporation taxes amounting to at least £2 billion in preceding years. According to the BSA, the average rate of corporation tax paid by the banks in recent years demonstrates that the alleged tax advantage of societies over the banks is more apparent than real; they also point out that there is legislation which prevents the building societies from offering leasing facilities and thus reducing their effective rates of taxation in the manner enjoyed by the banks (20).

Adjudicating on the relative merits of these arguments may be thought to take a consumer organisation beyond its proper limits. However, given the emphasis we have placed on enabling building societies to compete on equal terms with banks, we believe that it is appropriate for us to recommend that the Inland Revenue should take steps to see that the corporation tax treatment of banks and building societies should not inappropriately favour either.

TAXES ON BANKS

The Co-operative Bank represented to us that it had been unfairly treated by the Special Tax on Banking Deposits introduced in the 1982 Budget. The relevance of this to consumers, and more specifically to Co-operative Bank customers, is that the tax allegedly inhibited the Bank's ability to compete effectively with its rivals by means of the arbitrary imposition of a disproportionate levy.

Although the tax has frequently been described as a tax on 'windfall profits', in the event the amounts levied were related not to profits (and by implication ability to pay) but to the size of a bank's non-interest bearing deposits. The result was that the Co-operative Bank was obliged to pay a sum in tax equivalent to 88.9 per cent of its pre-tax group profit for 1981 – in percentage terms three times more than the Midland and six times more than Lloyds.

Taxes levied were as follows:

	pre-tax profits 1981 £m	special tax on deposits £m	% of profits
National Giro	5.5	7.3	*
Co-operative	3.6	3.2	88.9
Midland	232.2	65.1	28.0
Nat West	494.0	97.0	19.6
Barclays	566.6	94.1	16.6
Lloyds	385.6	58.6	15.2
Yorkshire	23.4	3.3	14.1
TSB	77.1	10.7	13.8
Williams & Glyn's	56.1	6.9	12.3
Average all above			18.8

* Subsequently the government injected £7.3m into the National Girobank.

It is no part of our remit to advise the government on the level of tax it chooses to levy on banks. We will, however, observe that the Co-operative Bank appears to have a strong point.

References to section 9

1. *Economist*, 16 October 1982.
2. National Consumer Council, *Consumers and Credit*, NCC, 1980.

3. The Royal Bank of Scotland was the first major clearing bank to stop giving new mortgages completely in May 1983. The proportion of new mortgages being offered by the clearing banks as a whole fell from one in three to one in ten between June 1982 and June 1983.
4. The Co-operative Bank was an exception, claiming that the costs incurred by their major competitors are greater than is necessary to run efficient money transmission systems.
5. See Appendix IV.
6. Banking Information Service, press release, 18 December 1982.
7. See also pp. 65–71.
8. No such agreements are registered with the Office of Fair Trading under restrictive trade practices legislation. We must therefore assume that agreements are informal.
9. *Retail Banker International*, 25 January 1982.
10. Agreement no. S271 was subject to a section 21(2) direction under the Restrictive Trade Practices Act 1976 in May 1983.
11. For an interesting insight into plastic card fraud, see Laurie Taylor, 'How to rob banks with a pen', *New Society*, 11 November 1982.
12. Price Commission, *Banks: charges for money transmission services*, HMSO, HC 337, para. 6.11.
13. The three other qualifications for admission (as identified by the CLCB in 1975) were: an existing branch network; the ability to conform to the functional requirements and timetable of the clearing system; acceptance of the costs of participation.
14. Price Commission, *op. cit.*, para. 6.13.
15. *Report of the Committee to Review the Functioning of Financial Institutions* (the Wilson Report), HMSO, Cmnd 7937, para. 1337.
16. Agreements S649 and S201, referring to the operation of the clearing systems in London and Scotland respectively, were subject to section 21(2) directions in July 1982.
17. The Bank of England has the expertise to make judgments about the technical competence of applicants to clearing arrangements and would, we believe, welcome the responsibility.
18. See appendix VI.
19. This recommendation was also made by the Wilson Committee; *op. cit.*, chapter 8.
20. BSA Bulletin, no. 33, January 1983, pp. 19–20.

Section 10 / Northern Ireland and Scotland

The terms of the government remit on which this report is based asked us to report on banking services in the United Kingdom as a whole. There are, however, sufficient differences of law, practice and context in Scotland and Northern Ireland to merit separate discussion.

Northern Ireland

The four Northern Ireland banks, the Northern Bank, the Ulster Bank, the Bank of Ireland and the Allied Irish Banks, offer deposit, lending, money transmission and other services to personal customers very much as in the rest of the UK. Between them, the four banks have some three hundred branches and over one hundred sub-branches and agencies in Northern Ireland serving the needs of some one-and-a-half million people — much the same number of outlets per head of population as the clearing banks have in England and Wales. Northern Bank and Ulster Bank are wholly-owned subsidiaries of the Midland Bank and the National Westminster Bank respectively: both subsidiaries declined to make independent submissions to us. (The Clydesdale Bank in Scotland is also a wholly-owned subsidiary of the Midland Bank but did submit evidence independently.) The Bank of Ireland and Allied Irish Banks are incorporated in the Republic of Ireland. All four banks have substantial branch networks in the Irish Republic, some 950 branches in total; and the Bank of Ireland and Allied Irish Banks have over fifty branches in Great Britain. Thus the four Northern Ireland banks operate within three distinct legislative jurisdictions, though the legislative position of the banks as regards their activities in Northern Ireland and Great Britain has been brought much closer together by the Banking Act 1979 and need not concern us further except in respect of rights of note issue.

Under the Bankers (Ireland) Act 1845, the Bankers (Northern Ireland) Act 1928 and the Coinage Act 1971, the four Northern Ireland banks are empowered to issue their own bank notes. (Scottish banks enjoy similar powers, but there are no comparable arrangements in England and Wales.) There is a small fiduciary issue for each bank which does not have to be covered by holdings of specific assets, but beyond this amount every bank note must be covered, pound for pound, by Bank of England notes – the latter may be held at the Bank of England. The fiduciary issues of the four banks amount to just over £2.1 million.

The significance of these arrangements to Northern Ireland consumers is difficult to gauge but probably marginal. In practice a mixture of local bank notes and Bank of England notes circulate side by side in Northern Ireland and exchange on a 'pound for pound' basis. In November 1982 the amount of Northern Ireland bank notes outstanding was £86 million, whereas there were probably some £200 million of Bank of England notes outstanding. The issue of the relatively small fiduciary issue is undoubtedly highly lucrative to the four banks, since they have to pay only production, transport and administrative costs plus a duty of one per cent per annum on their average circulation to the Inland Revenue. The cost implications of the issue of own bank notes in excess of the fiduciary issue are more complicated but such issues are generally less profitable, and after a certain point unprofitable, because of the need to maintain cover with the Bank of England (1).

Northern Ireland has fewer bank accounts per head of population than the rest of the UK. One estimate for 1982 put the proportion of the adult population who have current accounts at only 25 per cent compared with 54 per cent in Great Britain (2). However, far more people have credit union accounts – there were some 112,000 subscribing members by the end of 1982. Credit union expansion in recent years has been faster than that of the banks (just under one hundred unions by the end of 1982) and about the same as that of the building societies, although in money terms the credit union sector is still relatively small. Building society growth accelerated sharply in 1982; by the end of the year there were approximately eighty full branches plus a number of agencies. The Trustee Savings Bank of Northern Ireland now provides very strong competition for the established banks as, to a lesser extent, does the National Girobank. Total account holding, however, remains low by Great Britain standards.

The Irish Banks operate a cartel covering opening hours, charging tariffs and interest rates. At the request of the Northern Ireland Bankers' Association (NIBA), the supply of banking services in Northern Ireland was exempted from the operation of the Restrictive Trade Practices (Services) Order of 1976 issued under the Fair Trading Act 1973; this exemption is kept under review by the Department of Trade and Industry in London.

Opening hours are subject to agreement with the Irish Bank Officials Association (IBOA); current opening hours are therefore the consequence of collective bargaining between the IBOA and the cartel.

Banking services in Northern Ireland are less accessible to bank customers than in the rest of the UK. The agreement operated by the banks dictates that opening hours are limited from 10.00 am to 12.30 pm and 1.30 pm to 3.30 pm, Monday to Friday. On two days a week, security considerations permitting, banking hours are extended by opening at 9.30 am. The most significant feature of these arrangements is lunch-hour closing.

As we have noted elsewhere, the inconvenience of limited opening hours in the UK as a whole (Scottish consumers are less well served than their counterparts in England and Wales) has been mitigated by the development of extensive ATM programmes. This is particularly important for access to cash, but also for up-to-date information on account balances.

It should therefore be noted that the Irish banks are some way behind the English and Scottish banks in the application of new technology in general and in the installation of ATMs in particular. For almost two years the operation of ATMs was blacked by the IBOA, a dispute which seriously disadvantaged Northern Ireland consumers by comparison with consumers elsewhere in the UK. The banks are now engaged in a big push to make up lost ground, and the Bank of Ireland, Ulster and Northern banks were discussing plans to share their machines at the time of writing.

Money transmission arrangements in Northern Ireland continue to rely heavily upon expensive manual paper processing. The computerisation programmes of the banks are several years behind those of the London and Scottish clearing banks. The formal approval of the IBOA is required before new technological procedures can be introduced. We were informed that incomplete computerisation programmes are a critical factor in the banks' lack of enthusiasm for acquiring new current accounts amongst cash-paid workers. It is claimed that the banks cannot profitably handle greater volumes of paper transactions on comparatively low credit balances until transmission processes have been fully automated.

This helps to explain why the most effective competition for money transmission business has come from the Trustee Savings Bank of Northern Ireland. The TSB's computerisation programme is a long way in advance of the four commercial banks'; one consequence of this is that a customer, on proof of identity, can effect a transaction at any of the branches of the Bank, all of which are linked to instantly retrievable and up-to-date information on individual credit balances. No other banks supply this service. The TSB also opens at lunchtimes.

The banks' cartel on charging tariffs and selected interest rates is operated under the auspices of the Northern Ireland Bankers' Association (NIBA). These arrangements cover all fees and abatements arising from the operation of current accounts including the conditions on which 'free' banking is offered. Thus in August 1982 the customers of all four banks were instructed that 'due to rising costs, the member Banks of Northern Ireland Bankers' Association have found it necessary to increase the Scale of Minimum Charges, as indicated below . . .' (revised schedule of current account fees). Interest rates paid on deposit accounts are generally in line with the recommendations of NIBA, though the cartel is now less ubiquitous than it once was in respect of bank lending and borrowing. In particular, recent services like home mortgages and notice deposits have been introduced outside the cartel.

The cartel was investigated by the Price Commission in 1978. The Commission was informed by NIBA that exemption from cartel registration requirements had been requested on four grounds:

'(i) Its members conduct banking operations in the Republic, and it is economically necessary to harmonise the terms upon which business is transacted in both territories. As a cartel exists in the Republic, the removal of a similar forum in Northern Ireland would lead to the involuntary operation of a cartel due to influences emanating from the Republic;

(ii) present disturbances and depressed level of economic activity in the Province;

(iii) stability of costs engendered by the arrangements;

(iv) instability and consequential adverse effect on resources caused by open competition between banks in a small economy.' (3)

The Commission rejected arguments (i), (iii) and (iv) but felt unable to reach a judgment on the relative importance of (ii) – the security argument. The Commission was most dismissive of argument (i), commenting that '. . . it cannot be right that cartel arrangements in the Republic should dictate banking practices in part of the UK' (4).

Five years have elapsed since the publication of the Price Commission's observations, and the cartel, though diminished, remains intact. We believe that the argument for removing NIBA's exemption under fair trading legislation is now stronger than it was in 1978. The fact that some new banking services, as we have noted, are offered outside the terms of the cartel strengthens the case for withdrawal on grounds of logic and consistency. The argument previously advanced to the Price Commission that open banking competition in a small economy might have (unspecified) destabilising consequences has subsequently been invalidated by the stringent prudential provisions of the Banking Act 1979.

The defence of the cartel on grounds of security is no longer convincing. First, the TSB and the building societies have demonstrated that financial institutions are capable of opening their doors to the public for more than four-and-a-half hours per day without suffering adverse consequences. Secondly, we cannot recognise any connection between considerations of security risk and the imposition of fixed current account fees and abatements. There remains the argument based on arrangements in the Republic. This too has been weakened by the separation of the two currencies, the pound and the punt. In principle, we agree with the Price Commission that it is wrong for Northern Ireland consumers to be denied the advantages afforded by open competition amongst the banks elsewhere in the UK as a consequence of the cartel which exists in the Republic.

We therefore recommend that the Department of Trade and Industry should withdraw the exemption order referred to above, and that the four Northern Ireland banks should be required to engage in open competition on all matters concerned with pricing and interest rate policy. We hope that one result would be banking hours which do not put Northern Ireland consumers at a disadvantage compared with the rest of the United Kingdom.

Scotland

Personal banking services in Scotland are dominated by the three Scottish clearing banks, the Bank of Scotland, the Clydesdale Bank and the Royal Bank of Scotland. There are a number of shareholding links between these banks and the traditional London clearers: Barclays owns 35 per cent of the Bank of Scotland; the Clydesdale Bank is owned by the Midland; and Lloyds has a 16 per cent interest in the Royal Bank of Scotland group, which also includes Williams and Glyn's. Between them, the three Scottish clearers operate more than 1,500 branches. Their strongest competitors are the TSBs and, more recently, the building societies.

The total level of bank account holding in Scotland in 1981, at 77 per cent, outstripped that in England and Wales at 72 per cent. However, these figures conceal an important disparity in the pattern of bank account holding between England and Wales on the one hand and Scotland on the other. In 1981 current accounts were held by only 44 per cent of the adult population in Scotland compared with 63 per cent in England and Wales; conversely deposit/savings accounts were held by 50 per cent in Scotland as against only 30 per cent in England/Wales (5).

These figures reflect the stronger traditional attachment of Scottish people to personal savings (the Trustee Savings Banks have their origins in Scotland) and the response of the Scottish banks to this propensity to save. This was to develop the distinctive Scottish bank deposit account, which differs from the bank deposit account south of the border. Scottish bank deposit accounts are on demand, while those of the English banks are technically at seven days' notice, a requirement which is normally waived (with interest paid adjusted in lieu of notice). In practice, many Scots have used their deposit accounts as current accounts without cheque books; these accounts have permitted cash withdrawals on demand, more recently by plastic card, the payment of wages/salaries payments by automated credit and the application of standing order payments. They are traditionally passbook-based and have not been liable to service charges.

There have been some recent changes in the way Scottish bank deposit accounts work that are designed to minimise the high cost of updating passbooks manually, but their main features have been kept intact and they remain popular. Indeed all the Scottish clearing banks operate more deposit accounts (in the Scottish sense) than current accounts. Clearly, many customers are happy to do without a cheque book in return for modest payment of interest, these being the most obvious distinguishing factors between the two forms of account.

This choice between two basically different types of bank account gives Scottish consumers an advantage compared with the customers of the London clearing banks; traditional English bank deposit accounts are relatively inflexible and limited, and consequently less popular. Scottish bank deposit accounts are distinctive in two other respects. First, they compete more directly with building society, TSB and other outlets for small savings than the generality of English bank accounts. Secondly, their popularity means that Scottish banks are less dependent than their English counterparts on current account balances which, as we note elsewhere, are highly vulnerable to movements in interest rates (6). One Scottish clearer told us that they would expect to be able, as a consequence, to maintain their branch network more or less intact even if interest rates fell to approximately 3 per cent. No London clearer would venture such a claim.

It has been suggested to us that competition for personal banking business in Scotland is keener than that experienced elsewhere in the United Kingdom. One reason for this is the historic strength of the Scottish Trustee Savings Banks. It is estimated that one person in four in Scotland has an account with the TSB compared with one in eight for the UK as a whole.

Secondly, the historic build-up of branch offices in Scotland appears to have had the effect of providing more competition in many of the small towns and rural areas of Scotland than occurs in England and Wales. On a straight population comparison, Scotland has some 1.44 bank branches per 5,000 people against 1.13 for England. Thirdly, in spite of the fact that the development of personal sector banking in Scotland has tended towards the interest-bearing deposit account rather than to the interest-free current account which predominates elsewhere in the UK, competition to acquire new current account business is very intense. This is reflected in the fact that Scottish current account bank charges are generally more favourable than those enjoyed by many English clearing bank customers. The Scottish TSBs, unlike their counterparts in England, have for many years maintained a system of zero charging for current accounts which are kept in credit. So too has the Clydesdale Bank. The combined market share of these two institutions in Scotland is significantly higher than that held by the Co-operative Bank, the National Girobank, the Yorkshire Bank and Williams & Glyn's which offer a similar facility in England and Wales, giving them comparatively greater scope for influencing the rest of the market.

Competition between the Scottish clearing banks was further enhanced in the early 1980s by the withdrawal of a number of agreements on, for example, opening hours and inter-bank agency charges, formerly lodged with the Office of Fair Trading. However, the question of opening hours, as in Northern Ireland, does give cause for concern. Most branches of the three major banks open from 9.30 am to 12.30 pm and 1.30 pm to 3.30 pm on Monday to Wednesday with extended hours on Thursday evenings and Friday lunchtimes. These hours are longer than equivalent opening times in Northern Ireland (generally by half an hour per day), but shorter than those in England and Wales, because of lunchtime closing on four days per week. A few city centre branches open regularly during lunch-hours, but they are exceptional. The extensive development of ATMs in Scotland does go some way to reducing the inconvenience of these hours; and as in Northern Ireland the Trustee Savings Banks and other competitors are open when the clearing banks are not. Nevertheless, lunchtime closing is undoubtedly a serious deprivation for Scottish bank customers and compares unfavourably with practice south of the border. We therefore urge the Scottish clearing banks to amend their opening hours so that their customers are at least as well served as the generality of bank customers in England and Wales.

It was put to us by two of the Scottish banks that another aspect of access-ibility – the maintenance of rural or semi-rural branch networks – may be positively influenced by the clearing banks' right of note issue. These arrange-ments, established under the Bank Notes (Scotland) Act 1845 and the Currency and Bank Notes Act 1928, are comparable to those enjoyed by the Northern Ireland banks already described. The Scottish banks' fiduciary issue is similarly small, at approximately £2.7 million. All other Scottish bank notes in circulation have to be covered by Bank of England notes or coin. In November 1982 the value of Scottish notes in the hands of the public was £591 million. The argument of the two banks is that because the notes of an issuing bank which are kept in tills and strongrooms are in effect just pieces of paper and do not have to be matched in the same way as notes in circulation, the banks are able to cut down on costs and minimise loss of interest. The claim is that this 'free money' in tills helps to maintain marginally viable branches. We are unable to judge just how significant this factor might be in sustaining small branches – the tradi-tionally strong personal savings base of the Scottish banks is clearly another factor, though one which is increasingly threatened by competition from the building societies. Nevertheless we do recognise that rights of note issue, in both Scotland and Northern Ireland, bestow some financial benefits upon their respective banks, and by extension in theory at least to their customers; we therefore endorse the Price Commission's view that there is a strong case for retaining those rights (7). Scottish consumers may also welcome locally issued notes as a manifestation of national identity.

Finally, there are two legal issues peculiar to banking services in Scotland, the first of which requires minor statutory amendment. Section 53(2) of the Bills of Exchange Act 1882, which applies only in Scotland, has several implications for Scottish consumers, the most important of which relates to stopped cheques. On receiving instruction to stop a cheque, banks in Scotland do not pay the cheque to the creditor's account but do debit the customer's account by the value of the cheque. The sum is then transferred to a suspense account which does not bear interest. The money can only be returned to the customer with the consent of the cheque holder, or by means of a time-consuming, complicated and expensive court procedure or, assuming that the dispute between the two parties has not been resolved, after the expiry of a five-year period when the cheque holder's rights lapse. The use of the stopped cheque as a sanction in dispute with traders therefore carries a possible penalty for Scottish consumers. It is not clear how many managers are aware of this provision, or whether they all choose to apply it; nevertheless a number of cases have been reported to the Scottish Consumer Council.

Another consequence of section 53(2) is that if a customer draws several cheques at the same time and there are insufficient funds in the account to meet the total sum, the bank may not pay out on some of the cheques up to the value of the balance in the account. Instead the bank is obliged to refuse payment on all these cheques and to transfer the money in the customer's account to a suspense account. Again the customer is able to free this money only with the co-operation of all the people to whom he or she has made out cheques.

There are two points to note. The first is that such provisions are inherently unfair to consumers whose funds may be effectively locked up and deprived of interest earnings for considerable periods of time, even in disputes where the consumer's stance is ultimately vindicated. Secondly, the statutory provision in question does not apply elsewhere in the United Kingdom and therefore discriminates against consumers with accounts in Scotland. Both the Committee of Scottish Clearing Bankers (CSCB) and the Scottish Consumer Council have therefore called for the amendment of section 53(2) so that the same procedures could be operated in Scotland as currently apply in England, Wales and Northern Ireland. We support this recommendation.

A second legal matter peculiar to Scotland arises from the lack of recognition in Scots law of the concept of the equitable mortgage, the availability of which in the remainder of the UK facilitates simple, secured lending procedures which can be dealt with by bank staff alone. In Scotland, a bank requiring the security (or heritable security) of a property before lending to a borrower must acquire rights under a registered standard security requiring the attention of a solicitor and consequent additional fees. This difference between the two sets of legal requirements does not extend to house purchase loans. This problem is mitigated in practice in personal, as distinct from business, lending by the fact that the requirement of heritable security is rarely invoked by the banks. The Scottish Consumer Council has therefore concluded that there are insufficient grounds for advocating any major reform of the law of conveyancing; that would be necessary if this disadvantage were to be removed. We therefore make no recommendation.

References to section 10

1. Norman J. Gibson, *The Financial System in Northern Ireland*, Northern Ireland Economic Council, April 1982, Annex 1.
2. *Ibid.*, p. 6.
3. Price Commission, *Banks: Charges for Money Transmission Services*, HC 337, HMSO, 1978, para. 9.17.
4. *Ibid.*, para. 9.18.
5. Inter-Bank Research Organisation, *Research Brief*, October 1982.
6. See Appendix IV.
7. Price Commission, *op. cit.*, para. 8.7.

Executor and trustee services are provided by banks through separate departments or subsidiary companies: we use the general phrase 'bank trust
corporations'.

Bank trust corporations may be appointed as executor by a person making a
will (the testator) to wind up his or her affairs after death. They may be
appointed a sole executor, but they often act jointly with an individual chosen by
the testator. In some cases, the named executor may ask the bank trust corporation to act on his or her behalf. The most important tasks of any executor are to
obtain the formal grant of probate (obtain confirmation, in Scotland), to gather
in the assets of the deceased, to pay liabilities and to distribute the estate in
accordance with the will. In some cases continuing trusts may be created by the
will, in which case the bank acts as sole or joint trustee.

Trusts appointing a bank as trustee may also be established by a living person
known as a settlor. (In Scotland, a trust is established by a 'truster', which is
included within our use of the term 'settlor'.) A trust – whether arising on death
or during a lifetime – can be a convenient method for a person who wants to
make provision for family or dependants but who is either unwilling or unable
(for whatever reason) to make absolute transfers of property. There may often
be important tax considerations. When acting as executor or trustee, the bank is
providing a commercial service and its remuneration, as we shall see, is received
in the form of charges for the services which it provides. Amongst the most
important reasons for the appointment of banks are (in the words of selected
banks' publicity)

* their permanence and continuity ('. . . because the Trust Company never
  dies, it offers complete continuity . . .');
* their impartiality ('. . . you can be certain your wishes will be carried out
  with absolute fairness and impartiality. This spares your friends and family
  from the strain of having to make difficult decisions at a time when through
  sheer grief, they may not be able to think clearly . . .')

Banks also attach considerable importance to their investment and administrative skills.

There is some ambivalence on the part of banks about their attitudes to executor and trustee work. The clearing banks promote this activity in advertisements and in material provided for their customers. Nevertheless some bankers appear to regard it as no more than an ancillary activity which has to be provided in order to make a comprehensive package of services available to customers. On the other hand, there are others who see it as an important source of commercial activity in its own right. But, to keep the issue in perspective, the Committee of London Clearing Bankers pointed out to us that in 1981 less than fifteen thousand applications for Grants of Representation of England or Wales would have been dealt with by bank trustee corporations. This comes out of the total of 203,192 applications made by solicitors (1), which indicates that the private legal profession enjoys well over ninety per cent of the professional market.

Executor and trustee services prompted the largest source of complaint from members of the public who responded to our requests for views on bank services. We cannot say how representative these comments are of the views of all those who use such services, and we understand that letters such as these give only one side of the story and may be incomplete in themselves. We point out below that similar complaints have been levelled at others – particularly solicitors – who carry out these services. We also know that there must be far more members of the public who are entirely satisfied with the services provided by bank trust corporations. National Westminster Bank, for example, supplied us with a selection of letters received from members of the public and charitable organisations which included praise for its probate and trust services. These letters included such comments as:

'. . . I think of you as a personal friend quite apart from all your superbly efficient and kindly help in sorting out my sister's estate and our family problems . . .'

'I cannot refrain from telling you how delighted we are that you have brought the administration of this estate to a close within 4½ months of the death of the testator . . . How I wish that all executors of estates in which we [a large charity] have an interest acted with your despatch and efficiency.'

'Your management of the whole affair has been absolutely marvellous, and we are so grateful to you for the way you have dealt with it, so swiftly and for us painlessly. Please will you also thank the appropriate powers that be in the Bank who waived the administration costs; it is a kind gesture, and I'm sure my father would have appreciated it.'

The letters of complaint we received often revealed deeply felt grievances. And some of the charitable bodies who wrote to National Westminster Bank included such phrases as:

'[A full explanation] . . . is not typical of some of the solicitors and trustee departments with whom we have dealings from time to time.'

'As an organisation we frequently benefit from legacies administered by a variety of firms of solicitors, trust companies and banks. Experience shows, sadly, that [efficient and speedy] service cannot be taken for granted these days . . .'

The main criticism voiced to us about executor services concerned their cost, especially when banks acted as executors of small estates involving less than about £50,000. With trustee services, our correspondents were more concerned with a decline in the value of the trust, and the way banks handled the trust's affairs, though complaints were made about costs as well.

Solicitors, through the (English) Law Society and the British Legal Association, have further raised the possibility that in the provision of these ancillary services, banks may be caught in conflicts of interest, as bankers on the one hand and as executor/trustees on the other. In such a situation, solicitors claim that banks cannot give impartial advice. Some are also aggrieved at the freedom of banks to advertise their services without restriction while individual solicitors (who compete for the same business) may not.

Should banks act as executors and trustees?

It was put to us that banks cannot be independent and impartial in the initial advice they give to the testator or settlor. The suggestion is that the relationship between banker and customer makes it difficult, if not impossible, for the bank to give, and for the customer to receive, the best objective advice about the selection of an executor or trustee. This may be a reflection of the trust that banks widely enjoy from their customers. But it does raise the possibility that conflicts of interest could arise, directly or indirectly, from the different roles of the bank or its various divisions, departments or subsidiary companies. This conflict may carry over into the manner in which the administration of the trust is carried out. The various roles assumed by the 'corporate' bank might include:

* banker (and possibly lender) to the original testator or settlor;
* banker to the estate or trust fund;
* possible banker to some of the beneficiaries;
* sole or joint trustee of the trust fund;
* manager of the bank's unit trusts.

The Law Society raised this point in general terms, but did not pursue it in its evidence to us:

'It is not for the Law Society to examine the philosophical question as to whether, from a consumer's viewpoint, it is beneficial to be beholden to a bank for anything but banking services . . . There is however an argument that a consumer must be protected from a situation where unnecessary conflicts of interest are resolved in such a way as to be detrimental to his interests.'

The Society went on, however, to express specific concern in connection with the initial advice about choice of executor or trustee:

'Advice given has to be independent and impartial. In the case of a customer, particularly one who is a borrower seeking advice from the bank, it is unlikely if not commercially impracticable (since the manager owes his first duty to his employers and the company's shareholders, unlike a solicitor whose first duty is always to his client) for such advice to be given.'

The British Legal Association (BLA) said, in relation to conflicts of interest, that:

'The activities of the banks in this connection are objectionable.'

The BLA went on to propose, amongst other things, that a bank should not be able to benefit as executor/trustee without satisfying the Probate Registrar that the testator had had the advice of an independent solicitor; that banks or their employed solicitors should not be able to draft wills for profit; and that banks should be prohibited from advertising their executor and trust services.

We recognise the theoretical conflicts of interest that could arise. Banks are commercial organisations which are accountable to their shareholders; they do not have the same professional obligations as solicitors who are explicitly bound to act in the best interests of their clients. On the other hand, solicitors, too, are commercial men and women who must make a profit from executor and trust work. They also have a quite legitimate interest in encouraging clients to instruct them in connection with trust and probate matters. We do not believe that the profit motive of banks disqualifies them or calls for new restrictions on their ability to act as trust corporations. Nor does the mere fact that the prospective executor or trustee is also the testator's or settlor's banker of itself affect its qualifications for appointment. Trust departments or companies are run as separate operations from the parent bank. Moreover, no one forces a bank customer to seek advice from a bank about the choice of executor or trustee.

Restrictions on the lines proposed by the BLA would act as a considerable fetter on competition and could in our view be justifiable only if there was clear evidence that the potential conflicts of interest were in fact acting to the serious detriment of consumers. To give solicitors in private practice a virtual statutory monopoly in this respect might well amount to a cure far worse than the supposed ill. The Law Society, which speaks for many more solicitors than the BLA, did not urge us to introduce new restrictions on the freedom of banks to undertake executor or trust business and recognised the value of competition. Commenting on the level of charges, it said:

'[The level] is higher than in the case of a solicitor who may fulfil a similar function. No complaint is made of this because, if nothing else, *it does favour the legal profession in competition in the market place for the privilege of performing such services.*' [emphasis added]

We do not believe, therefore, that actual or potential conflicts of interest require any new restrictions on the appointment of banks as executors/trustees or on their ability to act in that capacity. We are reinforced in this general conclusion by the commitment to increased competition implicit in the recommendation of the Royal Commission on Legal Services in England and Wales that section 23 of the Solicitors Act 1974 should be amended to permit trust corporations to apply for probate of a will without the intervention of a solicitor (2). It is not clear to us why, in 1982, the Lord Chancellor rejected demands by the banks to implement this recommendation.

An important point remains, however. There is some scope for a conflict of interest to arise during the administration of an estate or trust. A bank trust corporation is in a position to make a profit for its parent bank as a result of investment decisions. We return to this specific point later, when we turn to the standards of service and conduct which should be expected of bank trust corporations. In that context, we argue that certain safeguards may be desirable in acknowledgement of potential conflicts of interest. Subject to those safeguards, however, we see no reason why banks should be compelled to scale down their involvement in this market.

Attracting business

The way in which bank trust corporations attract business provides a more concrete target for those who are uneasy about their involvement. Some lawyers are clearly unhappy at some of the promotion techniques adopted by bank trust corporations. The Law Society claimed in evidence to us that:

'The banks advertise their Executor and Trustee services extensively. Plainly the person most likely to notice this fact is the customer of the bank concerned. He visits his bank regularly. The pressures of advertising today are intensive . . . Because of the nature of the competitive advertising and the pressure from the head offices of all the major banks upon all their managers of ordinary as well as trust branches, there are far too many cases occurring where wills are prepared making appointments of a trust corporation, where they are plainly unnecessary, highly expensive and particularly damaging to the close relatives remaining behind . . .'

ADVERTISING

The implicit accusation of the legal profession is of course that the freedom of banks to advertise gives the banks an unfair competitive advantage. In a submission made in 1981 to the Lord Chancellor's Office, the Law Society successfully argued against an attempt by the banks to be allowed to obtain grants of representation. In arguing that unnecessary appointments of bank trust corporations were being made, the Society said:

'Trust corporations are commercial institutions which use their considerable resources to advertise for probate and trust work and are not restricted by any professional code of conduct from persuading the public to use their services . . .' (3)

In its evidence to us, the British Legal Association went further with its call for:

'legislation [to be] enacted forbidding the advertising of the services of bank trustee departments or companies or the solicitation of business therefor . . .'

If the legal profession believes that advertising gives the banks an unfair advantage, then the remedy is in its own hands. The solicitors' profession is completely free to engage in 'institutional' promotion – and, indeed, has done so in various forms, including advertising to persuade people to instruct solicitors in connection with wills and probate. A leaflet from the Law Society suggests that solicitors should be appointed as executors and claims – 'provocatively', according to the Committee of London Clearing Bankers – that this 'will almost certainly cost your estate less than appointing a bank'.

It is true that individual solicitors or firms are not allowed to advertise, but this rule is effectively self-imposed through the Solicitors' Practice Rules. Solicitors cannot therefore complain when competitors attract business through advertising. Restrictions on advertising by solicitors have been the subject of two Monopolies Commission reports. In the first, published in 1970 (Cmnd 4463), the Commission suggested that restrictions on advertising should not prevent 'publicity by individual practitioners that is informative in the sense that primarily it provides information about the availability of services' (4). The second report, published in July 1976 (5) – exclusively concerned with advertising by solicitors – went further by suggesting that advertising could promote competition, providing that it did not make claims of superiority over other practices, was not inaccurate or misleading, and did not bring the profession into disrepute.

The Royal Commission on Legal Services in England and Wales reviewed the arguments for and against these recommendations, and largely endorsed the Monopolies Commission conclusion. It said, 'a solicitor who is in direct competition with non-solicitors, such as banks who are themselves permitted to advertise, should be enabled to compete on equal terms' (6).

We do not, therefore, accept that the fact that banks can advertise constitutes unfair competition with solicitors.

Unnecessary appointments

We recognise that it is difficult to define occasions when the appointment of a bank trust corporation is inappropriate or unnecessary. Nevertheless, the initial enquiry from a bank customer must on occasions lead to an appointment where the work could have been handled more cheaply by a solicitor or by an executor acting in person. As we have seen, the Law Society claimed that there are 'far too many cases where appointments of a trust corporation are plainly unnecessary'. The response of the CLCB was:

'There can only be few cases where a professional executor may be regarded as unnecessary as even in the most simple estates, there are many testators, who for a variety of reasons wish an independent and reliable executor in the form of a trust corporation to wind up their affairs.'

We believe that the banks themselves should be concerned to have genuine regard to the customer's best interests when discussing the possibility of a bank appointment. This means a full discussion of all the options with enquirers. Banks are, of course, fully entitled to stress their own particular advantages, but it may be that, particularly in the more straightforward cases, they could more actively consider proposing alternative arrangements, including (where appropriate) personal application for a grant of probate. In many cases, the estate will not be at all complicated and may well not need a professional executor or a professional doing everything for a family executor. A personal application, with limited and inexpensive professional guidance, may be all that is needed. We understand that some bank trust corporations do offer this sort of 'hand-holding' service, but their literature does not draw much attention to it. We hope that banks and solicitors will develop this sort of service, for appropriate cases, more fully. In most cases it would be preferable for the bank to discuss the various options at the outset, rather than wait for the renunciation of appointment which can happen when the estate proves too small or the beneficiaries are reluctant to have the bank involved.

It is clearly in the interests of consumers to discover as much information as possible before deciding upon an appointment. We also believe that there is a clear need for better, non-promotional information for the public. In many straightforward cases, for example, there may well be no need for either a bank or a solicitor to be involved. The Probate Registries enjoy a high reputation for the way in which they handle 'Personal Applications'. In 1981, over 62,000 grants were issued to personal applicants in England and Wales – nearly a quarter of the total. We suspect that, whether or not there is a will, many more families could save hundreds of pounds by opting for this do-it-yourself approach.

The Probate Registry issues a helpful booklet, *Personal Application for Probate or Letters of Administration*, and the citizen's advice bureau service provides its bureaux with fuller information about the tasks of personal representatives. The Scottish Home and Health Department, in conjunction with the Scottish Association of CABx, publishes a booklet called *What to do after a death*. A number of books are also on sale to the public.

Conflicting statements by both bankers and solicitors underline the necessity of completely independent and impartial advice, both in general terms (for example, on the question of whether the services of a professional, whether bank or solicitor, are necessary for small, simple estates) and for an individual faced with the choice of appointing an executor.

The need for advice was recognised by the Royal Commission on Legal Services in Scotland which had noted that the administration of estates was made easier if the dead person's affairs were left in good order, and that making a will would greatly assist this. The Royal Commission recommended the production of a leaflet describing the steps that citizens should take to leave their affairs in order so that, when they die, others will be saved needless worry and expense. The leaflet should include a list of the documents necessary for the tidy settlement of an estate; advice about the importance of a valid will; warning against the use of pre-printed will forms; advice about choosing an executor; sources of legal advice and so on. This is information that every citizen should have at his or her disposal. The leaflet should be made widely available through such outlets as solicitors' offices, advice centres, social work departments, social security offices, hospitals and libraries (7).

We endorse this recommendation of the Scottish Royal Commission. The provision of such advice cannot be left to those with a financial interest in winding up a person's estate after death. The problem, of course, is who should prepare it. The task might fall to a government department or to voluntary organisations. The National Council for Voluntary Organisations, for example, published a leaflet giving advice on what to do when someone dies (*Dealing with Death*, Bedford Square Press, 95p – soon to be out of print).

There is one final issue concerning the way by which bank trust corporations come to be appointed as executors. Banks sometimes refer their customers to private solicitors to have a will drafted. It has been suggested that there may be pressure on the solicitor to ignore his duty to have regard exclusively to the best interests of the new client and to ensure the appointment of the bank as executor in the will. The inter-dependence of many solicitors and their local banks is a complex field, and it is not difficult to see how subtle forms of pressure may be perceived. The solicitor may fear that if he advises an alternative to the appointment of the bank, then he may expect to receive fewer or no further instructions or favours from that bank.

This complaint has been raised by solicitors in correspondence to their professional journals. One solicitor wrote of a local bank manager's expressed displeasure when he had prepared wills for a couple referred by the bank which – at the clients' request – did not appoint the bank as executor:

'he was clearly not pleased. Had it not been understood that the bank was to act? I replied that the couple had been referred to us so that we could act for them, not for the bank . . . His reaction was, to me, astonishing. He said "This is why I usually make a point of coming along with people I introduce but on this occasion I was unable to do so".' (8)

Complaint is also made that the banks sometimes refer customers to a solicitor other than the one who previously acted for that client. The suggestion is that such new solicitors will be 'tame' enough not to question the appointment of the bank. It has been suggested (9) that, to deal with this problem, the Law Society should more strictly enforce its *Guide to Professional Conduct* which states that solicitors who accept instructions on the introduction by a third party should, 'before taking any step on that person's behalf, obtain written confirmation from him that he wishes him to act and that he has no other solicitor whom he wishes to instruct'.

Much of this will doubtless be regarded as special pleading by members of the legal profession, and we doubt that it is a widespread problem. We would, however, deprecate any attempt – however subtle or indirect – by a bank to influence the solicitor/client relationship, even when the bank has directly introduced the client to the solicitor.

But this disguises two further points. First, many of the complaints made by solicitors on this specific point would disappear if they could make their own services more directly accessible and so avoid relying on banks and similar sources of referral. Secondly, the fact that solicitors also cannot claim total disinterest indicates the need for a source of independent guidance.

Are bank trust corporations' charges too high?

Bank literature advertising executor and trustee services often (but not always) includes information about charges that may be levied once the bank is required to act. There is sometimes a flat-rate acceptance fee, and an administration fee charged as a percentage of gross capital value of the estate. There is sometimes also an activity or service fee related to the amount of work involved. For trust services, there will also be an annual management fee, again charged as a percentage on value. Such charges are termed 'ad valorem' – that is, they relate to value rather than to the extent and complexity of work involved. There is usually a minimum charge, and some banks say there may be 'reasonable' additional discretionary charges, but that the administration fee may be reduced if the bank considers the administration unusually simple in relation to the value of the estate.

These charges are given as guidelines only. By the time the testator dies they may have been superseded in which case the new fees are charged.

As an example of charges currently in force, National Westminster Bank's Trustee Department lists the following fees for acting solely or jointly as the executor of a will or as administrator (for instance, under an intestacy):

Administration fee based on gross value of the estate:

On the first £50,000	5 per cent
On the next £50,000	3 per cent
On the excess over £100,000	2 per cent

A minimum fee will apply in estates of less than £10,000.

The National Westminster booklet makes it clear that VAT is added to all fees. It goes on to provide for 'a reasonable additional charge according to the work involved' to be made, on a discretionary basis, where complicated or demanding work is involved. There is also provision for Fee Concession – a reduction in the administrative fee which may be made where the administration was unusually simple in relation to the value of the estate. This is particularly likely to be applied where the main asset is the testator's residence which is to be passed to beneficiaries.

National Westminster's Standard Terms and Conditions provide that all charges and expenses incurred in employing solicitors, stockbrockers, accountants and other professional agents are payable in addition to the Bank's fees. The same is true for 'general expenses', including postage, telephone calls, stationery and travelling expenses. Although the Standard Terms and Conditions are set out in the Bank's booklet, none of these extra charges is mentioned in the section on fees.

Several people who wrote to us about executor services told us about the actual charges made by the various banks. The late Mrs H, for example, left an estate with a gross value of approximately £17,000. The main asset was a house which was sold for £13,950. The administration expenses amounted to £1,984.61p, which broke down as follows:

Fees for obtaining probate (court fees, solicitors' fees, insurance premiums, etc.)	£81.00
Fees connected with sale of house (estate agents, solicitors, etc.)	£703.77
Bank Trust Company Charges:	
to clear tax	£28.75
fees	£981.77
disbursements	£36.64
VAT	£152.68
	£1,984.61

In this case, the bank's fees (£981.77) represented nearly 6 per cent of the total gross value of the estate, before taking into account VAT on these fees and additional disbursements.

Another correspondent, the son of a bank manager and the son-in-law of another, said that he started with a prejudice in favour of banks. However, his experience in dealing with an aunt's will led him to conclude that 'banks "milk" this market for all they can . . .' He told us that his aunt's estate, worth £41,000, was in simple investments, there being no house or chattels. There were 9 legatees, including 3 residuary legatees. Where necessary, all addresses had been supplied by the family. The charge for dealing with this estate was initially £2,086 plus VAT. 'When asked to detail work done and how the charge was arrived at they "waffled" but after 3 or 4 letters they reduced it by about £150.'

In another case a bank trust corporation's charges totalled £2,175.93 (including their fees of £1,908.39). We were told that this was a gross estate of £33,456.03 where the widow was the sole beneficiary. The estate consisted of securities, for which all certificates were handed over, and an insurance policy. Apart from the legal aspects, our correspondent told us that the work done by the bank resulted in recovery of state pension arrears, income tax repayment and death grant.

In a case submitted to the Office of Fair Trading (OFT) by the British Legal Association, administration expenses of £2,239.23 were levied on an estate with assets of £34,743.79. The main asset was again a house, transferred to the widow. The administration expenses broke down as follows:

Costs connected with probate	£97.50
Solicitors' fees for obtaining probate	£86.25
Solicitors' fees for transferring property	£34.50
Trust company charges	
fees	£1,724.74
disbursements	£32.64
VAT	£263.60
	£2,239.23

In this case the bank's fees (excluding VAT and disbursements) amounted to just under 5 per cent of the gross value of the estate.

In correspondence with the OFT, the British Legal Association claimed that banks charge substantially more than solicitors for their executor services, 'usually of the order of 3-4 times' (10)*. Solicitors' fees in England and Wales are governed by the Solicitors' Remuneration Order 1972 which requires remuneration to be fair and reasonable having regard to all the circumstances of the case and, in particular, to a number of specified aspects. These include complexity, the skill, labour and specialised knowledge and responsibility involved, the time spent, the nature of the documentation, the amount or value at stake, and the importance of the matter to the client. The English Law Society's notes for guidance suggest a number of yardsticks, stressing that the ultimate test remains that the charge should be fair and reasonable, not an arithmetical calculation. The yardsticks are:

* an expense element, calculated by reference to the time taken by the solicitor or his staff member;
* a percentage 'service increment' on the expense element (normally in the range of 25–35 per cent); and
* a value percentage, which for non-contentious probate and administration of estates where the solicitor acts as executor is 1½ per cent or more of the gross value of the free estate. (The value of the deceased's home 'may' be

---

* The BLA had approached the Director General of Fair Trading about the allegedly high charges of bank trustee departments. The Association felt that these justified action by the Director General under Part III of the Fair Trading Act 1973. This gives the Director General the power to seek assurances from traders who have carried on a course of conduct with their consumer customers which is detrimental to their interests – either economic, health, safety or other interests. (The 'assurances' sought are that the traders will cease the offending cause of action.) The Director General concluded that the evidence provided by the BLA did not justify action under Part III which depends on proof of persistent breaches of the law, either civil or criminal.

discounted by half for these purposes and the notes suggest possible adjustment for large, small or complex estates.)

We set out below a very rough comparison of the charges likely to follow the administration of the straightforward estate of a reasonably prosperous, but by no means untypical person. These comparisons must be treated with very considerable caution. If the case had been complicated – for example involving the distribution amongst a wide class of beneficiaries, the transfer of a business, the administration of a life interest and/or tax complications – the solicitor's charge would probably have been significantly greater. In such cases the charges of a bank might also have increased – especially if solicitors or accountants had to be involved, but any proportionate increase would be likely to be smaller. The illustration does serve to show, however, that the value of the estate has an important influence on the charges of solicitors, as well as those of banks.

Mr Jones has died, leaving his entire estate under his will to his widow. The will appoints a professional executor – i.e. either a solicitor or a bank trust corporation. The estate comprises:

house in the south-east (in his own name)	£50,000
life insurance policies	15,000
cash in bank and building societies	10,000
personal chattels and car	3,000
	£78,000

A solicitor's charges might be:

* 10 hours' work (interview, correspondence documentation, telephone calls) at £30 per hour	£300.00
* 30 per cent 'service increment'	90.00
* 1½ per cent of estate (house at £25,000)	795.00
	£1,185.00

(*Note:* Hourly charge rates are likely to vary according to status of fee-earner and locality.)

Barclaytrust's charges (subject to discretionary reduction) would be:

* acceptance fee	£150.00
* administration fee (5 per cent × 78,000)	3,900.00
	£4,050.00

National Westminster Bank charges (subject to a discretionary fee concession) would be:

* administration fee	
5 per cent × first £50,000	£2,500
3 per cent × balance of £28,000	£840
	£3,340

Lloyds Bank Trust Division charges would be:

* acceptance and responsibility fee	
(3 per cent × £53,000 with house at ½ value)	£1,590
* 4 'units' at £7 for the ascertainment and handling of each asset (say)	£262
* 3 'units' at £7 for the ascertainment and handling of each liability (say)	£42
	£1,894

Midland Bank Trust Company charges would be:

* responsibility fee (3 per cent × £78,000)	£2,340
* activity fee ('reasonably commensurate with the work')	£345
	£2,685

Note: Barclaytrust advised us that their charges were under review. National Westminster Bank said that their fee in this sort of case 'would certainly attract a reduction of at least £500 and probably twice that sum'. Midland Bank Trust Company said that, for a case of this nature where the house represents a large proportion of the estate and passes to the surviving spouse, the responsibility fee would be reduced to 2 per cent giving a total of £2,185. Lloyds Bank also pointed out that their fee would be about £700 lower, if (as is increasingly the case) the house had been jointly owned, and reductions of the same order could be expected in all other cases in that event.

___

It is certainly true that in all these cases, it would (as we have indicated) be open to both solicitors and banks to reduce these charges, possibly quite considerably. The difficulty is that the consumer has no assurance of any such reduction. In any event, VAT and actual expenses are added in all cases. In the case of bank trust corporations, that will normally mean the addition of the fees of solicitors appointed to obtain the actual grant of probate. This last item appears to be the cause of some annoyance – both to consumers and to the banks themselves.

Others have drawn attention to the different charges which can be encountered. In May 1977, *Which?* estimated that on a £30,000 estate, a solicitor would charge about £925 including VAT and probate registry fees, whilst charges payable to banks varied between £913 and £1,680. In both cases, it was pointed out that the fee could be less for a simple estate. The bank's charges would, however, be increased by solicitors' fees, estimated then at £100 or more. *Which?* said, then, that the costs for an estate of this size would be £86 for the person who acted alone. Most of the 92 members who provided information about their own efforts spent somewhere between five and fifty hours on the task.

More recently in April 1983, *Planned Savings* magazine attempted a similar exercise for an estate (without a house) worth £25,000 and concluded as follows:

Barclays:	£1,400 + VAT
Natwest:	£1,250 + VAT
Lloyds:	£1,016 + VAT
Midland:	£1,200 + VAT
Devon solicitors:	£200 + VAT
London solicitors:	£500–£750 + VAT
Solicitor's charges estimate by Law Society:	up to £1,500 + VAT

This article stressed that all these figures should not be taken as unalterable, and that final charges could reflect concessionary rates and/or the amount of work involved and the time spent.

It is clear that there are likely to be considerable differences in costs and that the prudent consumer should shop around before deciding upon a professional executor. There are also substantial savings available for those prepared to act in person. It is also clear, however, that no simple comparison can be made between charges made by banks and those made by solicitors. For neither group is there a standard method of calculation, although as a very broad general rule the banks' charges are influenced to a greater extent by the value of the estate, whilst solicitors' charges include a stronger reflection of the complexity of the estate as represented by time spent on it.

Charges based upon value carry the advantage of certainty. It should be possible to obtain a reasonably accurate idea of the likely charge at the outset. This does depend, however, on knowing the value, or at least the rough value, of the estate. Such certainty can also be eroded by charging principles which can increase or decrease the final charge according to the complexity. Certainty may also prove expensive where – as can often be the case – a high value estate proves very straightforward.

By contrast, charges based on a time-charge should more fairly reflect the complexity of the particular case. The testator/settlor – or, rather, the beneficiaries – should have the satisfaction of knowing that the charges reflect actual work done. However, this method, too, has its drawbacks. A small estate may prove to be particularly complicated. There may be little or no control over the selection of the person who does the work, which may well affect the hourly charging rate and/or the number of hours taken. And, even where charges are based on time, an element of the final charge is likely to take account of the value.

Not surprisingly, the CLCB emphasised the benefits of certainty associated with percentage charges:

'To our minds, the need for a client to know the prospective charge as nearly as possible is paramount . . .'

One of the difficulties of this, of course, is that testators may have little idea of the worth of their final estate – 2 per cent or 3 per cent of an unknown figure is still unknown, even assuming that the bank makes no change in its charging method in the meantime.

Obviously neither approach to charging is perfect. How can dissatisfaction with charges be reduced? Our evidence prompts us to underline:

* the need for banks fully to disclose to their clients the likely level of charges to be made; and
* the establishment of some means by which banks' charges can be queried after the event if they appear too high.

When a bank customer makes a will appointing the bank as sole or joint executor, we suggest that the bank should give that client a rough estimate of the probable charges to be levied by the bank and others (for example, solicitors who act for it) depending on the approximate value and complexity of the estate. We appreciate that this can be no more than a rough guide: assets may appreciate in value, difficulties cannot be predicted, and charges may alter. But at least it would give clients a figure, rather than a list of percentages and vague references to additions or reductions.

Secondly, banks should devise procedures to inform customers who are known to have appointed a bank as executor or trustee, of any changes to their scale of fees.

Thirdly, when banks are called upon to undertake their executor duties (when their customer dies) they should – wherever this is possible – discuss with the beneficiaries of the estate the likely level of charges. In the case of small, uncomplicated estates, banks should make a point of raising the possibility that their services may not be necessary. The CLCB said that 'following long-established practice, the banks will always renounce probate if all the beneficiaries ask them to do so'. The trouble is that, in most cases, the beneficiaries are unlikely to know that they can do this.

We also believe that some means must be established to allow bank charges to be queried. If the work is done by a solicitor, for example, dissatisfied clients can seek the views of the Law Society on the level of charges or they can apply to have the costs 'taxed', a process by which the court examines the charges made, and fixes the amount of the bill. The Royal Commission on Legal Services in England and Wales recommended that the fees of all executors should be able to be taxed in the courts. The Royal Commission said:

'At present a trust corporation or any other person or organisation may draft a will in which it is nominated as executor with power to charge for its services. Except when a solicitor is so authorised, there is no check on the reasonableness of the charges made, which . . . may be quite different from those prevailing when the will is signed. This is particularly important because the testator, who authorised the charge, will not be alive when the charges are made. We consider therefore that there should be the same safeguards as would apply if a solicitor handled the administration. In short, an interested party should have the right to require the charges to be taxed by the court in the same way as solicitors' charges may be taxed at present. In cases where a bank, or a member of a banking group, acts as executor those safeguards should cover not only acceptance, administration and annual charges but also any associated bank charges and other financial advantages arising in the course of the administration.' (11)

A more recent report has recommended that beneficiaries – as well as executor clients – should be entitled to ask the Law Society to review the charges of solicitor-trustees and solicitor-administrators (12).

It may not be such a radical proposal that bank charges should be open to challenge. The courts have already shown that they have an inherent jurisdiction to increase a professional trustee's remuneration (13) and it has been suggested – but not yet tested – that this might mean that there is a parallel jurisdiction to reduce charges (14).

CLCB points out, quite rightly, that few solicitors' clients seek to have the costs taxed by the courts. A major deterrent is that if the costs claimed by the solicitor are reduced on taxation by one-fifth or less, the costs of the taxation itself fall on the applicants.

Therefore, although we support the principle that bank clients should be able to challenge charges made by banks for executor and trustee services, we do not consider that taxation of costs should be the only means. Something simpler and more accessible is needed. We return at the end of section 11 to how this might be provided.

The standards of bank trust corporations

As we indicated earlier, questions about 'quality' of service were raised most frequently about banks' trustee services, but were not confined to that aspect. Again, we must emphasise that we have no way of knowing whether complaints were justified, or whether the views expressed to us are representative of users as a whole. Many beneficiaries are doubtless entirely satisfied.

The problems which were reported to us divided into two main categories: complaints – obviously with hindsight – about the poor performance of trust funds and the dwindling of assets; and complaints about the way banks handled trust affairs – lack of consultation with beneficiaries, delays in replying to letters and so on.

Banks are not alone in facing criticism from clients about executor and trustee work. The Royal Commission on Legal Services in Scotland said:

'Our evidence suggests that it is in the area of administration of the estate following the grant of confirmation [the Scottish equivalent of probate] that dissatisfaction with the services provided by solicitors most often arises. The administration and winding up of estates by solicitors are the subject of a number of complaints each year to the Law Society – principally complaints about delay. It has been demonstrated to us by evidence from a number of individuals that some estates do take an unreasonable length of time to clear up. Sometimes the delay is not caused by the solicitor; other parties may take an excessive time to reply to his letters or to furnish necessary information. In some instances, however, delay is caused by solicitors themselves.' (15)

In England and Wales, successive reports of the Lay Observer – who monitors the handling of complaints by the Law Society – have made similar points. His report for 1982 said:

'My statistics show that administration of estates has again given rise to more of the complaints referred to me than any other single category. Many of these complaints are of delay by solicitors in completing the administration, or in paying income . . . or in paying legacies. Other complaints alleged failure to provide sufficient information to beneficiaries on their likely entitlement from the estate or failure to provide accounts.' (16)

The recent report of the Lord Chancellor's Law Reform Committee on the *Powers and Duties of Trustees* noted that:

'A common complaint by beneficiaries is that it takes a very long time to wind up an estate and that little, if any, information is provided on the progress of the administration. It seems that solicitors are the most frequent target for complaints though it is possible that other personal representatives, whether lay or professional, might well be open to the same criticism.' (17)

A comparative evaluation of the quality of service offered by all those who take on executor and trustee work – banks, solicitors, the Public Trustee and so on – goes well beyond the scope of this report. We cannot state whether banks perform any 'better' or 'worse' than others also providing such services. Nor can we deal here with complaints raised against solicitors or other professionals. What we are able to state with some certainty is that the letters we received from members of the public point to the pressing need for some realistic independent means by which complaints can be investigated and adjudicated, if necessary.

The following extract from a letter we received demonstrates the feeling of powerlessness expressed by many customers, trustees and beneficiaries. (It is by no means the most virulent in its criticisms.)

'My mother elected me as co-trustee with [the bank] on her death in 1971. Her money was put in trust to go to my children on my death – meanwhile to be invested (the income coming to me) and monies released for my children at the trustees' discretion. Each time I, as co-trustee, have required monies for them, it has been like getting blood out of a stone. This is of course particularly annoying, when due to inflation, money which could have been of some real use in the last few years, will soon be a pittance.

It has dawned on me that of course [the bank] is unwilling to release much money because thereby they lose a comfortable steady income, even though my mother's estate amounted to only approximately £18,000 or so. I have pointed out to the trust officer that the whole business is very one-sided. They receive a fee for doing very little – investing in gilt-edged security, and occasionally reluctantly releasing limited sums for my children's use – education mainly . . .

Last year I demanded to be paid at last for my telephone, postage and stationery expenses, and received £100. I then asked rather belatedly what fees they paid themselves and was horrified to note that they allotted themselves £35 for postage and stationery for one year alone – during which time I received at the most four letters. When I took this up with them they indignantly pointed out that internal memos etc. brought the cost up to £35.

I have worked out that from my late mother's relatively small estate [the bank] has received at least £1,758. The most galling aspect of the case is that my mother, when almost in her dotage, was talked into tying up her money in this way by a "friendly" and reassuring bank manager, who said that this way she would be safeguarding all our interests.'

Another correspondent gave us details of two small family trusts with which she had experience: one established in 1928 in which the original capital of £5,300 had increased in value by only £1,920 after 44 years (thus representing a huge decrease in real value); and the second established in 1940 with a capital of £7,722 which had grown by only £200 after 42 years.

Any assessment of complaints of this nature must be influenced by the balance that has been sought between income and capital. In any event, a bank which acts as trustee cannot be held responsible just because the trust investments perform poorly. No claim made by a beneficiary, or by anyone else, will succeed where the proper standards of behaviour have been observed. Over hundreds of years, the English courts have laid down and developed these standards through the rules of equity. In Scotland there is a separate statutory regime. The courts have – in those cases which reach them – been prepared to act vigilantly in the interests of beneficiaries to impose high standards on all trustees, in respect of their duties and the discretions available to them. The utmost diligence in the performance of the various duties imposed on trustees must be observed in order to escape liability for loss sustained by the trust fund. So far as the various discretions are concerned:

'. . . a trustee must act honestly and must use as much diligence as a prudent man of business would exercise in dealing with his own private affairs; in selecting an investment he must take as much care as a prudent man would take in making an investment for the benefit of persons for whom he felt morally bound to provide . . .' (18)

This well-known principle is applied even more strictly to banks and other professionals who act as trustees:

'A higher standard of diligence and knowledge is expected from paid trustees.' (19)

In the case of Bartlett v. Barclays Bank Trust Co. Ltd, Brightman J. said:

'. . . a higher duty of care is plainly due from someone like a trust corporation which carries on a specialised business of trust management. A trust corporation holds itself out in its advertising literature as being above ordinary mortals. With a specialist staff of trained trust officers as managers, with ready access to financial information and advice dealing with and sorting trust problems day after day, the trust corporation holds itself out, and rightly, as capable of providing an expertise which it would be unrealistic to expect and unjust to demand from the ordinary prudent man or woman who accepts, probably unpaid and sometimes reluctantly from a sense of family duty, the burdens of the trusteeship.' (20)

Subject to the terms of the trust, the law requires a bank, like any other trustee, to invest the trust funds properly and speedily so as to ensure that they are productive. Trust deeds appointing banks usually permit a wide range of investments. Trustees are also under a duty to keep accounts and to produce these to any beneficiary when required. Trustees must also, when required, give any beneficiary all reasonable information as to the manner in which the trust fund has been dealt with and as to the investments made.

It is also possible to require an investigation and audit of trust accounts by the English Public Trustee (section 13, Public Trustee Act 1906), although the risk of an order for the applicant to pay the costs of such an exercise may act as a deterrent in many cases. Although beneficiaries generally do not have the right to be consulted and cannot control a bank trustee, the beneficiaries can – so long as they are all adult, of sound mind and together entitled to the whole beneficial interest – jointly put a complete end to the trust. Of lesser significance, a person who is 'indefeasibly entitled to a share in divisible personalty' (such as a particular piece of furniture) is entitled to have that share transferred to him.

The Chancery Division of the High Court – in Scotland, the Court of Session – is available (at least in theory) to enforce these duties and to ensure that discretions are properly performed.* In highly exceptional cases, the court has jurisdiction to remove a trustee and appoint a new one (21). This can – at least in theory – be done wherever it is required for the welfare of the beneficiaries, even if the trustees have been guilty of no misconduct. Slightly less severely, a trust may be administered or executed by the court, which means that trustees cannot act without the court's sanction. More frequently – by virtue of the court's controlling influence over all trustees – the court has power to determine doubts or give rulings on virtually any question affecting trustees and beneficiaries. The jurisdiction cannot be ousted by the trust instrument.

These standards and controls might seem to be an adequate answer to any beneficiary who complains that a trust fund has not been well invested or that a bank trustee has otherwise given cause for complaint. However, the exercise of a discretion cannot usually be challenged and, as we shall see, there are many other factors at work. The 'protection' available to beneficiaries may prove to be more apparent than real. We believe that improvements can be made in four main areas:

*   improving the information available to testators, settlors and beneficiaries;
*   increasing the scope for consultation between bank trust corporations and beneficiaries;
*   reducing the scope for a bank to derive any direct or indirect profit from the investment of the trust estate;
*   avoiding the uncertainties and cost of litigation by the introduction of simpler, and more effective, means for beneficiaries to challenge the conduct of bank trustees.

IMPROVING INFORMATION

We suspect that many beneficiaries who feel aggrieved at the way in which a bank is administering an estate are ignorant or hazy about the rules which we have outlined. It is likely, also, that those creating settlements, by will or otherwise, do not know a great deal about the duties of trustees or the constraints on their conduct. Professional advice is unlikely to cover all these points unless specifically requested.

We believe that it would be beneficial for banks – either individually or collectively – to prepare a booklet outlining the main principles of law which affect the administration of estates and trusts. We do not think that this need be elaborate or comprehensive. It could include, however, such matters as:

*   the main duties of executors and trustees;
*   the ways in which they can exercise their discretions;
*   the extent to which they can consult with beneficiaries (see below);
*   the rights of beneficiaries to receive information about the trust, to receive accounts and to call for an investigation and audit;

* The County Court may act if the total value of the fund does not exceed £30,000 (£15,000 in Northern Ireland).

* the rights of beneficiaries to put an end to a trust;
* the rights of beneficiaries to apply to the court under the Variation of Trusts Act 1958 or equivalent legislation;
* the supervisory role of the court and the circumstances in which a beneficiary can apply to the court;
* other means of challenging the activities of a trustee.

Although this information would be of benefit in numerous cases where there is no bank involvement, we believe that the banks could take the lead in preparing this sort of information. We envisage that the booklet would be widely available through banks, and would automatically be given to all those considering the appointment of the bank as trustee. The booklet should also be sent to all identified beneficiaries – or their parents or guardians – as soon as the trust administration starts. Such a booklet would not be a substitute for personal professional advice, but it could, we believe, be an extremely useful supplement to give a fair and balanced idea of what can, and cannot, be expected of a bank trust corporation.

IMPROVING CONSULTATION

A number of people who wrote to us were clearly unhappy that they had not been consulted by the bank trust corporation, or that their wishes had been ignored. One 61-year-old widow complained about one bank's 'appalling track record' on investment decisions over many years. She objected in particular to 'their consistent refusal to consult either me or my (adult) sons', who, together, were said to be the sole beneficiaries.

The law does not help those who are unhappy at the apparent disregard (or ignorance) by a bank trust corporation of the wishes or hopes of beneficiaries. There is no obligation on a trustee to consult the beneficiaries, let alone to try to meet their wishes.

'In carrying out his duties a trustee must be guided by the trust instrument and the rules of equity. In the exercise of any power or discretion . . . he is bound and entitled to use his own judgment, and ordinarily he is not obliged to consult the wishes . . . of [beneficiaries].' (22)

Nor can a trustee be compelled to give reasons for exercising a discretion one way or the other. These rules may be entirely justifiable where there are actual or potential conflicts amongst beneficiaries, or where there is a danger of frequent or vexatious demands made upon executors and trustees. It was for these reasons that a recent report rejected the idea of a statutory right to information for beneficiaries (23).

Nevertheless, any inflexible adherence to the non-consultation rule in all cases could well be seen as insensitive or high-handed. Moreover, we suspect that there would be a higher risk of resentment at any strict application of this rule where a bank trust corporation is the trustee. Trustees who are members or friends of the family, or who are the family solicitor or accountant, will nearly always be more likely to know more about the personal circumstances of all concerned. One correspondent, who wrote to us complaining about the performance of two trusts, drew the general conclusion – indignantly, but inaccurately – that:

> 'Bank trust departments are, according to them, not accountable for their performance in "managing" trusts to any person or anybody at all, not even to the beneficiaries. They do not even accept the rights of beneficiaries to consultation about investments.'

It is beyond the scope of this report to discuss whether the non-consultation rule is satisfactory. The rule does not ban consultation and we are sure, in any event, that bank trust corporations will usually try to find out the wishes of beneficiaries and keep them informed about the administration of the trust. Nevertheless the evidence available to us suggests that there may be more scope for consultation between bank trust corporations and beneficiaries. Beneficiaries will often have competing interests and may sometimes be unreasonable or selfish or improperly motivated; but consultation does not mean control. We have in mind that banks should urge testators and settlors to include a provision obliging the banks as trustee to consult beneficiaries (or their parents and guardians) and, in so far as that is consistent with the general interests of the trust, to give effect to their wishes. (This bears some resemblance to section 26(3) of the Law of Property Act 1925 which obliges trustees of statutory 'trusts for sale' of land (for example arising on intestacy) to consult with adult beneficiaries.) We would like to see such a provision become the norm where a bank is appointed.

It must be stressed that this proposal would do no more than improve the flow of information; it would not bind the bank to any course of action. It would clearly be necessary to make due allowance for the interests of future beneficiaries and the bank as trustee would have to make its own decisions where the beneficiaries are not in agreement. Even if such a provision did not result in much more than present practice, we feel that a process of consultation in accordance with the trust instrument would ultimately benefit the banks by creating a better climate of confidence.

REDUCING THE SCOPE FOR DIRECT OR INDIRECT PROFIT FROM INVESTMENT DECISIONS

The third area for improvement returns to the debate about conflict of interest raised at the beginning of this section. We deal now with safeguards directed at possible conflicts of interest during the administration of the trust or estate. On this point we had fewer complaints than those concerning charges, delays or poor investment records, but it does raise an important issue of principle. It is necessary first to say a little more about the law.

One of the most fundamental rules of equity – 'the great principle' – is that a trustee should not profit from the trust:

'With certain exceptions, neither directly nor indirectly may a trustee make a profit from his trust. This rule is part of the wider principle that in order to protect a trustee against "the fallibility of human nature" he may not put himself in a position where his duty and his interest may conflict . . .' (24)

These rules can be traced back to the leading case of Keech v. Sandford in 1726 (25) where a trustee who took a personal lease of Romford Market had to hold it on trust for an infant beneficiary. The rule means that a trustee must refund to the trust, with interest, all personal profit made from such activities as using trust funds to support his own business, making a remunerative profit from the management of trust property, or purchasing part of the trust estate. The rule applies to the mere fact of a profit; it is not confined to cases of fraud or bad faith.

A recent case which discussed the rule that a trustee may not make a profit from his trust was Swain v. The Law Society (26). In that case Stephenson L.J. said that this rule:

'is part of the wider principle that in order to protect a trustee against the fallibility of human nature he may not put himself in a position where his duty and his interest may conflict . . .'

A major exception to this rule is that the trust instrument – such as the will or a trust deed – may expressly allow the trustee to derive a benefit from the trusteeship. Solicitors who act as trustees or executors cannot charge for their services without such express authority. And of course bank trust corporations will invariably ensure that wide charging and investment clauses are included in the will or deed. Without such clauses they will simply decline to act.

The usual procedure is for the bank trust corporation to ensure that the trust instrument refers expressly to its current terms and conditions. These tend to be wide. As well as allowing the bank to levy charges in accordance with its scale, they are entitled to hold trust funds in their own bank accounts, to charge bank fees, to invest in the bank's own unit trusts and so on. Apart from the general remuneration provisions, the terms and conditions for Barclaytrust, for example, state that:

'4. The company may without being liable to account for any profit thereby made:
   a) act as banker and transact any banking or allied business on normal banking terms;
   b) retain the customary share of brokerage and other commissions;
   c) perform any service on behalf of the estate or trust and make charges commensurate with the service rendered;
   d) employ at the expense and on behalf of the estate or trust any parent or associated or subsidiary company as banker or to transact any allied business or for any purpose for which a trustee is entitled to employ agents;
   e) retain any remuneration received as a result of the appointment of a

nominee as a director or other officer of any other company whose shares or debentures shall from time to time be held in the estate or trust.

5. The Company shall not be required, by reason only of the general rule preventing a trustee from deriving a profit from his trusteeship, to account to the estate or trust for any profit made in the ordinary course of business by the Company or any parent or associated or subsidiary company arising from the exercise of any power or discretion conferred by the will or codicil or trust instrument or by law.'

We must stress that the banks are operating perfectly legally in using such wide clauses, and in taking advantage of them. The booklet issued by Lloyds Bank Trust Division openly and properly includes, in a statement of its investment policy:

'In the smaller cases where an adequate spread of equities is required but cannot be easily obtained, advantage may be taken of one or other of the Bank's Unit Trusts.'

Nor do we suggest that, in practice, the banks have acted in any way improperly. Moreover, we do not raise any objection to the bank's right to impose charges for their services or to recover ordinary bank charges in respect of the trust fund's current account. Our concern arises specifically in connection with investment decisions made by the bank trust corporation, where we believe that the bank should not benefit and should be seen not to benefit. The bank must act in a way that is above reproach. This was recognised in the following case decided in 1952 by Mr Justice Harman.

In Re Waterman's Will Trusts, Lloyds Bank Ltd v. Sutton (27) a lady appointed a bank to be her executor. The will entitled the bank to remuneration 'in accordance with its published terms' and entitled the bank to keep any profit resulting from its services as banker. It transpired that in the four years since death, the estate – worth some £10,000 – had earned a very small income, and that for some considerable time £9,000 in cash had been deposited by the bank with itself. In the words of the judge:

'So that, during the year before the matter came before me, the estate as a whole had only earned one-half per cent interest. This was a startling state of things, and it seemed to me to call for some further investigation . . .

. . . If any private trustee having £9,000 of his beneficiaries' money in his pocket chooses to place it on deposit in his own business, in other words, to lend it to himself, the court will without hesitation charge him interest . . ., whether or not he made a profit, because he has employed trust money in his trade, and that the court will not allow. It is, therefore, conceded that this is not a thing which the bank could do unless the charging clause which it put before the testator dispenses with the usual penalties.'

Although the judge went on to say that it would be 'a shocking thing' for the bank to make a profit in this way at the expense of the beneficiaries, he went on to hold that the charging clause was indeed sufficient to entitle the bank to keep this profit. The failure to invest more profitably could not be attacked as no beneficiary had alleged breach of trust.

Returning to the present day, we have seen that despite the judge's stern criticism in 1952, wide charging and investment clauses are still in use. It is worth repeating that these are effective to overrule the principles that there should be no conflict of interest and that a trustee should not make a direct or indirect profit. We believe that it is understandable that beneficiaries who believe that a trust fund has not sufficiently maintained its value will feel doubly aggrieved where a bank has derived a direct or indirect profit from that investment decision.

A Scottish correspondent complained that too much money had been kept on current account even though 'much emphasis was given in one reply [from the bank] to it not being the bank's policy to keep large sums on current account'. He remained dissatisfied with this response to the loss of income, but he was pessimistic about doing anything about it:

'I foresee protracted – and vain – argument over this matter with the Bank, which I will lose. And who would sue a Bank for a mere £200–£300 on the basis that if they had handled matters different that sum might have been earned?'

An even more disturbing case was reported to us, via a member of parliament, where a dissatisfied constituent wrote:

'The one area where I think that [the bank] may have "sailed very close to the wind" involved their investment in equities. All the equity investment is in a number of [the bank's] unit trusts. There are hundreds of unit trusts, so presumably [the bank] consider that they are the only organisation who can run a successful investment programme – or is there another reason for their choice?'

The same correspondent also complained that as the bank's management fees are a percentage of the trust's book value, '. . . re-investment of the interest (such as it is) is more advantageous to them, than allowing the money to be used for the benefit of the [important beneficiaries]'. His general conclusion was that there 'was no way in which any checks or counterchecks could have been made on what they did. Putting it another way, they could simply write cheques to themselves.' This may be an exaggeration, but this, and similar cases, do demonstrate the need to avoid even a hint of conflict of interest in the course of executorship and trustee administration.

Bank trust corporations would undoubtedly argue that they can fully justify, on investment grounds, decisions which might benefit the parent bank. This is to miss the point of principle which, for centuries, has been a corner-stone of the law. Nor, in our view, is it a sufficient answer to point to the various commissions which may be received by other professionals.

We would like the bank trust corporations to review their overall investment policies. We have in mind that guiding principles might be laid down on the following lines:

* no fund administered by a bank trust corporation should be invested in the shares of that bank or in unit trusts managed by that bank;
* where it is decided that a deposit account is needed, that account should not normally be opened with the same bank;
* special care should be taken to ensure that any current account never contains an excessive balance;
* commissions earned (for example on insurance of trust property) should be added to the trust.

It may be desirable for banks to change their documentation specifically to ensure such practices. In any event, the explanatory booklets which we have proposed should spell out that these principles will be followed. We do not believe that banks or bank trust corporations will regard these proposals as unreasonable. If they do, we ask them to remember that it is only by virtue of their own documentation that they are able to derive any sort of income – direct or indirect – from the trust work in the first place. Our proposals do no more than seek a partial return to the rules of equity.

RESOLVING GRIEVANCES ABOUT THE ADMINISTRATION OF ESTATES AND TRUSTS

We turn finally to a point which has arisen several times in this section. This is the need for an effective procedure for disgruntled members of the public to pursue their grievances against a bank trust corporation. As we have seen, there are four main types of grievances which could be resolved by such a procedure. These are:

* dissatisfaction with the level of charges;
* complaints of non-consultation;
* complaints of delay;
* allegations of breach of trust, particularly where there is dissatisfaction resulting from investment decisions.

We believe that a new procedure is required. There is a measure of public dissatisfaction at the moment. Individual banks – whether at head office or any other level – cannot claim a truly independent role in resolving disputes. The courts have only a very limited role. They cannot for example deal with charges, complaints of non-consultation or (except in the very worst cases) with complaints of delay. In any event, the courts are remote, expensive and inaccessible. It will only be the very brave or the very foolish who (without full legal aid) will wish to challenge a bank trust corporation in court.

We have only been able to trace two reported cases since the war when a bank trust corporation has been sued. The second of these – Bartlett v. Barclays Bank Trust Co. – a complicated case involving a claim of over £½ million, demonstrated the difficulties of legal action, even for the wealthiest. At the end of that case, Brightman J. was critical of the vigour with which the bank had defended the case and said:

> 'This action has lasted well over 40 days . . . I think it is a pity that a large and responsible trust corporation should have put the Bartlett family to the expense and anxiety of a marathon court proceeding.' (28)

It is certainly in the interests of consumers of more modest means that there should be an effective mechanism for their legitimate grievances to be independently resolved. A new procedure would, therefore, allow three key features to be incorporated:

* it could be set up so as to be accessible and to achieve a fair balance as between banks and individuals;
* it could deal with issues which cannot be examined by the courts;
* issues capable, in theory, of being dealt with by the courts could be settled more simply and cheaply.

In section 7 we have proposed the establishment of an independent Banking Ombudsman, with power to recommend solutions to disputes between banks and their customers. Such a person could, we believe, legitimately deal with complaints involving bank trust corporations, as well as complaints arising from more regular aspects of the banker/customer relationship.

There are, of course, a number of special features which arise from executor and trustee services, but we do not believe that any of these present an insurmountable obstacle to this jurisdiction. It cannot be argued that our proposal would oust the power of the court to supervise all aspects of executor and trust work. The Ombudsman would only have powers of recommendation; it would remain open to any party to make application to the court where that is possible.

We accept that, out of a single estate or trust, there are likely to be more potential complainants than the single customer who is dissatisfied with his bank. Complainants who are actual or potential beneficiaries are not 'consumers' in the strict sense, but we do not see why they should not take advantage of a banking redress scheme when their grievances relate to the activities of a bank trust corporation. It would, of course, be necessary to take account of the identity of possible complainants in devising the Ombudsman's terms of reference. It would, for example, be necessary to include the parents or guardians of infant beneficiaries.

There will be some cases where different beneficiaries will have competing interests and it will be necessary to ensure that, in such cases, the Banking Ombudsman is able to take full account of divergent positions.

There remains the problem of defining the jurisdiction. One of the major attractions of a Banking Ombudsman would be that it would increase public confidence in the full range of services provided by banks. We therefore believe that the jurisdiction should be defined as widely as possible. Broadly, it should extend to:

(i)   review of all charges arising in the course of the administration of an estate or trust. The criterion should be that all charges should be 'fair and reasonable' having regard to the amount of work done, the complexity of the work and the value of the estate or trust (This recommendation does not negate the suggestion that the courts should also be able to 'tax' these charges; the recommendation is the counterpart of the Law Society's power to review solicitors' charges);

(ii) consideration of any complaint that a person with a legitimate interest in an estate or trust had not been adequately consulted by a bank trust corporation. (Our recommendation that a duty to consult should be included in bank trust deeds would mean that such a complaint would really be an allegation of breach of trust, under (iv) below);

(iii) consideration of any complaint of maladministration in the conduct of an estate or trust. This would, for example, allow the Ombudsman to deal with complaints of unnecessary delay which were not so extreme as to amount to breach of trust;

(iv) consideration of cases which involve an allegation of breach of trust. This would embrace cases where it was suggested that the trust instrument had not been observed and cases alleging breach of the rules of equity.

In all these cases, the Ombudsman – as described more fully in section 7 – would consider whether they fell within his terms of reference, investigate the case fully, consider the submissions of all interested parties and make a recommendation. We would expect the banks to observe such a recommendation in virtually all cases, but it would remain open for anyone to make an application to the court where that was possible. If a bank felt that a recommendation of the Ombudsman would (if observed) involve a breach of trust, we would expect the bank itself to make an application for the court's guidance.

Conclusion

The Committee of London Clearing Bankers, in evidence to us, wished to emphasise the clearing banks' 'high reputation in executor and trustee work which have been established and maintained through the high level of service that they have provided for over 70 years. They believe that their own internal procedures for ensuring the maintenance of that high level of service and for the investigation of fee complaints etc. fully meets their customers' requirements and expectations.'

The banks' procedures do not satisfy at least that tiny minority of customers who took the trouble to write to us – often at great length – in the course of our investigations.

We make the following proposals to deal with the specific problems we have identified:

* Although there are a number of actual or potential conflicts involved in the appointment of a bank trust corporation, we do not consider that it is illegitimate for them to do this work or that statutory restrictions are needed.
* Improved competition between bank trust corporations and others – particularly solicitors – is the best way to prevent the appointment of an inappropriate executor or trustee.
* To this end, the legal profession should improve the promotion of its services to the public, including the freedom for solicitors to advertise individually.
* An independent leaflet should be produced – by government or a voluntary organisation – to give people independent and impartial advice to help them leave their affairs in order after death.
* Banks should ensure that their literature and their advice does not lead to their appointment when there is no real need for it, and should actively develop services aimed at helping executors and administrators who are acting in person.
* Banks should give, at appointment, a rough estimate of probable charges and should devise a procedure to keep relevant customers informed of changes to their scales.
* When banks are called upon to undertake executor duties, they should, wherever possible, discuss the likely level of charges with beneficiaries and, in some cases, should themselves raise the possibility of renouncing the executorship.
* The charges of bank trust corporations should be subject to review. They should be 'fair and reasonable' having regard to the amount of work done, the complexity of the work and the value of the estate or trust.
* Banks – individually or collectively – should publish a booklet outlining the main principles of law which affect the administration of estates and trusts.
* Bank trust corporations should see that wills and trust deeds which appoint them should, where appropriate, oblige them to consult beneficiaries and, in so far as consistent with the general interest of the trust, to give effect to their wishes.
* We have suggested that bank trust corporations should consider restrictions upon their own investment policies to deal with the dangers of actual or apparent conflicts of interest during the administration of an estate or trust.
* The Banking Ombudsman should be empowered to investigate complaints against bank trust corporations and to make recommendations for their resolution. This should include reviews of charges, complaints of inadequate consultation, complaints of maladministration and allegations of breach of trust.

We believe that our specific proposals will go a long way towards alleviating the problems we have discussed. We have also made clear our belief that more effective competition between bank trust corporations and others, particularly solicitors, who provide similar services will, in the long run, do most to reduce consumer dissatisfaction.

We have had to look at executor and trustee services from the point of view of those relatively few cases where bank trust corporations are involved. It has become apparent to us that such problems as there are, are by no means confined to the banks. We have refrained from comment about the value for money which the public gets from those professionals – whether banks or solicitors – who are paid for their involvement with estate and trusts.

A full professional service rarely comes cheaply. We have mentioned the need for some form of 'hand-holding' help for straightforward cases where consumers wish to do most of the work themselves. There may also be a case for considerable simplification of law and practice to reduce the need for reliance upon professionals. This is well beyond the terms of reference of a report on banking services. But we are left in little doubt that the whole area of executor and trustee work is one which merits full investigation extending to an examination and comparison of the roles of all those involved.

References to section 11

1. *Judicial Statistics*, 1981. See also Welsh Consumer Council, *Probate; the Do-it-Yourself Way*, WCC, 1978.
2. Royal Commission on Legal Services in England and Wales, 1979, Cmnd 7648, paras. 19.25 and R19.3.
3. *Law Society's Gazette*, 11 November 1981.
4. Monopolies Commission, *A Report on the General Effect on the Public Interest of Certain Restrictive Practices*, 1970, Cmnd 4463, para. 347.
5. Monopolies and Mergers Commission, *Services of Solicitors in England and Wales*, HOC 557, 1976, chapter 5.
6. *Op. cit.*, para. 27.32.
7. Royal Commission on Legal Services in Scotland, 1980, Cmnd 7846, paras. 13.19–13.26.
8. *Law Society's Gazette*, 3 February 1982.
9. *Ibid.*, 28 October 1981.
10. Correspondence, Pettybridges and Best to Director-General of Fair Trading, 27 April 1982.
11. *Op. cit.*, para. 19.27.
12. 23rd Report of the Law Reform Committee, 1982, Cmnd 8733, paras 3.50–3.55.
13. Re Duke of Norfolk's Settlement Trusts (1981) 3 AER 220.
14. *Law Society's Gazette*, 24 February 1982, p. 217. See also: A. Kenny, Consumer Protection for the Beneficiary, 1983, unpublished, where it is pointed out that in the Duke of Norfolk case, Walton J. (at first instance) suggested, *obiter*, that '. . . if the Court has an inherent jurisdiction to increase the rate of a trustee's remuneration, the jurisdiction must exist to

decrease such remuneration.' The Court of Appeal went on to confirm the power to increase, but did not deal with a power to decrease.

15. *Op. cit.*, para. 13.18.
16. 8th Annual Report of the Lay Observer, April 1983, HC 323.
17. *Op. cit.*, para. 7.13.
18. *Snell's Principles of Equity*, 28th edition, p. 212.
19. Underhill, *Law of Trusts and Trustees*, 13th ed., 1979, p. 461.
20. (1980) 1 AER 139, p. 152.
21. Under Section 1(1) of the Judicial Trustees Action, 1896.
22. *Snell's Principles of Equity*, 28th edition (1982), p. 232.
23. 23rd Report of the Law Reform Committee, *op. cit.*, para. 7.16–17.
24. *Snell's Principles of Equity*, 28th edition, 1982, p. 244.
25. (1726) 2 W & TLC 648.
26. (1982) 1 WLR1717, p. 29.
27. (1952) 2 AER 1054, p. 1055.
28. (1980) 1 AER 139, pp. 155–156.

Appendix I / Some of the developments in consumer banking services during the time this report was in preparation (taken from contemporary newspaper reports)

DATE*	EVENT
10 Feb 1982	Clydesdale Bank and BP Oil introduce point-of-sale debit card scheme called Counterplus in Aberdeen
18 Feb	Lloyds offer 100% home loans
24 Feb	Leicester Building Society to introduce Citibank's Tandem Account and 'Leicestercard'
24 March	Kelloggs offer free cash to children who open bank accounts in conjunction with three banks
28 March	British Legal Association attacks banks for allegedly 'ripping off' the public over the services they offer as executors and trustees of wills
3 April	TSBs to be restructured; share ownership may be divided amongst eight million customers
12 April	Lloyds introduces automated bank statements in braille for blind customers
15 April	Clearing banks agree to keep customers' cheques for a minimum of three years
21 April	A second automated bank clearing centre opened in Dunstable
22 April	Rising fraud forces the banks to ban use of conventional cheque cards abroad from May 1983
	American Express and Lloyds merge sterling travellers' cheque operations
30 April	National Westminster launch monthly income account to meet the needs of retired people
12 May	Barclays to introduce new scale of customer account charges and increase minimum credit balance needed for free banking from £50 to £100 from 1 June
14 May	Barclays to re-open on Saturdays at selected branches
15 May	Lloyds to take over network of estate agents

* Of press report about the event.

DATE	EVENT
18 May	Co-operative Bank to clear cheques for Abbey National Building Society's planned cheque book service
27 May	Banking Insurance and Finance Union rejects Barclays proposals for Saturday opening
28 May	TSB and Debenhams join to provide banking facilities 6 days a week in a Sheffield department store
7 June	More than half the working population now paid by cheque or direct credit transfer
17 June	Midland offers new Access cash facility enabling customers to draw up to £100 from ATMs each week
19 June	Leeds Permanent Building Society to issue sterling travellers' cheques – commission free
9 July	National Westminster launches bonus interest rate scheme for customers who regularly deposit between £10 and £500 monthly
7 Aug	Lloyds to curb mortgage lending
25 Aug	Royal Bank of Scotland and Williams & Glyn's Bank to integrate operations more closely
9 Sept	National Westminster and Midland to link up their cash dispensers
10 Sept	Midland to curb mortgage lending
17 Sept	Midland to re-launch 'Save and Borrow' account – in effect an interest-bearing current account
13 Oct	Barclays launch premium credit card with overdraft facility of up to £7,500
2 Nov	Leicester Building Society is the first building society to introduce out-of-hours ATM
15 Nov	Nottingham Building Society to launch first UK electronic home banking service in conjunction with Prestel and the Bank of Scotland
24 Nov	National Westminster increases charges by up to 45%
30 Nov	Lloyds launch Black Horse young savers account – an extra-interest deposit account for young savers
4 Dec	Lloyds increase charges by more than one-third
31 Dec	Barclays increase charges by up to 50%
9 Jan 1983	Midland becomes the last of the big four to raise its current account charges
11 Jan	Midland and Nationwide Building Society, along with National Westminster and National Provincial Building Society, announce links to enable the two societies to make available Access credit cards
27 Jan	The Spalding Report from the Building Societies' Association advocates wide-ranging changes to building society legislation designed to give the societies wider lending and other powers
2 Feb	Midland to introduce new Eurocheque and Eurocheque guarantee card scheme in May
3 Feb	National Westminster launches *Moneycare*, the bank's free consumer finance magazine

DATE	EVENT
4 Feb	NCR launches the first talking ATM
9 Feb	Halifax Building Society re-launch interest-bearing account with cheque book facility
9 Feb	Western Trust and Savings introduces its 'Welcome-Plus' account – an arranged credit limit account charging 2% monthly interest on amount owing with no charge for writing cheques
16 Feb	National Westminster to charge customers of other banks, except Lloyds, 50p for cashing cheques
1 March	Barclays introduce 'Cashplan', an interest-bearing cheque account
8 March	Boston Trust and Savings to launch a free bank cheque cashing service in return for customers' names and addresses
15 March	Barclays, Lloyds, Williams and Glyn's, Royal Bank of Scotland and Bank of Scotland announce plan to link up their ATMs
9 April	Midland opens new-style shopper branch at Leamington Spa
28 April	Clydesdale and B.P. to extend their Counterplus point-of-sale debit card scheme in Scotland
29 April	Leeds Permanent Building Society to link with Yorkshire Bank and Barclaycard to provide their customers with a credit card
30 April	The Bristol and West Building Society to link up with Standard Chartered Bank to provide a wide range of current account services
4 May	The banks review plans to introduce photographs on cheque guarantee cards
6 May	Barclays and Trustee Savings Banks to link up their ATMs
9 May	Royal Bank of Scotland the first major bank to pull out of the market for new home loans
12 May	Britannia Group becomes the second unit trust group to offer an extra-interest account with cheque book facility for savers at the top end of the market
20 May	Barclays to raise charge for cashing cheques of other banks' customers on Saturdays from 50p to £1
24 May	National Westminster becomes the last of the big four to announce tough restrictions on new home loan lending
26 May	National Westminster launches Cash Wise, an interest-bearing current account aimed at the unbanked
27 May	Committee of London Clearing Bankers announces that it is to press ahead with a national point-of-sale electronic payments system

Appendix II / Research into consumers' attitudes to banking services, by Market Behaviour Ltd

Research objectives

The major objectives of the research are as follows:

1. To determine what consumers' perceptions are of their own needs for banking services, and to discover what their perceptions are of the various different types of banking services now on offer.
2. To establish what specific problems people experience, with a view to quantifying these and other attitudes in a full sample survey.

    In particular, we are concerned to discover:

    (i) What are the attitudes of the unbanked towards the alternative ways of payment for goods and the alternative services offered by the traditional clearing banks, other banks and by the building societies? What do they feel about such institutions? What has prevented them from acquiring a bank account?

    (ii) What are the satisfactions and dissatisfactions experienced and felt by banked consumers towards the service they are given in general and towards such specific features as accessibility, opening hours, standards of counter service, etc? What, moreover, do they know about the services that are available to them?

    (iii) What do consumers feel in an area, for example, like the West Midlands, where there has recently been new and competitive activity by the Western Trust and Savings Banks; how have new services like these affected attitudes?

    (iv) What impact are the microtechnological changes that are taking place in banks likely to have on consumer attitudes and behaviour?

    (v) What is the role played by different sources of information available to the consumer, including advertising in the various media?

    (vi) What is the extent of consumer awareness of and experience of what to do when things go wrong? In what ways do they need more information about this aspect of banking services?

3. To explore the banking needs and experience of selected ethnic minorities, in particular, those who are involved with the repatriation of earnings.

Method and sample

The sample was split into two sectors:

    (i) an evaluation of the attitudes amongst the banked and unbanked in England, including some of the ethnic minorities;

(ii) an evaluation of consumer attitudes in Scotland and Northern Ireland, in this case with a sample who are banked.

Note: The majority of banked respondents held a bank current account (for money which they spent, for paying bills) and a building society account (for saving). A few respondents held a bank deposit account instead of or in addition to a building society account.

1. THE ENGLISH SAMPLE

The methodology took into account the following factors and hypotheses:

(i) that attitudes between the unbanked, and between those who bank with the traditional clearing banks and those who bank at other institutions will be different and that the three types of consumer should be interviewed separately;

(ii) that the attitudes, levels of awareness and the priorities of consumers will vary according to their age and position on the life-cycle. We recommend therefore that the different age/life-cycle sectors be recruited into the same groups, but that the differences between them are clearly monitored;

(iii) that rural-dwellers will have different behaviour and possibly attitudes, because of the lack of accessibility. Thus, we propose to look at them separately by means of a small number of individual interviews;

(iv) that ethnic minorities will share attitudes and priorities, but because of within-group homogeneity, should be kept as distinct sectors, separated according to ethnic background;

(v) that consumers in the West Midlands should be contrasted with consumers in another part of the country in order to isolate whatever impact is being made by the activity currently taking place in that region.

Hence, the main base of the English research was 15 group discussions, quota controlled as follows:

Region	Sex	Unbanked	'Other' banked	Traditional clearer banked
West Midlands (10 groups)	male	1 group C1C2D	1 grp* BC1 / 1 grp C2D	1 grp BC1 / 1 grp C2D
	female	1 group C1C2D	1 grp BC1 / 1 grp C2D	1 grp BC1 / 1 grp C2D
Greater London area (5 groups)	mixed	1 group C1C2D	1 grp* BC1 / 1 grp C2D	1 grp BC1 / 1 grp C2D

* These groups proved impossible to recruit as stated, perhaps reflecting the more down-scale orientation of the second order banks. The social grading was therefore changed to C1C2D.

Unbanked respondents were defined as those who did not have a bank current account. They were allowed to have a deposit account with a bank or building society (although not with a traditional clearer bank).

All banked respondents had a personal bank current account.

Traditional clearer banked respondents held a current account at one of the following banks:

Barclays
Lloyds
Midland
National Westminster
Williams and Glyn's

'*Other*' *banked* were defined as those who held an account at one of the following:

Trustee Savings Bank
Co-operative Bank
Post Office/National Giro
Yorkshire Bank
Standard Chartered
Abbey National Building Society
Leicester Building Society
Citibank Trust
Boston Trust
Western Trust and Savings
Security Pacific
Bank America Finance
Bank of Credit & Commerce International
Allied Irish
United Bank
Muslim Commercial
Habib Bank
Bank of Ireland
Bank of Baroda
National Bank of Pakistan
Bank of India.

In fact, in England, all our 'other' respondents (with the exception of those in the ethnic minority groups) held accounts with either the TSB, the Co-op Bank, or the National Giro.

Each group consisted of 4 respondents aged 20–29 years, single and married without children, and 4 respondents aged 30–50 years, married with children.

In the mixed groups, 4 respondents were male and 4 were female.

The self-employed and small business owners were excluded.

No more than half the women in each group held a joint account; the rest had their own personal account.

In addition, 3 group discussions were conducted with members of *ethnic minority groups* – West Indians, Indians and Pakistanis. All groups took place in the Greater London area.

All respondents were of C1C2 social grade. The Indian and Pakistani groups were with men only but the West Indian group was mixed, half male and half female.

All groups consisted of 4 banked (either traditional clearer or 'other') and 4 unbanked respondents. There was a spread of ages between 20 and 50 years in each group. The Indian and West Indian groups included both immigrants and British-born respondents but the Pakistani groups consisted solely of immigrants (this was because we were advised that Pakistani immigration only really commenced in the 1960s and hence British-born respondents of the required age group would be practically impossible to find).

The Indian group included two linguistic sub-groups.

Finally *four individual interviews were conducted in rural areas*, relatively isolated from big towns. The respondents were required to live ten miles from any big town and at least three miles from the nearest bank/building society/post office branch.

Precise details of the individual interviews were as follows:

Female, 20–29, single, C1, traditional clearer
Female, 30–50, married with children, C2, traditional clearer
Male, 20–29, single, C2, 'other'
Male, 30–50, married with children, C1, traditional clearer

The interviews took place in Kent, and the Fen areas of Lincolnshire and Cambridgeshire.

It had been originally intended to interview 2 traditional clearer and 2 'other' banked respondents. However, 'other' respondents proved extremely difficult to find in rural areas.

2. THE CELTIC SAMPLE

Four group discussions were conducted, 2 in Scotland (Edinburgh) and 2 in Northern Ireland (Belfast).

In Scotland one male group and one female group was conducted.

4 aged 20–29 – 2 'other' banked
            2 traditional clearer
4 aged 30–50 – 2 'other' banked
            2 traditional clearer

In Northern Ireland it was thought necessary to split the group by religion. Hence, there was one group of Catholics and one group of Protestants. The groups had similar quotas to those of the Scottish groups, except that in each group half the respondents were men and half were women.

In Scotland the traditional clearer banks were defined as the Royal Bank of Scotland, the Bank of Scotland, and the Clydesdale Bank.

In Northern Ireland the traditional clearer banks were defined as the Ulster, the Northern, and the Allied Irish.

Discussion guide

The topics discussed in each group were as follows:

BANKED GROUPS

Warm-up introduction: what types of accounts held (all types) at which institutions, what prompted choice, how long held?

Current accounts with cheque book
What prompts choice of institution, extent of shopping around for first or subsequent choices? Awareness of alternative institutions available, extent of conscious thought about them, attitudes and imagery. Future plans for current account.

Current account services
Which services have ever and currently take advantage of, which others aware of? Services = statements, SO, DD, O/D, loans, cheque cards, cash-dispenser cards, any others. Attitudes to obtaining cash from counter v. dispenser.

Any problems encountered through use of a current account, attitude to service given by bank and problem solving.

Use of money transferral v. cash
Extent of using cash and in what amounts v. cheques, direct payments and credit cards. Criteria for choice of payment and perceived accessibility of cash through banks, post offices, building societies, cash in hand or combinations of these and other methods. Attitudes to the implications of possible future developments by banks covering costs of money transferral by increasing cheque charges.

Use of and attitudes to provision of peripheral services (if available) e.g. insurance, wills, investment advice and purchasing/selling, travel and foreign exchange, mortgages etc. Any problems.

Use of and attitudes to savings and deposit accounts at *any* institutions. Awareness and comparison of interest rates available. Criteria for choice of account and institution. Extent of 'shopping around' and opening/closing accounts.

Imagery and attitudes towards the general services offered by institution *types* i.e. banks, building societies, National Giro, 'money shops' (Citibank etc.) and perceived differences between them. In particular awareness, imagery and attitudes towards the growth of and services offered by Citibank, Western Trust and Avco.

Credit cards–awareness and use of services, awareness of true interest rates in comparison with other forms of borrowing.

UNBANKED GROUPS

How they manage money, particular needs and methods of solving financial problems.

Ever considered using a current account at an institution? Reasons for rejection. Ever considered a savings/deposit account at any institution? Criteria for choice or rejection. *Users*: satisfaction with service, problems encountered.

Awareness of services and imagery of institutions offering banking services. Awareness of market changes.

Future money management plans.

The 'ideal' institution for their needs.

ALL GROUPS

Future implications
The ideal financial services desired – what is good now and what is missing?

Introduce visual prompt material, covering micro-technological developments.

Discuss increased automation – further automatic dispensers, fewer tellers.

Discuss potential growth of 'money shop' outlets such as Citibank v. traditional outlets such as banks and building societies.

Discuss the current competitive moves (e.g. Abbey National cheque book accounts, banks offering mortgages), which are breaking down traditional demarcation lines.

Awareness, use of, attitudes to and needs of available 'information' on banking services, e.g. advertising and publicity from commercial institutions in media – 'editorial' programmes on tv/radio, articles in press, 'objective' advice from commercial institutions.

Timing

The group discussions were conducted between 28 June and 29 July 1982.

Summary of main findings

CONSUMER SATISFACTION WITH SERVICES

Consumer satisfaction with banking services can be divided into two areas: firstly, satisfaction at an objective, factual level, with the standard and relevancy of the services provided; secondly, a more subjective satisfaction derived from the degree of involvement and rapport that people feel with the bank and its staff.

Dealing first with the factual standards of service it did appear that many respondents had experienced at least one bank error, for example a statement mistake, a mix-up between two accounts or alternatively a mistake on a standing order. It was clear that people generally acted quickly to have mistakes rectified. They chose various methods of informing the bank of their mistake (some wrote, some phoned and some went in person) but it did appear that they succeeded in having the error rectified. Respondents clearly experienced no difficulty in complaining where *their* money was concerned.

Some people appear to be satisfied with the banks' handling of the error and subsequent apology; others appear to react in anger and may close their account, transferring it to another bank.

The major dissatisfaction with banks is centred around their opening hours. Inconvenience on this point is clearly minimal to many people; if they work in town they probably have easy access to banks. Some see the cash-dispenser machine as the solution to the problem. However, it does seem likely that it might particularly inconvenience some C2D households with longer and inflexible working hours. Certainly many people see opening hours to be an indication of poor service to the public overall and to reflect a lack of concern for non-business customers (to some extent this criticism of banks may well be linked with an emotional feeling of a lack of interest on the part of the banks with an individual's account).

Respondents criticised the queues at lunchtime resulting from a combination of inconvenient opening hours and the practice of the counter staff of taking their lunch break at the time when the public most need their service.

Bank charges are of course another area of criticism but it is important to note that not all respondents who paid them complained about them. People who don't complain recognise that the bank is providing them with a service in giving them a cheque book and paying their bills by standing order. People who do complain appear to have lost view of the fact that banks provide a service. There appear to be two categories in this latter group: people who have had a bank account imposed upon them by their firm; and people who accept an account as being so much a part of their daily lives that they have forgotten that it does provide them with a service. A bank account appears to many to be seen as an essential part of life and it is one that they no longer appreciate.

This leads us to the question of the more emotional satisfaction with banks. Among people who have been forced to join or who have merely joined because a bank account was seen as part of the process of growing up, it is perhaps not surprising that they do not have particularly positive reactions towards banks. This attitude may partly explain why so many people appear to become annoyed with banks when they make mistakes; they do not appear to be willing to *forgive* their bank for its mistakes; and some may instead react in rage and close their account.

In addition it was clear that many respondents felt ill at ease in their bank. The people who appeared to be most satisfied with their banks were those who had a close, friendly relationship with the banks and the managers. Such people were mainly BC1 men, respondents living in rural areas, or a few people who, by chance, had achieved such a relationship by e.g. working above the bank and knowing the staff well. However, for many respondents it did appear that the bank atmosphere (and in particular a perceived intimidating attitude on the part of the bank manager) did not encourage a feeling of closeness to the bank. It appeared that many people *felt* that they were not treated as equals in a bank; that there was one standard of service for the rich and one for the poor; and that their manager was off-hand, rude, and unsympathetic.

There does appear to be evidence to suggest that individual managers might well discriminate in their treatment between customers. It should not be forgotten, however, that the bank manager is 'only human'. Hence, he might well treat a professional man as an equal; due to common tastes and interests, a conversation about a bank might well turn into a friendly 'chat'. Alternatively, a nervous young person approaching the manager for the first time might well be treated with what seems to his young customer to be a lecture. Members of the ethnic minorities accuse managers of racial prejudice; this may well be true in certain cases but it is perhaps worth pointing out that in some cases communication difficulties might lead to exasperation on both sides. It is perhaps relevant that some of the most satisfied bank customers were banked with the National Giro. If they wanted a loan they had merely to fill in a form; there was no personal communication between the manager and his customer. (They did, however, complain about the counter staff.)

It should also be noted that some respondents appeared to have an attitude towards banks, concerning the purpose of banks, that was probably not shared by the manager himself. Some appeared to regard the bank almost as a social service. They expected a loan merely because they had been a customer for a long time, not because they would necessarily have the money to pay it back. It can be seen that conflicting attitudes would always be likely to produce friction between manager and customer.

Of course, because a manager is 'only human' and is dealing with a fellow human being, it would seem to be impossible to eliminate all causes of complaint. It would also appear to be a mistake to presume that the majority of the customers would like to see a manager replaced with a detailed set of rules that would govern whether or not a loan would be given. There were several instances of complaint concerning letters about a 'petty' overdraft, letters that had been sent out automatically. Recipients of such letters appeared to think that the manager should have looked at the history of their account and stopped such a letter going out; or at least sent a more personal, polite note himself. The majority felt very strongly that personal service was important (this opinion is dealt with further in the section below on Micro-technology).

It was clear that many respondents did not feel encouraged to ask questions or to ask to see the manager. This leads to a situation in which many people are perhaps unaware of the full extent of the facilities that they could make use of in the bank; this lack of information may or may not be supplemented by advice from family, friends and associates.

It is important to note that, while some people are content with the atmosphere and the information services provided by the banks, there are many who are not. Those who are not may well be those who are being drawn into the banking system by the forces of change; because they are now paid by cheque they have been obliged to open an account, although they may have preferred to have remained without a bank account.

It appears from the research that for many people the ideal bank would have a manager who was easily accessible to all customers. Ideally he would be always visible; at the very least the customer should have met him when he/she opened an account. The bank should take the initiative of informing customers about all their services in a comprehensive and easy-to-understand booklet (and preferably in verbal terms as well, perhaps at the initial meeting with the manager, when the booklet could be explained and all the facilities pointed out with reference to the customers' needs). It appears that, at the moment, few people approach the bank for general advice about services of their own volition (although the exception to this rule might be in small branches where the manager is more likely to be known personally to the customer).

Some respondents appeared to be very happy with the fact that they were using very few services; however, others would like to be better informed. They appreciated the information that they received from friends, information that enabled them to make better use of their accounts and which they would not have thought of approaching the bank to find out about. People do not, however, want to feel pressurised into accepting services that they do not need.

In summary it appeared that some dissatisfied respondents in fact required a friendly advice centre. And it was clear that many would prefer to have this service performed by an established bank rather than by a new institution. Respondents were clearly worried about what might happen to *their* money in an unestablished institution.

As far as the unbanked are concerned it would appear that, for the majority, the banks could do little to encourage their custom. This section of the community is largely happy with the idea of dealing in cash; these people have no need of a bank account. However, there were indications that some of the unbanked might have been interested in an account had they had more information on the subject. However, they appeared to feel too embarrassed to go into a bank and to enquire about an account. A simple introductory leaflet and an encouraging atmosphere would appear to alleviate some of their problems on this point.

MICRO-TECHNOLOGY AND PLASTIC MONEY

People appear willing to accept micro-technology, provided that they have a choice about whether or not they have to use it; and provided that it does not threaten their present life-style. The British people in general appear to be very anxious not to follow what they believe to be the ways of the United States and to become a nation of credit card holders. They also have a fear of an Orwellian nightmare in which they do not leave the home and instead sit in an armchair pushing buttons.

Many people accept change provided that it is in moderation. Hence, they accept the idea of the shop till-card – provided that it is not in every shop. They accept the concept of the tv bank – provided that it is largely confined to business use. They also accept the idea of perhaps greater use of machines such as the cash dispenser at banks – provided that the counter staff are still available. In particular, some people appear to dread the idea of the end of personal service; they regard it as part of the general quality of life.

Finally, it should be remembered that a significant minority of people still do prefer to deal solely in cash, and that these people should continue to be catered for.

Details of main findings

1. Use of and attitudes towards banks

REASONS FOR OPENING A CURRENT ACCOUNT

1.1 The opening of a current account was commonly regarded as an automatic occur-rence in the natural course of events, typically related to starting a job which did not pay wages in cash.
1.2 For certain C2D respondents, however, it was not an automatic step but was a direct result of their terms of employment.
1.3 Others had opened a current account specifically for the payment of bills.
1.4 Some married women had opened a personal current account as a means of indepen-dence from their husband and separate from the joint husband-and-wife account.

CHOICE OF BANK

The traditional clearers
1.5 Choice of bank emerged largely as a matter of convenience in terms of proximity to home or work. There was minimal discrimination between the services offered by different banks.

1.6 Barclays, Lloyds, National Westminster and Midland were the best known. Williams and Glyn's was rarely mentioned, and the Trustee Savings Bank and the Co-op Bank were not regarded as providing the full range of services.

1.7 Choice between the banks was generally determined according to the following factors:

* proximity to work or home
* convenience of choosing the firm's bank
* personal recommendation, usually from the family
* (in a few cases) professional recommendation e.g. by a lawyer
* specific services and advantages offered
* emotional reasons/first impressions.

'Other' banks

1.8 'Other' banks, such as TSB or National Girobank, were usually chosen for specific reasons other than proximity. Firm and family influence were more important. One woman went to the TSB in order to keep her own account; and professional advice was also mentioned.

1.9 Convenient opening hours were another attraction of the TSB and the Giro, as was interest on current accounts for the Co-op.

PERCEIVED ADVANTAGES OF HAVING A BANK CURRENT ACCOUNT

1.10 Safety and convenience of a cheque book.

1.11 Paying bills: by standing order, posting cheques, paying by giro transfers at the bank, post office giro. Budget accounts were used for bills by one or two respondents. There was some confusion and anxiety about direct debits.

1.12 Bank statements as a way of checking on finances. The Girobank in particular was praised for the frequency of its statements.

1.13 Overdrafts: by prior arrangement; without arrangement; by writing a cheque which would not be cleared until after pay-day; wrong-dating of cheques; non-signing – 'forgetting to sign' – of cheques.

1.14 Loans: cheaper but less quick and easy to procure than hire purchase.

1.15 Cash cards: fast and convenient.

1.16 Advice from the manager: particularly for BC1 respondents. Some people were reluctant to seek advice from their bank manager.

PERCEIVED DISADVANTAGES OF HAVING A BANK CURRENT ACCOUNT

1.17 Opening hours: perceived to be short and inconvenient.

1.18 Queues.

1.19 Bank charges: attitudes to these varied between willing acceptance and resentment, usually according to the perceived usefulness of the bank's services.

1.20 Lack of discretion/flexibility/common sense, concerning automatic charges without full consideration of the individual account holder's situation.

1.21 Phone call charges.

1.22 The charge for cashing cheques of other banks.

1.23 £50 cheque card limit: considered unrealistic nowadays.

1.24 Mistakes and computer errors.

1.25 The imposition of 'dangerous' services upon customers, e.g. credit cards, large loans.

1.26 Girobank: £100 daily withdrawal restriction; lack of overdraft facility; reluctant acceptance of Girobank cheques by small stores.

1.27 TSB: undesirable changes resulting from increased competition with the 'big four', e.g. obligatory current account in order to use deposit account for payment of bills and computer break-downs; inflexibility in comparison to the traditional clearers, lack of cash dispensers in England and Scotland.

COMPLAINTS AND BANK SWITCHING

Individuals varied as to whether they complained to the bank or actually switched banks as a result of the following:

1.28 'Petty' letters about small overdrafts.
1.29 Account mix-ups.
1.30 Mistakes on standing orders.
1.31 Poor service.
1.32 Manager's attitude over credit facilities.

(Specific reasons for switching banks):

1.33 Moving job or home.
1.34 Different levels of bank charges.
1.35 Convenience of opening hours.

GENERAL ATTITUDES AND FEELINGS CONCERNING BANKS AND BANK STAFF

1.36 *The bank* – generally perceived to be in business to make money. Some, particularly women, accepted this while others, particularly C2D, resented it.
1.37 Banks were believed to be most helpful towards businessmen or people with a lot of money, with the possible exception of the TSB.
1.38 The respondents felt that the banks were not particularly accommodating to less affluent people in terms of general attitude, opening hours and bank charges.
1.39 Banks were commonly regarded as hard, inhumane and unsympathetic.
1.40 *The manager* – recognised as influencing individuals' image of a particular bank.
1.41 Respondents with a good relationship with their manager were most positively disposed towards bank services and tended to be the following people:

* BC1 men;
* people who had a very long-term relationship with a particular bank;
* people who knew the manager personally;
* people who felt they had a particularly pleasant manager.

1.42 Those who were ill at ease with their managers tended to be women, some young people, some C2Ds, and ethnic minorities.
1.43 Respondents felt that managers were particularly well disposed towards people in a sound financial position.
1.44 Many people, particularly in Northern Ireland, were in awe of bank managers and were reluctant to approach him for advice. The absence of a manager on the premises in Girobank was not seen as a problem.
1.45 *The staff* – the attitude of the staff was more important to women than to men. There was general satisfaction with counter staff apart from a few complaints about rudeness or inefficiency, notably in Scotland. Post office staff had the poorest reputation.

2. Use of and attitudes towards building societies

REASONS FOR JOINING

2.1 Building societies were primarily associated with saving, in contrast to banks which were seen as places to keep ready cash and through which to pay bills.

2.2 The majority of respondents held a building society account in order to save and because it was considered the best way to save for the following reasons:

2.3   * high interest level

2.4   * interest is tax-paid

2.5   * mortgage availability

2.6   * safer from withdrawal than a current account

2.7 Some respondents had a bank deposit account, which was felt to have certain advantages.

CHOICE OF BUILDING SOCIETY

2.8 Commonly chosen for reasons of convenience or family influence.

2.9 Large building societies were considered more secure.

2.10 Savings were often placed in building societies which had given respondents their mortgages.

2.11 Shopping around for the most favourable interest rate was generally only considered worth while for longer-term deposits in high-interest share accounts.

2.12 Men were better informed about interest rates than women.

2.13 There was little usage of high-interest longer-term deposit accounts.

GENERAL ATTITUDES TO BUILDING SOCIETIES

2.14 Generally seen as brighter and more friendly than banks; orientated towards people saving for a house as opposed to the banks which were orientated towards business people.

2.15 Smaller branches of both banks and building societies were expected to be friendly.

2.16 Respondents' image of building societies and banks was influenced by their familiarity with the institution and its procedures.

3. Attitudes of the unbanked towards financial institutions

REASONS FOR NOT HAVING A BANK ACCOUNT

3.1 Those who were paid weekly saw no need for a bank account, since they used their income up each week.

3.2 Younger respondents who had no responsibilities or regular outgoings felt they did not need a bank account.

3.3 Those who had a spouse with a bank account felt they did not need a bank account themselves even if they had full- or part-time earnings.

3.4 Most of the unbanked respondents preferred to use cash as a way of keeping track of their finances.

3.5 The problem of opening hours.

3.6 Bank charges.

3.7 The perceived inefficiency of banks.

3.8 Keeping personal finances secret from wives (Scotland).

3.9 Avoiding tax inspection.

3.10 Banks are designed more for businessmen than for the general public.

3.11 Ignorance or lack of confidence.

ATTITUDES TOWARDS BUILDING SOCIETIES AND OTHER FINANCIAL INSTITUTIONS

3.12 The majority of unbanked respondents held a building society account for savings.

3.13 Some saved bill money in a building society.

3.14 Higher interest rates and longer opening hours gave building societies a more favourable image than banks among many respondents.

3.15 Some women held building society accounts to keep their money safe, both from themselves and from robbery, or, alternatively, from their husbands.

3.16 Building society cheques were considered useful for paying large bills.

3.17 Unbanked respondents were generally satisfied with building societies' service.

ATTITUDES TO LOANS

3.18 Most unbanked respondents avoided using credit of any kind, preferring to save up.

3.19 There was confusion over the relative interest rates of bank loans and hire purchase. Finance companies and store credit accounts were considered to have very unfavourable rates.

3.20 A minority accepted that credit was sometimes necessary, and hire purchase was regarded as a convenient method. Provident cheques were favoured by some women.

FUTURE ACCOUNT PLANS

3.21 Some unbanked respondents expected to open a bank account in the future.

4. Money management

PREFERRED METHOD OF PAYMENT

CASH V. CHEQUE

4.1 Most of the unbanked and many banked respondents preferred using cash to cheques.

4.2 Most banked respondents used cash for small items and cheques for larger items.

4.3 Cheques were most frequently used by the higher social grade or by respondents who had difficulty getting to a bank.

4.4 The majority of respondents felt that cash payment was easier to control than cheques, but some held the opposite view.

4.5 Cheques were felt to reduce the risks of theft, and people appeared to carry less cash on them than they had formerly.

CREDIT CARDS

4.6 Many people were afraid of over-spending with credit cards and felt it was more difficult to keep track of finances with them than with cheques.

4.7 Users found credit cards convenient for purchases when they did not have the money on them; to save writing cheques; for delaying final payment; on holiday abroad; in an emergency.

4.8 Some users paid the full amount off each month.

4.9 Respondents, who had received a credit card automatically because it also served as a cheque guarantee card, varied according to whether and how often they used it as a credit card.

ALTERNATIVE METHODS OF PAYMENT

4.10 Store accounts which had to be paid in full at the end of each month were favoured, whereas some respondents rather regretted opening store accounts where interest was charged on the outstanding balance.

THE RETURN OF CASH?

4.11 Cash dispensers meant that some men were using cash more frequently nowadays.

4.12 Cash was considered quicker and more convenient to pay and carry around than cheque books, and had the additional advantage of a potential discount.

CONTROL OF FINANCES

4.13 Joint husband-and-wife accounts were common for household expenses. Individuals varied as to whether the husband, wife, or both jointly, had responsibility for household management and payment of bills.

USE OF THE BANK

4.14 Women tended to go more frequently to the bank than men, owing to bank opening hours, with the exception of Edinburgh. Once a week was the average for most people.

4.15 Some respondents rarely went into their bank, either because of cash dispensers, or because they had moved away from the area, without changing to another branch.

FACILITIES USED OUTSIDE OF THE BANKING SYSTEM

4.16 Respondents obtained cash outside the bank system in a number of ways: cashing cheques at work, local pubs, garages, borrowing off the family.

5. Use of information and knowledge of banking services

AWARENESS OF INFORMATION SOURCES

5.1 Television advertising was the most frequently mentioned source of information, perceived as promoting bank loan facilities in particular.

5.2 Newspaper advertising was also important, especially in relation to building society interest rates.

5.3 Friends and relatives were also a source of information.

5.4 At the bank itself, leaflets and, for BC1 men in particular, the manager himself were sources of information.

5.5 Newspaper articles were also informative.

DEGREE OF USE AND ATTITUDES TO INFORMATION SOURCES

5.6 There was some ignorance and a lack of interest concerning the range of services offered by banks.

5.7 This was apparently due to confusing information from leaflets and bank staff; an excessive amount of information; and a perceived lack of encouragement on the part of the bank combined with respondents' reluctance to approach bank staff.

THE ADVANTAGES AND DISADVANTAGES OF POSITIVE ADVICE

5.8 People were reluctant to seek advice but generally receptive when it was given.

5.9 Bank magazines (such as Girobank's) and personal letters were well received but circulars tended to be ignored.

5.10 There was some interest in a personal approach from the bank manager, although some respondents were wary of this.

5.11 Ideally, a personal approach giving simple information in layman's terms, without any pressure, appeared to be desirable.

MISINFORMATION AND LACK OF KNOWLEDGE

5.12 Many respondents held mistaken beliefs about certain banking services.

6. New developments in the financial market

AWARENESS OF NEW DEVELOPMENTS

6.1 Respondents were aware of new activities in the financial market from their reading of newspapers.
Developments mentioned were Saturday opening, mortgages, store credit schemes, in-store banks, 'Cash Line' in a Scottish bank, increased competition between the finance companies and banks and building societies.

ATTITUDES TOWARDS NEW DEVELOPMENTS

6.2 Respondents were generally positively disposed towards the new developments, since they indicated improvements as a result of competition.

6.3 Differences between banks were considered marginal, due to competition between them.

6.4 Banks and building societies were felt to be moving closely together in terms of services offered.

NEW BANKING INSTITUTIONS

6.5 Awareness of Citibank, Western Trust and Savings, and Avco was limited, Citibank being the best known, mainly due to shop credit accounts.

6.6 Some expected these institutions to be finance houses, which aroused suspicion.

6.7 Some had seen shop or newspaper advertising for them.

6.9 Perceived advantages were Saturday opening, interest on current accounts, a friendly atmosphere.

6.10 Perceived disadvantages were lack of long-term establishment which gave security fears; over-friendly/less professional approach leading to fear of money's safety; lack of cheque acceptability due to newness.

6.11 Respondents generally lacked interest in these institutions.

MICRO-TECHNOLOGY AND PLASTIC MONEY

GENERAL REACTIONS TO CHANGE

6.12 There was awareness of increased use of computer technology by financial institutions.

6.13 The respondents were wary of moving over to 'plastic money', which they associated with America.

6.14 Men were more receptive than women to the idea of mechanised banking with no counter staff.

6.15 There was general wariness of total mechanisation and computerisation, with the exception of younger respondents of about 20 years.

AUTOMATED TELLER MACHINES

6.16 Users were generally satisfied with ATM cards, apart from the occasional machine break-downs.

6.17 Perceived fears/disadvantages were:

* machines 'swallowing' cards
* other people keying in one's number and drawing from one's account
* cheques
* robbery after obtaining money
* impersonal
* general mistrust of machines
* forgetting one's number.

THE SHOP-TILL CARD SYSTEM

6.18 This system was felt to be an inevitable step for large stores.

6.19 Perceived advantages were speed of transaction and reduced need to carry cash with its risk of theft.

6.20 Perceived disadvantages/suggested improvements were: difficulty of keeping track of one's money; personal balance available to be shown on a screen before making a transaction; fear of losing one's card; loss of cheque's four-day advantage before withdrawal from account.

6.21 Interest in the system varied between individuals.

TV BANKING AT HOME

6.22 Received a generally negative response due to:

* bank accounts revealed to spouses or, by mistake on neighbours' screens;
* security fears for cash sent through post;
* science fiction nightmare.

6.23 Suggested advantages were for the disabled; for businessmen; a useful source of information; overcomes opening hour inconvenience.

7. The ethnic minorities

WEST INDIANS

7.1 Their views generally reflected those expressed in the main series of group discussions, although they were particularly anxious about being mugged.

7.2 Black people found it difficult to obtain loans, particularly for business.

7.3 West Indians tended to feel more at ease in building societies than banks.

7.4 They were reluctant to approach the bank manager, and obtained information from other people.

7.5 Barclays had a good international reputation, supported by its popular International Money Orders.

7.6 Cash was preferred to cheques by some, for similar reasons to the other respondents mentioned earlier. HP was not used due to its perceived expensiveness.

7.7 West Indians lent money to friends more freely than the white respondents, and participated more in joint saving schemes with friends.

THE INDIANS

7.8 The Indians favoured standing orders more strongly than other groups.

7.9 They regarded a cheque book as safer and, in many ways, more convenient than cash, and they appeared to pay great attention to detail in keeping check of their finances.

7.10 Like the white respondents, they found bank opening hours inconvenient; they were reluctant to deposit money by means of a machine; they felt that banks were more orientated towards businessmen; and they welcomed the idea of more positive advice.

7.11 Like the West Indians, the Indians recognised Barclays as having a good reputation for international dealings.

7.12 The unbanked respondents generally had building society accounts, as did most of the banked.

7.13 Unlike the West Indians and Pakistanis, the Indians did not appear to save together, but lending within the community was important.

THE PAKISTANIS

7.14 The Pakistanis appeared to be the least involved with the British banking system, and were confused over the services offered.

7.15 Possible causes for this were language difficulty, low wages, and perceived colour prejudice.

7.16 There was some awareness, through the press, of recent developments, and some advantages were acknowledged in having a bank account. The main disadvantage was felt to be the inconvenient opening hours.

7.17 The Habib Bank was preferred to the International Money Order for sending money home.

7.18 Like the other minority groups, the Pakistanis found building societies more friendly and polite than banks.

7.19 They also lent money, interest free, to friends and participated in a 'committee' savings system.

8. The rural interviews

8.1 Rural respondents were the sectors of the population generally most satisfied with their banks.

8.2 Getting to the bank was not perceived to be a problem, and alternative cheque-cashing facilities at local shops were used. Cash dispensers were not considered necessary in the country.

8.3 Cheque cards were often not required for cheque payments in the country.

8.4 These respondents were not interested in a Girobank account, in spite of the post office's relative proximity.

8.5 Reactions to new technology generally reflected those expressed by the majority of respondents in this study.

Appendix III / Research into attitudes of consumers with bank accounts, by Market and Opinion Research International

Introduction

This report contains the results of a survey conducted by MORI (Market & Opinion Research International) on behalf of the National Consumer Council. The purpose of the survey was to examine the attitudes of current account holders to the services provided by their banks. The questionnaire was included as part of our quarterly GB omnibus survey.

In all, 2,028 interviews were conducted with a representative quota sample of adults aged 15+ in 171 constituency sampling points throughout Great Britain. Interviewing took place in respondents' own homes between 6 and 12 January 1983. Details of the sampling, fieldwork and weighting methods used are shown in the technical appendices, along with a profile of the sample (pages 229–30).

Of the 2,028 respondents interviewed, 1,284 held a current account with a branch (either in their own or joint names). The results contained in this report are based on the answers provided by these respondents.

Throughout the report, an asterisk (*) signifies any value less than one half of a percent. Where answers do not add up to 100%, this is due to computer rounding or multiple answers.

Main findings

Table 1   Current account holding

Over three-fifths of the adult population now have a bank account, either in sole or joint names. More men than women have accounts and men are more likely to have their account in their own name. Account holding is highest in the 25–54 age range. People in the upper socio-economic groups AB and C, are much more likely to hold a bank account, although it is interesting to note that account-holding amongst the DE group is 42%.

Q. Do you have a personal current account with a cheque book at a bank, either in your own name alone, or jointly with another person?

	(Base)	Any account	Own name	Joint names	No account
		%	%	%	%
All respondents	(2028)	63	38	27	36
Sex: men	(968)	68	44	25	31
women	(1060)	59	33	29	40
Age: 15–24	(394)	45	36	9	54
25–34	(377)	74	38	40	25
35–44	(366)	75	39	39	24
45–54	(233)	77	47	33	23
55–64	(326)	63	38	27	37
65+	(327)	50	35	17	49
Class: AB	(337)	87	59	35	12
C1	(467)	82	49	35	18
C2	(636)	59	31	29	41
DE	(588)	42	27	15	58
Region: North (inc. Scotland)	(739)	60	33	28	44
Midlands	(501)	57	33	25	42
South	(788)	75	48	30	25
England and Wales	(1836)	65	40	28	34
Scotland	(192)	43	26	17	57

BASE: All adults

Table 2   Period for which current account has been held

Five per cent of all current account holders have opened their first ever current account in the past twelve months. Nineteen per cent opened their account within the past five years, and about a quarter of customers have held an account for no more than six years.

Inevitably, younger respondents will have opened their accounts the most recently and 37% of 15–24-year-olds opened their first account within the past two years (79% within six years). However, the expansion in the number of bank accounts in the country has not been confined to the younger generation; 10% of over-65-year-olds with accounts have held these accounts for no more than six years.

The banking habit appears to be spreading through all social classes. Although DE respondents are noticeably less likely than higher social groups to have an account, they are noticeably more likely to have opened an account recently. Seventeen per cent of DEs have opened an account in the past two years, and 33% in the last six years.

Q. How long ago did you open your first personal current account with a cheque book at a bank?

	%	Cumulative %
Within last 12 months	5	5
Over 1–2 years ago	5	10
Over 2–3	3	13
Over 3–4	2	16*
Over 4–5	3	19
Over 5–6	5	24
Over 6–10	17	42
Over 10–15	19	61
Over 15–20	10	71
Over 20	29	100

	(Base)	Within last 2 years	Within last 6 years
		%	%
All	(1284)	10	24
Age: 15–24	(172)	37	79
25–34	(283)	10	24
35–44	(276)	5	13
45–54	(181)	5	15
55–64	(207)	3	11
65+	(165)	4	10
Class: AB	(293)	5	14
C1	(376)	8	21
C2	(373)	11	29
DE	(242)	17	33

*Figures do not exactly add up due to re-percentaging.
BASE: All with current accounts

Tables 3 and 3a Reasons for opening account at branch chosen

The main reason why new customers (i.e. those having opened an account in the past six years) chose the bank and branch they chose is its convenience – either to home or work. Over half (54%) gave this as their reason. Given that people are usually reluctant to admit the effect of advertising on their actions, it is, perhaps, surprising that over a quarter attributed their choice to the power of advertising.

There is clearly a strong tendency for new account holders to choose a bank used or recommended by their employer and 21% said they chose the bank that their employer deals with. A further 18% chose a bank that they had dealt with before (for example, they might have held a deposit account there) or one that had been recommended by family or friends. Fifteen per cent chose a bank that offered specific services that they found appealing (for example, interest on current accounts). Older new account holders tended to be more influenced by their employers' policy (presumably a switch to cashless payment was their motivation for opening an account). Younger respondents (and the middle classes) were more likely to ascribe their choice to the influence of advertising.

Q. Why did you open an account with . . . (1st bank) and why did you open the account at that particular branch of . . . ?

(unprompted answers)

(Individual numbers are small, and answers have been grouped together under broad headings)

	All %
1. *Convenience* most convenient for home/work/*only* convenient bank	54
2. *Advertising*	26
3. *Employment link* company deals with it/pays wages into it	21
4. *Familiarity* previous dealings/recommendation of family, friends/work for them	18
5. *Specific services* interest on current accounts/low or no bank charges/Saturday opening	15

BASE: All 'new' current account holders, i.e. within past six years [300].

Table 3a

	Base	Convenience	Advertising	Employment link	Familiarity	Specific services
		%	%	%	%	%
Sex: all	300	54	26	21	18	15
men	136	52	28	23	15	19
women	164	56	25	19	20	12
Age: 15–24	134	52	40	12	12	15
25–34	65	56	16	14	28	19
35–54	61	56	14	41	19	13
55+	40	55	15	32	20	13
Class: ABC1	117	50	38	14	16	15
C2	111	60	21	25	14	18
DE	80	52	17	25	25	12

BASE: all those who have opened an account within past six years (300)

NOTE: care should be taken in interpreting these results due to small bases.

Tables 4 and 4a Awareness of services provided by banks

Customers appear very well aware of the range of services offered by their banks and 59% knew (or assumed) that their own bank provides all of the services we listed. With the exception of cash dispensers (which, of course, some banks do not provide) those services that customers doubted were provided, tended to be in areas which the public does not associate with clearing banks, e.g. tax advice, insurance and stocks and shares. Newer account holders were slightly (but not significantly) less aware of the range of services offered.

Q. Which of the following services do you think your bank does NOT provide the customers?

(As a means of measuring awareness of the services provided by banks, respondents were asked to identify from a showcard those services which they thought their bank did *not* offer.)

	%
Cash dispenser card	10 (29% TSB)
Tax advice	10
Life assurance	9
Managing/buying stocks and shares	7
Insurance (non-life)	6
Unit trust	5
Barclaycard/Access	4
Budget account	3
Bridging loan	3
Mortgage	3
Home improvement loan	2
Standing order	1

Continues overleaf

	%
Direct debit	1
Saving and deposit account	1
Direct transfer of wages	1
Overdraft	1
Personal loan	1
Cheque guarantee card	1
Travellers' cheques	1
Foreign currency	1
Provides all these services	59 (38% TSB)

BASE: All current account holders [1,284]

Table 4a

	Bank provides all these services	(Base)	%
	All respondents	(1284)	59
Bank:	Barclays	(224)	68
	Lloyds	(151)	67
	Midland	(141)	67
	Nat West	(254)	67
	TSB	(133)	38
First opened account:	in past 6 years	(300)	53
	6–10 years ago	(226)	59
	over 10 years ago	(758)	62

BASE: All current account holders

Table 5 Was information provided when the account was opened?

Two-thirds of new customers (those having opened an account in the previous six years) said that their bank provided them with leaflets on services available when they first opened their account. Men were more likely to recall receiving such information.

Younger new account holders were also more likely to recall having received information from their bank, suggesting, possibly, that many older account holders might have opened their accounts without their banks realising that they were, in fact, new to banking. It should be remembered that many of this group seemed to have opened their accounts because their employers changed to cashless payments, and the necessary information may have come from the employer, not the bank.

Q. When you opened this first account, did your bank provide you with any leaflets or printed material telling you about the particular services that they provided?

	%	
Yes	66	
No	26	
Can't remember	8	

	Yes, provided information	
	(Base)	%
All	(300)	66
Sex: men	(136)	71
women	(164)	63
Age: 15–24	(134)	73
25–34	(65)	68
35–54	(61)	54
55+	(40)	28
Class: AB	(39)	77
C1	(75)	65
C2	(109)	71
DE	(77)	57

BASE: All 'new' current account holdings

Table 6 Usage of bank services

Virtually all of the current account holders we interviewed had used at least one of their bank's additional services. Only 7% had never used such services and only 11% had not done so in the past twelve months. In general, most of those who had ever used one of their bank's additional services had also used them within the previous twelve months.

The services most commonly used were standing orders and cheque guarantee cards (used in last twelve months by 51% and 49% respectively). Forty eight per cent claim to have ever 'used' direct transfer of wages into their account (38% in the past twelve months) but we suspect that this is an underestimate and that many respondents may have misunderstood what we were referring to.

The services most rarely used tended to be those relating to insurance and investments which, as we have seen, respondents tended not to associate with banks.

Q. Which of the banking services on this list have you ever used?
Q. Which, if any, of these services have you used in the past twelve months?

	Ever used	Used in past 12 months
	%	%
Standing orders	59	51
Cheque guarantee card	54	49
Direct transfer of wages to account**	48	38
Savings/deposit account	40	29
Travellers' cheques	38	21
Direct debit	36	31
Barclaycard/Access	36	31
Foreign currency	36	20
Personal loans	32	16
Cash dispenser card	31	25
Overdraft	24	15
Home improvement loan	9	4
Bridging loan	7	2
Budget account	7	6
Mortgage	5	3
Managing/buying stocks and shares	4	2
Life assurance	4	2
Other insurance	3	2
Unit trusts	2	*
Used none	7	11

**We suspect that this is an underestimate due to misunderstanding of the question.
BASE: All with a current account [1,284]

Table 7   Usage of bank services – details

Having recorded which particular services respondents had ever used, we then allocated them to one of three groups according to the number of different services that each had ever used. Those who had used 7 or more of the 19 services listed were classified as 'heavy' users, those who had used between 3 and 6 were called 'medium' users and the remainder we have called 'light' users.

Men tend to use a greater number of banking services than women and the middle classes use considerably more than working-class account holders. Similarly, home owners make greater use of their bank's services than do people living in rented accommodation – though this will, in part, reflect the higher number of home owners among the middle classes.

The account holders who make the greatest use of banking services appear to be those in their late twenties to mid-forties. At this age, many people will have taken on a wide range of financial commitments which then tend to be reduced as they age. Only 15% of those aged 65+ are classified as 'heavy' users of bank services compared with 42% of 25–34-year-olds. Younger respondents (aged 15–24) are also fairly unlikely to have used many financial services – though they tend to be as likely as their elders to have used cheque guarantee cards and are more likely to use cash dispenser cards. Inevitably, newer account holders tend to have used fewer services than customers who have held their accounts for more than six years.

	Base	Usage of services		
		heavy	medium	light
		%	%	%
All respondents	(1284)	30	40	30
Sex: male	(656)	33	40	27
female	(628)	26	40	34
Age: 15–24	(172)	22	42	37
25–34	(283)	42	40	18
35–44	(276)	38	39	23
45–54	(181)	30	43	27
55–64	(207)	20	45	35
65+	(165)	15	31	54
Class: AB	(293)	50	33	17
C1	(376)	33	43	24
C2	(373)	23	44	34
DE	(242)	11	39	49
Opened first account				
in past 6 years	(300)	12	40	48
over 6–10 years ago	(226)	34	40	25
over 10 years ago	(758)	35	40	25
Home ownership				
owner occupied	(942)	35	41	25
other	(342)	17	38	46

BASE: All with a current account

Table 8   Experience of bank errors

Twenty-nine per cent of account holders could recall ever having experienced any of the banking errors listed on the following table and 15% said they had experienced such errors in the previous twelve months.

Inevitably, the service where the most errors were recalled tended to be services that were widely used. Thus, noticeably more customers had experienced errors in the payment of standing orders (a service used by 59% of respondents) than had noticed errors in their budget accounts (only 7% had ever had a budget account). The most common errors fall into two categories, those involving money transmission, such as direct debit, standing order and giro transfer, and those involving bank statements, such as delays, inaccuracies and bank charges.

Virtually everybody who had experienced an error in the previous twelve months had pointed the error out to the bank. Only in the case of delays in the provision of statements and errors in calculating interest on loans did less than 90% point out the error. Presumably in the former case the statements arrived (late) but before a complaint could be made and, perhaps, in the latter case the error was in the customer's favour.

Q. Which, if any, of these problems have you ever experienced with a bank?
Q. And which, if any, of these problems have you experienced in the past twelve months?
Q. The last time there were . . . did you point out the error to the bank?

	Ever experienced	Experienced in past 12 months	% of all experienced in past 12 months who pointed error out to bank
	%	%	%
One or more error	29	15	na
Detail of error:			
errors in payment of standing orders	10	5	100
inaccuracies in your bank statements	9	4	99
delays in providing statements requested	7	4	80
errors in transferring money to your account	7	3	90
errors in payment of direct debits	5	2	96
bounced cheques when money in account	5	3	95
errors in calculating bank charges	3	1	96
failure to pay bills through budget account	1	1	100
errors in calculating interest on loans	1	1	86
None of these	71	85	na
Any payment (transmission) errors	20	10	na
Bank statement errors i.e. delays/inaccuracies/charges	16	8	na

BASE: All with a current account [1,284]
na = not analysed

Table 9   Experience of bank errors – details

As one would expect, and as the laws of probability dictate, heavier users of bank services are more likely to have experienced errors in the provision of these services than are lighter users of banking services.

In addition, those respondents aged 25–44 appear to have experienced a greater number of errors than older respondents. Possibly this is due to their higher usage of banking services.

Interestingly, nearly a quarter of those who have paid bank charges in the past twelve months report that their bank has made at least one error during that period, and not necessarily errors in the calculation of bank charges. For some reason, customers who pay bank charges appear more conscious than other customers of their bank making a whole range of errors, possibly because they keep a much closer watch on their account details.

		Ever experienced errors	Experienced in last 12 months	Any payment (transmission) error	Bank statement errors i.e. delays/ inaccuracies/ charges
		%	%	%	%
All respondents	(1284)	29	15	20	16
Age: 15–24	(172)	27	20	18	17
25–34	(263)	41	22	30	23
35–44	(276)	32	22	23	18
45–54	(181)	26	10	17	17
55–64	(207)	22	6	16	10
65+	(165)	16	6	8	9
Class: AB	(293)	33	17	21	19
C1	(376)	31	15	22	18
C2	(373)	27	15	19	14
DE	(242)	24	14	16	13
Bank charges in last 12 months:					
paid	(567)	39	23	29	21
not paid	(533)	22	9	14	12
Usage of bank services:					
heavy	(388)	42	24	32	24
medium	(517)	28	14	19	17
light	(379)	16	9	10	9
Home ownership:					
owner occupier	(942)	30	15	21	18
other	(342)	25	15	18	12
Opened account:					
in past 6 years	(300)	26	20	17	14
over 6–10 years ago	(226)	28	17	19	16
over 10 years ago	(758)	30	13	21	17

BASE: All with current account

Table 10 Satisfaction with bank's handling of complaint

As Table 8 indicates, 15% of our respondents had experienced or reported errors to their banks in the year prior to our study. In consequence, the results of the subsidiary question we asked of such respondents are based on extremely small samples. Nonetheless, it seems that, in general, about three-fifths of customers were at least fairly satisfied with their bank's handling of their complaint, whilst about one-third were dissatisfied.

Such bad experiences do, it seems, little to alter the overall favourable image that customers have of their banks; for example, 80% of those having experienced such errors in the previous twelve months were at least fairly satisfied with their bank's services overall, whilst only 13% were dissatisfied. One mistake, especially if it is satisfactorily handled, does not necessarily destroy a customer's opinion of a bank.

Q. How satisfied or dissatisfied were you with the way the bank handled the error you pointed out to them in . . .?

	Very satisfied	*Fairly satisfied*	*Neither/ nor*	*Very/fairly dissatisfied*
	(Base)%	%	%	%
Errors in calculating bank charges	(17) 37	23	6	34
Inaccuracies in bank statements	(51) 36	28	6	31
Errors in transferring money into account	(35) 34	27	3	36
Errors in payment of standing order	(57)) 30	36	2	33
Errors in interest calculations on loan	(10) 28	30	11	31
Bounced cheques when money in account	(31) 26	22	3	49
Errors in payment of direct debit	(28) 21	43	3	33
Delays in statements	(43) 16	39	3	41
Failure to pay bills through budget account	(7) 14	46	0	40

BASE: All having pointed out an error to their bank within the past twelve months
NOTE: Care should be taken in interpreting these results due to extremely small bases.

Table 11 Frequency of receiving statements

Just under half (44%) of account holders say that they receive bank statements monthly, but significant proportions receive them quarterly (29%) or six-monthly (17%).

Younger respondents and those making most frequent use of their accounts tend to receive statements monthly, as do the higher social groups. Interestingly, bank customers in Scotland are significantly more likely to receive monthly statements.

Q. How often do you receive bank statements on your main account?

	%	
Once/week	1	⎫
Once/fortnight	1	⎬ 47*
Once/month	44	⎭
Once/quarter	29	
Once/six months	17	
Less frequently	2	
Don't know	5	

	(Base)	Received once/month %
All respondents	(1284)	47
Age: 15–24	(172)	56
25–34	(283)	60
35–44	(276)	52
45–54	(181)	41
55–64	(207)	33
65+	(165)	26
Class: AB	(293)	60
C1	(376)	48
C2	(373)	44
DE	(242)	34
Use of bank services:		
heavy	(388)	63
medium	(517)	46
light	(379)	31
Region:		
England and Wales	(1204)	45
Scotland	(80)	77

BASE: All with a current account.

*Discrepancy due to computer rounding.

Table 12 Satisfaction with bank statements

Three-quarters (74%) of customers are satisfied with the frequency with which they receive their bank statements, whilst 20% are dissatisfied. Interestingly, it tends not to be those who receive monthly statements who want a more frequent provision of statements, but those who receive their statements less frequently. Only 8% of those with monthly statements want a more frequent service (which banks might be reluctant to provide). On the other hand, 31% of those receiving less frequent statements are dissatisfied – yet presumably their bank would be willing to provide at least a monthly statement.

There is also a correlation between experience of banking errors and a desire for more frequent statements. In part, this may be because the former included errors related to the provision of bank statements, but it undoubtedly also reflects the desire of the customer to keep a closer track on his finances.

Whilst 20% were unhappy with the frequency with which they received their statements, only 10% of customers were dissatisfied with the amount of detail contained in their bank statement and only 3% had concerns about its accuracy. Looking at these figures the other way around, this gives 83% and 91% (respectively) satisfied with the amount of detail contained in their statement and with the accuracy. However, as we see later, when prompted customers were keen for their bank to provide more information on the calculation of bank charges in their statements.

Only those who have experienced errors and those who have paid bank charges in the previous twelve months were noticeably dissatisfied with the detail provided or with the accuracy of the statement.

Q. **From this card, could you tell me how satisfied or dissatisfied you are, overall, with ... ?**

d) **the frequency with which you receive your bank statement.**
e) **the amount of detail contained on your bank statements.**
f) **the accuracy of your bank statement.**

	d) frequency		e) amount of detail		f) accuracy	
	%		%		%	
Very satisfied	37 }	74	37 }	83	54 }	91
Fairly satisfied	37 }		46 }		38 }	
Neither satisfied nor dissatisfied	3		4		2	
Fairly dissatisfied	14 }	20	7 }	10	2 }	3
Very dissatisfied	6 }		3 }		1 }	
No opinion/does not apply	3		3		4	

Percentage dissatisfied with:

	(Base)	d) frequency	e) amount of detail	f) accuracy
		%	%	%
All respondents	(1284)	20	10	3
Bank charges in last 12 months				
paid	(567)	21	13	4
not paid	(533)	19	5	2
Users of bank services				
heavy	(388)	19	11	3
medium	(517)	21	10	3
light	(379)	19	8	3
Errors				
in last 12 months	(198)	33	24	14
longer ago	(172)	26	10	3
never	(892)	16	6	1
Statements received				
once a month	(600)	8	10	3
less frequently	(624)	31	10	4

BASE: All with a current account

Table 13 Payment of bank charges

Just under half (44%) of customers said that they had paid bank charges in the previous year, whilst a similar proportion had not paid them. When we pushed those who were unsure to make a guess, a total of 48% reckoned they had paid, compared to 45% who had not. It would be interesting, if possible, to compare these figures with the clearing banks' own internal records.

The segments of the population most likely to believe that they pay bank charges tend to be those who make the greatest use of their bank accounts. For example, about two-thirds (64%) of those with a high usage of their accounts say they paid charges, compared with only a third (34%) of those who use few of their bank's services. Similarly, the higher a customer's social class, the more likely he is to be aware that he pays bank charges. Respondents in the 25–44-year age group, the age at which many people start taking on financial commitments, were also noticeably likely to be aware that they pay bank charges. Those who receive monthly statements are also more aware of paying charges.

Q. Have you paid any bank charges during the past twelve months? If don't know: Would you say you are more likely to have paid them or more likely not to have paid them?

		%	
Definitely paid		44 ⎫	48*
Think likely to have paid		5 ⎭	
Think unlikely to have paid		4 ⎫	45*
Definitely not paid		42 ⎭	
Don't know		6	

	(Base)	*All paid* %	*All not paid* %
All respondents	(1284)	48	45
Age: 15–24	(172)	48	42
25–34	(283)	63	33
35–44	(276)	62	33
45–54	(181)	46	50
55–64	(207)	33	59
65+	(165)	23	70
Class: AB	(293)	58	33
C1	(376)	49	45
C2	(373)	48	47
DE	(242)	38	52
Users of bank services:			
high	(333)	65	32
medium	(517)	47	48
light	(379)	34	55
Receive statement:			
once/month +	(600)	57	37
less often	(624)	42	54

BASE: All with a current account
*Discrepancy due to computer rounding.

Table 14   Perceived method of calculating charges

The most striking feature is that one-third of respondents (34%) do not know how their bank charges are arrived at. On the whole, more customers were aware of the need to maintain a sufficient balance (to avoid charges altogether) than were aware of the method by which charges were calculated if they were due. In all, 51% said that the balance of the account was a determinant, whilst 22% mentioned usage of the account.

A minority were aware of the need to maintain a minimum balance in the account (£50 and £100 were the most commonly mentioned limits) whilst rather more were more vaguely aware of the need to maintain a certain balance. Sixteen per cent, however, seemed to feel it was sufficient simply to keep out of the red.

Regarding transactions-related charges, 15% were aware that these could be charged for cheques cashed, whilst 6% referred to charges for standing orders.

Q. Could you tell me what factors you believe your bank takes into account when calculating what bank charges you should pay?

	%	
Amount in the account (unspecified)	18	
Whether overdrawn/loans	16	
Minimum balance (unspecified)	6	account balance 51%
Minimum balance of £100	9	
Minimum balance of £50	5	
Average balance	1	
Charge for cheques used/cashed	15	
Charge for standing orders	6	transactions 22%
Number of transactions/withdrawals/deposits	5	
Time spent on account	8	
Charge per statement	1	
Personal/social contact with bank/manager	1	
Don't pay	3	
Don't know	34	

BASE: All with a current account [1,284]

Table 15   Perceived method of calculating bank charges – details

Awareness of the means by which bank charges are calculated appeared to be directly related to the customer's financial sophistication and experience of banks.

Thus, those who made use of a larger number of banking services were noticeably more likely to be aware that both the account balance and the number of transactions could affect the charges paid. Conversely, about half (51%) of rarer users of services had no idea how such charges are calculated. Similarly, those aged 25–44, and those in the higher social grades, tended to be more aware of the mode of calculation. Men, who still tend to have the main responsibility for financial matters, were also more aware of the method of calculation than were women.

Those customers who had paid bank charges in the previous twelve months were more aware of how those charges had been worked out than other customers but, nonetheless, a quarter (24%) of this group had paid these charges whilst being unaware of how they had been calculated.

| | Based on: | | |
	account balance	*number of transactions*	*don't know how calculated*
	(Base)	%	%	%
All respondents	(1284)	51	22	34
Sex: male	(656)	54	25	29
female	(628)	48	19	40
Age: 15–24	(172)	49	22	34
25–34	(283)	60	31	27
35–44	(276)	54	25	32
45–54	(181)	50	20	36
55–64	(207)	46	16	37
65+	(165)	40	11	46
Class: AB	(293)	62	28	25
C1	(376)	55	26	29
C2	(373)	49	20	38
DE	(242)	39	13	47
Usage of bank services:				
high	(388)	68	35	19
medium	(517)	54	21	33
light	(379)	30	10	51
Paid bank charges in last 12 Months:				
yes	(567)	61	32	24
no	(533)	46	15	38

BASE: All with a current account

Table 16 Do banks explain charges?

Less than a quarter ever recall having been told by their bank how their charges are calculated. Significantly, those who had most recently opened an account (within the past six years) were the least likely to have been provided with (or to recall receiving) such information. Women and those in the lower social grades were also less likely to recall having been provided with such information.

Q. Has your bank ever explained to you the basis on which they calculate bank charges?

Yes:	22%
No:	73%
Don't know:	5%

Continues overleaf

	(Base)	*Have explained charges* %
All respondents	(1284)	22
Sex: men	(656)	24
women	(628)	19
Age: 15–24	(172)	18
25–34	(283)	23
35–44	(276)	24
45–54	(181)	23
55–64	(207)	20
65+	(165)	17
Class: AB	(293)	32
C1	(376)	21
C2	(373)	17
DE	(242)	17
Usage of bank services		
heavy	(388)	35
medium	(517)	20
light	(379)	11
Bank charges paid in past 12 months		
yes	(567)	25
no	(533)	21
Statement received		
once/month+	(600)	26
less often	(624)	18
Opened first account		
in past 6 years	(300)	15
over 6–10 years ago	(226)	19
over 10 years ago	(758)	25

BASE: All with a current account

Table 17 Satisfaction with bank charges

Despite the high regard in which customers generally hold their banks, many customers resent paying bank charges for the services provided. Although 91% say they are satisfied generally with the service they receive from their banks, only 48% are satisfied with the amount of bank charges they pay (and 22% are dissatisfied).

Even fewer customers (39%) are satisfied with the way in which bank charges are calculated, though fewer are also dissatisfied. In many cases, charges were not seen as a problem as the respondent did not pay any. The main cause of dissatisfaction was, however, the failure of banks to give sufficient information on the manner in which charges are calculated. Nearly as high a proportion (32%) of customers were dissatisfied with the information banks give on how bank charges are calculated, as were satisfied (35%).

Dissatisfaction on all three counts tended to be higher among respondents who made heavy use of their accounts (who also tended to be in the 25–44-year-old band). Those who received monthly statements also tended to be less satisfied than those receiving statements less frequently.

Inevitably, those who had paid charges in the previous twelve months were particularly dissatisfied – with the amount they paid, the way in which these payments were calculated and the amount of information provided on this mode of calculation. In all, over half (51%) of those having paid bank charges (in the past twelve months) felt that banks provided insufficient information in this area. Those who had experienced banking errors in the previous twelve months were even more critical; 56% of this group were dissatisfied with the information provided on how their bank charges are calculated.

Q. **From this card, could you tell me how satisfied or dissatisfied you are, overall, with . . . ?**
   a) **the amount of bank charges you have to pay.**
   b) **the way in which your bank charges are calculated.**
   c) **the information you are given on how your bank charges are calculated.**

	a) *amount paid* %		b) *way calculated* %		c) *information given* %	
Very satisfied	17	} 48	12	} 39	11	} 35
Fairly satisfied	31		27		24	
Neither satisfied nor dissatisfied	10		15		11	
Fairly dissatisfied	13	} 22	13	} 20	19	} 32
Very dissatisfied	9		13		13	
No opinion/does not apply	20		26		23	

Percentage dissatisfied with:

	(Base)	% a) *amount paid*	% b) *way calculated*	% c) *information given*
All respondents	(1284)	22	20	32
Age: 15–24	(172)	25	19	37
25–34	(283)	32	28	46
35–44	(276)	27	25	39
45–54	(181)	18	17	26
55–64	(207)	14	15	19
65+	(165)	6	9	17
Bank charges in last 12 months				
paid	(567)	39	35	51
not paid	(533)	6	7	15
Usage of bank services				
heavy	(388)	30	30	43
medium	(517)	23	19	32
light	(379)	12	12	21
Errors				
in last 12 months	(198)	47	45	56
longer ago	(172)	23	26	44
never	(892)	16	13	24
Statement received				
once a month	(600)	27	23	37
less often	(624)	18	19	29

BASE: All with a current account

Table 18   Should banks explain charges?

A large majority (82%) felt that banks should show calculation of bank charges on each statement containing such charges – only 9% felt that they should not (8% had no opinion on the matter). People hold this opinion whether they had paid bank charges in the past twelve months or not.

Q. Do you think banks should show the calculation of bank charges on each bank statement containing such charges?

Yes: 82%
No: 9%
Don't know: 8%

	(Base)	*Should show calculation on statement* %
All respondents	(1284)	82
Sex: men	(656)	82
women	(628)	83
Age: 15–24	(172)	87
25–34	(283)	85
35–44	(276)	85
45–54	(181)	82
55–64	(207)	78
65+	(165)	73
Class: AB	(293)	77
C1	(376)	84
C2	(373)	85
DE	(242)	80
Usage of bank services		
heavy	(388)	81
medium	(517)	86
light	(379)	77
Bank charges paid in past 12 months		
yes	(567)	85
no	(533)	81
Statement received		
once/month+	(600)	83
less often	(624)	82
Opened first account		
in past 6 years	(300)	85
over 6–10 years ago	(226)	86
over 10 years ago	(758)	80

BASE: All with a current account

Table 19   Satisfaction with banking services

Despite the criticism that is sometimes levelled at the clearing banks, their customers are generally satisfied with the service they receive. As many as 62% of account holders are *very* satisfied with the service they receive from their bank and a further 30% are at least 'fairly' satisfied. Only 5% are dissatisfied.

Inevitably, customers who had been the victim of banking errors during the previous twelve months tended to be the most dissatisfied group but, even then, only 13% of this group claimed to be dissatisfied with their banks. Interestingly, younger customers tended to be little more dissatisfied than older customers. Whether this is due to poorer service (an unwillingness on the part of the bank to provide cheque or credit cards, perhaps) or a lack of empathy with banks, is difficult to tell; probably both play some part.

Q. Overall, how satisfied or dissatisfied are you with the service you receive from your bank?

	%	
Very satisfied	62	
Fairly satisfied	30	
Neither satisfied nor dissatisfied	3	
Fairly dissatisfied	4	} 5%
Very dissatisfied	1	

	(Base)	Dissatisfied %
All	(1284)	5
Age: 15–24	(172)	10
25–34	(283)	7
35–44	(276)	6
45–54	(181)	4
55–64	(207)	3
65+	(165)	1
Bank charges: paid in last 12 months	(567)	7
not paid	(533)	4
Errors made: in last 12 months	(198)	13
longer ago	(172)	8
never	(892)	3

BASE: All with a current account

Table 20   Desired changes in banking services

Although most customers are satisfied with the services provided by their banks, this is not to say that they do not see room for improvement. Significantly, the call was not for an increase in information from the banks but for the provision of a more convenient service. Half (51%) would like to see their bank open on a Saturday and for 41% this would be the most welcome change that their bank could introduce. A further 28% wanted longer opening hours on weekdays, and 27% would like their bank to have more tills open at lunchtime. In all, 67% of customers mentioned at least one of these three improvements.

Several of the other popular choices were also changes that would make the withdrawal of money from the banks more convenient – for example, an improved system of queuing, more cash dispensers and an end to the charge for cashing other banks' cheques.

Although a quarter (25%) would like to see an increase in the £50 limit on cheque guarantee cards, there was comparatively little demand for changes that would give customers access to greater quantities of money. Few wanted an increase in the limit on cash dispenser withdrawals, few wanted easier access to loans or a higher limit on credit cards, and few wanted credit cards to be more readily available. The call was for easier access to the customer's existing funds, not access to greater funds.

On the whole, customers seem fairly satisfied with the information provided by their banks but a quarter would like details on how their bank charges are calculated and 21% would welcome more frequent bank statements (the latter figure drops to 12% among those receiving monthly statements).

On the whole, variations in the requirements of different groups of customers tended to be predictable. Heavy users of banking services tended to be more likely to want most of these improvements, as did the middle classes (who tend to be heavy users).

Younger respondents were noticeably more eager to see an increase in the provision of cash dispensers (especially outside banks). Significantly, they were also eager to receive more information about how their bank charges are calculated. The 25–34-year-olds were the most likely to have paid such charges in the past twelve months and the most eager to obtain information on how these charges are calculated. Forty per cent of those having paid bank charges in the past twelve months would like their bank to provide more information on these.

QA. Which, if any, of these changes would you like to see your bank introduce?
QB. Which three or four would you most like to see introduced?

	Most liked introduced (QA)	All liked to be introduced (QB)
	%	%
Saturday opening	41	51
Longer weekday opening	21	28
Improved system of queuing	21	29
Increase £50 limit on cheque guarantee cards	18	25
More tills open at lunchtime	18	27
End charge for cashing other banks' cheques	18	29
Details of how your bank charges are calculated	16	25
More cash dispensers outside banks	16	23
More frequent bank statements	14	21
Easier access to your manager	6	11
More information on banking services	4	9
Increase limit on cash dispenser withdrawals	4	7
Easier access to loans or overdrafts	3	5
More cash dispensers inside banks	3	5
Higher limit on credit cards	2	5
Credit cards more readily available	1	2
Longer hours/Saturday opening/more tills at lunchtime	59	67
None of these	19	11

BASE: All with current account [1,284]

Table 21   Holding of building society accounts

Nearly two-thirds (64%) of bank current account holders also hold an account with a building society. There is clearly, therefore, considerable overlap in the clientele of the two types of institution.

Building society account holding is spread fairly evenly across all age groups (though it drops among those aged over 55). Building society accounts are commoner among middle-class bank account holders than among their working-class equivalents – possibly due to the higher level of home ownership among the former group. Building society accounts are also more common among heavy users of bank services (who tend to be home owners) and among those who have held their bank account for some time.

Q. Do you have an account with a building society?

		(Base)	*Have account at building society* %
All respondents		(1284)	64
Age:	15–24	(172)	62
	25–34	(283)	71
	35–44	(276)	69
	45–54	(181)	61
	55–64	(207)	64
	65+	(165)	53
Class:	AB	(293)	74
	C1	(376)	72
	C2	(373)	60
	DE	(242)	49
Usage of bank services:			
heavy		(388)	76
medium		(517)	67
light		(379)	49
Opened first account:			
in past 6 years		(300)	52
over 6–10 years ago		(226)	65
over 10 years ago		(758)	69

BASE: All with a current account (at a bank)

Table 22   Building societies v. banks – service

Despite the fairly high opinion that customers have of their banks, customers who have both a bank and a building society account tend to have a higher opinion of some aspects of the service provided by the latter than of the service provided by their banks.

As we have seen, bank customers are fairly critical of the opening hours of their banks and rate their building society's opening hours as considerably more convenient – 74% rate the building societies more highly compared to only 7% who find their banks more convenient.

In addition, 39% feel that building societies offer the quicker counter service, whilst 25% feel the reverse – nearly a third, however, see little difference between bank and building society in this area. Younger customers (15–24) feel that banks offer a quicker service but, as we have seen, they are significantly more likely to use cash dispensers. (Thirty-nine per cent of the 15–24 age group had used a cash dispenser in the last twelve months, compared with the average of 25%.)

Another area where the building societies have a lead is for the friendliness of their staff. Thirty-two per cent see building society staff as being the more friendly, whilst 18% feel that the banks' staff are the more friendly. To a considerable degree, this must reflect the different functions of the two institutions and, hence, the customers' experience.

The young are less convinced of the building societies' lead in all areas but the societies' staff are particularly more highly noted by those in the DE social classes and by those who make little use of their bank's services.

Q. Comparing your bank with your building society, which do you think. . . ?

	Building society	Bank	No diff.	Don't know
	%	%	%	%
has the most convenient opening hours	74	7	15	4
offers the quickest counter service	39	25	31	6
has the friendliest staff	32	18	46	5

Percent mentioning building society less percent mentioning bank (i.e. building soc lead)

Building societies lead		Convenient hours	Quickest service	Friendliest staff
	(Base)	±%	±%	±%
All respondents	(834)	67	15	14
Sex: male	(422)	66	18	19
female	(412)	69	11	10
Age: 15–24	(108)	55	−6	7
25–34	(204)	63	8	16
35–44	(190)	74	23	17
45–54	(111)	79	19	12
55–64	(134)	71	26	16
65+	(87)	56	13	12
Class: AB	(218)	64	8	11
C1	(276)	69	12	11
C2	(224)	73	23	15
DE	(116)	60	15	24
Opened first account (at a bank):				
in past 6 years	(159)	55	8	7
over 6–10 years ago	(148)	74	9	21
over 10 years ago	(527)	69	18	14
Work full-time	(474)	67	19	18
Usage of bank services:				
heavy	(295)	70	13	9
medium	(319)	67	14	14
light	(190)	65	17	22

BASE: All with both a current account (at a bank) and a building society account

Table 23   Additional services desired from a building society

Although the individuals we questioned all held both bank accounts and building society accounts, a surprising number of them would welcome their building society providing a range of more sophisticated banking services. Presumably, many could see some advantage in this and no discernible disadvantage for the customer. It should be remembered that we asked which services customers would like to see their building society provide, not which services they would actually use.

The new facility that would be most widely appreciated would be the introduction of building society current accounts, i.e. cheque book facilities – 56% would like to see their own building society offer such a facility. Next in order of popularity (but mentioned by considerably fewer) was the ability to pay standing orders from a building society account – 39% would welcome this facility. A third (32%) would like to see their society introduce cash dispensers, 28% would welcome building society personal loans and 26% would appreciate building society travellers cheques. At the bottom of the list, 20% would like to see their building society introduce overdraft facilities.

Twenty-three per cent did not wish any of these services from their building society. In general, those who already made fair use of their bank's facilities tended to want their building society to offer the same service.

Q. If building societies were able to offer a range of banking services such as those listed on this card, which, if any, would you like your building society to be able to provide you?

	%
Cheque book facilities	56
Payment of standing orders	39
Cash dispensers	32
Personal loans	28
Travellers' cheques	26
Overdraft facilities	20
None of these	23
Don't know	3

		None of these
	(Base)	%
All respondents	(834)	23
Age: 15–24	(108)	16
25–34	(204)	22
35–44	(190)	22
45–54	(111)	20
55–64	(134)	28
65+	(87)	36
Class: AB	(218)	27
C1	(276)	22
C2	(224)	21
DE	(116)	23
Usage of bank services:		
heavy	(295)	22
medium	(349)	23
light	(190)	26

Continues overleaf

	(Base)	*None of these* %
First opened account:		
in past 6 years	(159)	19
over 6–10 years ago	(148)	21
over 10 years ago	(527)	25

BASE: All with both a current account (at a bank) and a building society account

Table 24   Building societies v. banks – tax advantages

Although it is doubtful that the public has much detailed knowledge of the subject, it seems clear that they tend to see building societies as being the better place to save – in many cases regardless of the individual's tax position. Nonetheless, they appear more certain that this is the case for those paying standard rate tax than for those paying no tax.

Seventy-one per cent of respondents feel that a standard rate taxpayer would be better advised to invest with a building society whilst only 7% feel that a bank would offer the better deal. This view seems to be held more strongly by those who tend to have the greater knowledge of financial affairs – the middle classes, those who have held their accounts for some time, and those who make heavy use of their bank's services. Men also seem more likely to feel this than do women.

The more financially aware are, however, less convinced that building societies offer the better deal for those who fall outside the tax-man's net. Indeed, AB respondents tend to see the bank as a better bet for such an individual's savings. Nonetheless, on balance, more would still rate the building society (probably incorrectly) as the better place to save. Forty three per cent say the building society would be a better bet compared to 34% who would recommend a bank.

Q. Comparing your bank with your building society, which do you think. . . ?

	Building society	Bank	No diff.	Don't know
	%	%	%	%
. . . is the better place to save for people who pay the standard rate of tax	71	7	7	15
. . . is the better place to save for people who do not pay tax	43	34	7	16

Percentage mentioning building society less percentage mentioning bank (i.e. building society lead)

	(Base)	For people not paying tax ±%	For people paying standard rate of tax ±%
All respondents	(834)	9	64
Sex: male	(422)	8	71
female	(412)	9	57
Class: AB	(218)	−12	64
C1	(276)	13	68
C2	(224)	14	61
DE	(116)	22	60
Usage of bank services:			
heavy	(295)	1	70
medium	(349)	7	69
light	(190)	21	46
Opened first account:			
in past 6 years	(159)	27	55
6–10 years ago	(148)	14	61
over 10 years ago	(527)	1	68

BASE: All with a current account (at a bank) and a building society account

Table 25   Need for an ombudsman

Just over half our respondents (51%) saw either a great or slight need for a banking ombudsman. One-third of those who had experienced errors in the past twelve months saw a great need for such an agency.

Q. How much of a need do you think there is for an independent agency (such as an ombudsman) to whom a customer can complain if he is dissatisfied with his bank's response to a complaint?

	%	
a great need	24 }	51%
a slight need	27 }	
not much of a need	23	
no need at all	19	
don't know	7	

	(Base)	A great need	No need at all
		%	%
All respondents	(1284)	24	19
Sex: male	(656)	26	22
female	(628)	21	16
Age: 15–24	(172)	29	13
25–34	(283)	24	16
35–44	(276)	26	20
45–54	(181)	27	19
55–64	(207)	18	23
65+	(165)	15	27
Class: AB	(293)	22	22
C1	(376)	20	21
C2	(373)	26	17
DE	(242)	28	17
Opened first account:			
in past 6 years	(300)	29	14
6–10 years ago	(226)	26	15
over 10 years ago	(758)	20	23
Errors in last 12 months	(368)	33	19
Usage of bank services:			
heavy	(388)	22	24
medium	(517)	24	15
light	(379)	25	20

BASE: All with a current account

Technical appendix to Appendix III

Sample design

A two-stage sampling design was used; a random sample of sampling points and a quota sample of respondents within these sampling points.

1) CONSTITUENCIES

There are 623 parliamentary constituencies in Great Britain. Two of these (Western Isles and Orkney & Shetland) were excluded from the sampling frame as being too remote to cover. The remaining 621 parliamentary constituencies in Great Britain were classified into the Registrar General's ten new standard regions. Within each standard region, constituencies were classified into four types:

a) metropolitan county
b) other 100% urban
c) mixed urban/rural
d) rural

Within the resultant cells, constituencies were listed according to the percentage level of heads of household who were within the upper socio-economic grouping, according to the 1971 census data. Four systematic samples of 55 constituencies were selected, with probability of selection proportional to the size of the electorate in each constituency. Using one of the samples of 55, 15 constituencies were drawn out by means of a stratified random delete. This gave a total sample of 180 constituencies [(3 × 55) + 15].

2) RESPONDENTS

Within each sampling point, 12 respondents were to be interviewed. Respondents were selected by means of a 12-cell quota with which the interviewer had been provided. The quotas used were:

class: (AB/C1/C2/DE)
age: (15–24/25–39/40–59/60+)
sex/working status: (full-time male/full-time female/other male/other female)

These quotas were devised by an analysis of a full year's data on the National Readership Survey. Quotas were set to ensure that the demographic profile (in terms of the 12 cells described above) of the sample in each standard region matched the actual (NRS) profile in that region. Because of its small size, East Anglia was merged with East Midlands when the quotas were devised. The total sample set was therefore 12 × 180 = 2,160. The sample is representative of all adults in Great Britain (excluding the Western Isles and Orkney & Shetland) aged 15+.

FIELDWORK

All interviews were conducted in the home, with only one interview per household. Interviewers were instructed to leave at least five doors between each call. Half the interviews conducted by each interviewer were carried out in the evenings or at the weekends. Fieldwork was carried out by our sister company, Survey Research Associates.

WEIGHTING

The data were weighted by an 84-cell weighting matrix (2 sex × 2 age × 3 class × 7 regions). This was to adjust for any discrepancies in the coverage of individual sampling points.

Profile of the sample

	All current account holders			
	unweighted	*weighted*		
All	1284	100%	1297	100%
Men	656	51	659	52
Women	628	49	620	48
Age: 15–24	172	13	175	14
25–34	283	22	282	22
35–44	276	21	274	21
45–54	181	14	182	14
55–64	207	16	205	16
65+	165	13	161	13
Class: AB	293	23	281	22
C1	376	29	367	29
C2	373	29	387	30
DE	242	19	245	19
England and Wales	1204	94	1201	94
Scotland	80	6	78	6
Northern England	330	26	327	26
Midland	285	22	284	22
South	589	46	590	46

Definitions of sub-groups used in the analysis

North England:	Registrar General's standard regions – Northern, N.W. and Yorkshire and Humberside.
Midlands:	Wales, W. Midlands, E. Midlands, E. Anglia
South:	South West, South East, Greater London
Building society account:	All with account at a building society (and, of course, also with a bank)
Working full time:	30 hrs/week+
Working part time:	8–29 hrs/week
Not working:	work 7 hours or less per week

Usage of bank account
heavy:	Used 7 or more services ⎤
medium:	Used 3–6 services ⎬ see Table 6
light:	Used less than 3 services ⎦

Errors
any	⎤
in last 12 months	⎬ refers to experience of any errors (see Table 8)
none	⎦

Appendix IV / The economics of branch banking: a consumer perspective

The word 'branch' as used in retail banking conceals a wide variety of types, sizes and functions. A large, traditional city clearing bank branch might be twenty times as large as a small provincial TSB branch in terms of transaction values, running costs and staff complement. In economic terms, such variables as the balance of different types of business, deposit-taking base, automated facilities, staff-customer ratios and variety of ancillary services available are all crucial determinants of a branch's overall profitability. All statistical measures across financial institutions are crude and must be treated with care.

Generalisation is difficult even for the big clearing banks. The major banks each operates a wide variety of branch and sub-branch outlets. These range from the large, sophisticated city-centre bank office, through the familiar high street branch to the small village sub-office open only on market days. No bank structure is exactly typical, but the make-up of one of the big four serves as an example of what comprises an English/Welsh network. In mid-1982, this bank had approximately 1700 branches and 740 sub-offices. 5.8 per cent of its branches were situated in the centres of cities having a population of over a quarter of a million; a further 49 per cent were sited in conurbations with between 25,000 and 250,000 inhabitants. The remaining branches were largely situated in resort or market towns supported by a network of rural outlets. The total branch network included a number of specialist branches including 64 located in factories and office blocks, 26 in hospitals, 35 in universities, colleges and polytechnics, 13 at defence establishments and two permanent showground/exhibition centre branches. In addition five mobile branches served 105 locations in less populated rural areas. The bank told us that the commonest-size branch is one of nine staff, whereas the average-sized branch has thirteen staff in which eight people are primarily concerned with the personal sector – that is, individual consumers. The average number of staff per branch for all UK banks was 14.2 in 1981.

The fact that such an 'average' big four branch has five persons dealing with non-personal business immediately sets it aside from any TSB or building society branch where virtually all business is personal business. Another difference is indicated by comparing the number of customers serviced by branches of the various institutions. In 1981 the average number of personal current accounts administered by all banks was 2,200. Individual figures for the major clearers were significantly lower; for example, the Midland Bank average per branch was 1,700. Some Co-operative Bank branches however, being far fewer in number and heavily involved in postal banking techniques, administer as many as 20,000 personal accounts. Building societies do not administer current banking accounts in the traditional sense, but it is interesting to note that in 1982 the largest of them, the Halifax, serviced some six million investors via a network of 550 branches and 1,700 agencies, an average of approximately 10,900 investors per branch.

Building society branching operations are much simpler to maintain than the banks', reflecting a far narrower range of business. More importantly, building societies are not yet engaged to any significant extent in money transmission business, which is where much of the banks' heavy branch expenditure lies. As is shown below banks generally do not make an economic charge for the provision of money transmission services, a fact which has far more serious implications for the traditional clearing banks with their heavy branch networks than it has for some of their competitors.

All the banks, but particularly the big four, have discovered in recent years that branches are very expensive to run. Precise figures on costs have been difficult to come by. Indeed, it seemed that many of the banks have a surprisingly vague idea of how their costs break down. According to Mr. Vander Weyer of Barclays, however, the average running cost of a 20-person branch in England was about £250,000 in 1982. It is estimated that overheads, including a branch manager's time, can now cost over £30 per hour (1). Unit costs have risen steadily. One of the London clearers reported to us that 'there is probably only limited scope for achieving reductions in unit costs through staff savings. Reductions can be made though through achieving greater efficiency and by utilising automation to enable greater volumes of work to be handled without any increase in staff numbers.' Considerable improvement in operational efficiency along these lines has already been achieved. Between 1972 and 1981, although staff numbers rose in all but two years they did so at a lower rate than the increase in the volume of transactions handled. According to the Committee of London Clearing Bankers, the number of staff employed by the London clearers rose by 16 per cent between 1975 and 1982 while the number of transactions rose by 53 per cent (2). These figures reflect the introduction of new technology, including head office giant reader/sorting machines which can now handle up to 2,400 cheques a minute.

Although automation has had some effect in reducing branch costs in real terms, these costs are still high. Many basic handling activities are still manually conducted, although some of the burden of cheque encashment has been reduced by the introduction of automated teller machines. Capital equipment is very expensive. Total transaction volumes continue to rise steeply. Cheque writing, the most expensive way of effecting a transaction, increases by about four per cent per annum (until recently the rate of increase was approximately seven per cent) and is a particular burden upon the branches. Income from charges has generally not matched expenditure on costs in recent years, as we show below. The building societies are not exposed to these losses. Also, the traditional clearing banks have been less successful than the building societies in using their branches to obtain deposits. Bearing in mind the differences in the opening hours of bank and building society branches, the customer's impression is one of high-cost, low-access branches competing with comparatively low-cost, high-access branches (3). To understand why a question mark hangs over the future of branch banking, however, it is useful to look more closely at the factors which affect the profitability of retail branch banking, beginning with the losses that the banks appear to have been making on the operation of current accounts, narrowly defined.

The profitability of current accounts and transmission services appears to have declined substantially since the mid-1960s. Transaction volumes have risen enormously, but current account balances have fallen in real terms. The costliness of these developments has been offset over the last fifteen years or so by rising interest rates, but in 1982 these rates took a sharp tumble, a significant trend when we consider that for most of the clearers, the cost of providing money transmission services in 1982 was equivalent to around ten per cent of current account balances. In mid-1982, one clearer told us that:

'the profitability of current accounts is very sensitive to the level of interest rates; with base rates currently below 10 per cent the endowment effect may well have been eliminated and it is highly likely that personal current accounts are now making a negative contribution to profits . . .'

The precise impact of interest rate changes on particular banks is very variable, but the point nevertheless has a general application. This is why all the clearers began to raise their charges so sharply in the second half of the year; the big banks increased their charges for using cheques by up to 45 per cent.

Money transmission costs constitute a large part of the total costs of running branch networks. In 1978, the London clearers told the Price Commission that between 1972 and 1977 branch system costs had trebled to £1.5 billion, of which £900 million represented the cost of running a money transmission service (4). Between 1977 and 1979, money transmission costs rose by another third to around £1.2 billion, of which an estimated £600 million related to personal customers. We have been unable to update these figures, but there is no reason to doubt that the upward trend has continued.

A major reason for rising costs is the expansion in the volume of personal sector banking business. According to the Committee of London Clearing Bankers, automated clearings increased by over two hundred per cent between 1972 and 1981. More expensively, the volume of paper vouchers (mainly cheques) cleared rose by more than seventy-five per cent over the same period. In 1982, paper-based transactions still accounted for 82 per cent of the total number of cleared items. The clearing process for most of these transactions begins in a branch bank and ends in a branch bank.

The processing of paper transactions is expensive. The seventy-five per cent growth figure referred to above has serious implications for branch costs. It has been estimated, for example, that 25 per cent of an average cashier's time is taken up in cashing cheques (5). The more successful the banks are in attracting new current account business the greater the number of transactions that branches have to deal with. Automation has eased some of these problems, but in the absence of cheque truncation the handling and movement of cheques are still both labour-intensive and costly.

The real dilemma for the banks (and a major reason for their previous lack of enthusiasm in recruiting lower-income customers) is that on the basis of existing charging structures, many of the new accounts which are responsible for increased cheque writing are either unprofitable or only marginally profitable if considered as self-contained business, unless interest rates are high. This is the major reason why the banks are increasingly keen to cross-sell other services, some of which, like personal loans, are very profitable.

Since the 1960s the rapid growth in transaction volumes has obliged the banks to invest heavily in new forms of automated processing. The banks could not have coped with current volumes of transactions without the computers now in use. 'Back office' regional and branch banking electronic technology has been developed to speed up handling and accounting procedures by linking into centralised record-keeping systems. Most of this is invisible to the customer. Automation has moved more recently to 'front-office' with the emergence of automated teller machines and branch counter terminals. All the banks have moved heavily into information technology; the total investment of the London clearing banks in this area rose from £257 million in 1975 to £749 million in 1981 (6).

Costs, of course, form only one side of the equation. The important point is that increased costs have not been matched by increased income from charges on anything like the same scale. Between 1972 and 1977, according to a survey conducted by the *Economist*, total income from bank charges – that is from both personal and business customers – rose from £135 million a year to only £217 million, an increase of 62 per cent as against a 300 per cent increase in costs (7). Most of these increased charges were apparently borne by business. It was the evidence of this kind of arithmetic that led the Price Commission to conclude in April 1978 that the banks would be justified in increasing charges to their personal customers. The banks have since put up their charges but, until recently at least, not in line with rising costs. Thus in 1979 of the £600 million or so attributable to personal sector transmission costs, the banks were recovering only £50 million in charges. Even after the most recent and very considerable increases in charges, some of the banks claim that they are not even close to recovering their costs on money transmission services. According to Barclays, following the latest increases, personal account charges are unlikely to cover more than a fifth of the costs with which they are associated.

One explanation of these losses is that under the conditions of 'free' banking operated by the major clearers, a high proportion of personal customers pay no charges at all. Barclays, for example, in their submission to us, said that in each quarter an estimated 63 per cent of its personal customers benefit from 'free' banking in this way. And as explained in Section 3, when direct charges are imposed by the banks, they are abated by a 'notional' interest allowance calculated on average credit balances maintained. It is significant that as interest rates fell this allowance was halved by the banks between April and October 1982.

The falling notional interest allowance, no less than the rise in charges, spells bad news for all customers who do not qualify for 'free' banking. But even those customers who do pay the new higher charges appear not to be paying the full cost of providing the services in question, at least where paper transactions are concerned. Most banks are currently (Spring 1983) charging about 28p for the use of cheques for example whereas the cost to the banks of clearing cheques is claimed by most of the banks to be perhaps twice this sum.

The third factor involved, after money transmission costs and income from charges, is the volume of the balances held by the banks on which interest is earned. In real terms this figure has fallen almost every year since 1971, possibly reflecting a growing financial sophistication on the part of consumers who, when interest rates are high, are more likely to transfer their funds from current accounts to interest-earning deposit accounts. Current account balances are therefore sensitive to interest rate changes. Comparatively low interest rates at the level reached in Spring 1983 could favour the banks by acting as a deterrent to those customers thinking of moving funds out of current accounts. Declining interest rates therefore have both a positive and a negative effect on the profitability of current accounts: on the one hand they may persuade customers to leave their money where it is; on the other, such funds will have a reduced earning capacity.

Putting all three factors together – transmission costs, income from charges and volume of balances – gives us figures for *unrecovered costs per pound of current account balances*. These costs have risen substantially in recent years, though as we can see from Table IV.1 expressed as implicit rate of interest the trend has been uneven (8).

It is clear from these figures (and also from a comparable and very detailed set of statistics supplied to us by one of the Scottish clearing banks), that the pricing strategy adopted by the big banks has not seriously been designed to recover transmission costs out of income from transmission charges. This does not mean, as some of the banks have implied to us, that current accounts as a whole are unprofitable, *providing* unrecovered costs are lower than interest earnings on current account credit balances – which they have been and still are. (This might cease to be true if interest rates fell to, say, 5 per cent

Table IV.I   The unrecovered costs of money transmission: in £million

	1975	1976	1977	1978	1979	1980	1981
A. Money transmission costs	657	772	881	994	1 170	1 458	1 675
B. Income from money transmission charges	129	166	217	265	320	375	486
C. Unrecovered costs (A–B)	528	606	664	729	850	1 083	1 189
D. Average cleared balances on current accounts	7 660	8 545	9 733	11 841	13 000	13 298	14 448
E. Implicit rate of interest (C÷D × 100)%	6.9	7.1	6.8	6.2	6.5	8.1	8.2

Source: Price Commission and unpublished accounting data for Barclays, Lloyds, Midland and National Westminster

depending on how the banks adjusted their charges.) There is another reason, however, why the banks have been prepared to run up unrecovered costs on money transmission business by keeping their charges down – it provides a market in which to cross-sell profitable business like personal loans, credit cards and insurance operations and, equally importantly, to stave off competition from newer and smaller institutions. It may be argued that this kind of price strategy has benefited large numbers of customers by subsidising basic current account activity in conditions of 'free' banking.

There is a trade-off to be considered, however, between the recovery or non-recovery of transmission costs and the ability to sustain extensive networks. The statistics presented above provide one explanation, albeit a qualified one as we shall see below, for current doubts about the viability of some of these networks. In terms of customer access to branches therefore, it is possible that the consumer could ultimately be the loser by such a pricing strategy.

For most customers the provision of facilities for making personal payments is what distinguishes banks from other financial institutions, and branches are an integral part of that perception, hence the importance of the preceding discussion. From the point of view of the banks, however, the importance of the branch network has traditionally been located within a different perspective – the need to borrow from personal customers in order to lend to industry. The performance of the banks in the personal deposit-taking market is therefore an equally significant factor in explaining the vulnerability of branch structures. For a variety of reasons, the banks collectively have failed to maintain their market share although the largest drop in the market share over the last twenty years or so was registered by National Savings, the years 1963–72, showing a decline of 16.3 per cent, being particularly disastrous. Since the late 1970s National Savings have been making something of a recovery, but over the whole period the biggest threat to banks has come from the building societies. In the period 1963–79 the building societies increased their share of personal deposits by 25.2 per cent. In the pre-1972 period this was almost entirely at the expense of National Savings, but the crucial years were between 1974–77. Having performed well between 1972–4 in this market, registering a gain of 5.5 per cent in market share, the banks proceeded to lose an 8.5 per cent share during the succeeding three years. During the same period, the building societies chalked up a gain of 9.5 per cent. Over the whole period of 1963–79, the banks suffered a loss of 2.3 per cent in market share while the building societies gained 25.5 per cent, an advantage which they have retained (9).

These statistics are important in any consideration of the future of branch networks. Much of the recent expansion in building society networks took place as a means of improving deposit-taking performance, rather than as a means of promoting mortgage business. Similarly, in the past the banks have financed much or all of their lending from deposits gathered through their branches. The decline in the banks' share of deposit-taking business has obliged them to raise more and more of their finance on the wholesale money markets. Apart from the fact that the interest payable on wholesale money is higher than on personal deposits, it can be argued that progressive recourse to the money markets undermines the point of having branch systems. Both the banks and National Savings have in the past benefited from what could be described as 'cheap money', the availability of which in more recent years has been depressed by competition from the building societies paying better rates. This development has been much less critical for National Savings than for the banks because the National Savings movement does not have to support branch networks from income earned in a way which bears any real comparison with the operations of the commercial banks.

The performance of the banks *vis à vis* National Savings and the building societies can partly be excused by reference to a number of objective disadvantages over the period concerned. Governments have not dealt even-handedly with different types of financial institution. For example, between September 1973 and February 1975, the government prohibited banks from paying more than 9½ per cent interest on bank deposits of less than £10,000 in order to encourage a greater inflow of funds to building societies, allegedly in the interests of potential home buyers. (It is sometimes forgotten that governments have exercised controls over bank borrowing as well as bank lending.) Similarly, differences of financial structure and financial criteria have been and continue to be a factor in differential performance between institutions. Commercial banks are required to subscribe to higher capital/liabilities ratios than are building societies and savings institutions. In their evidence to us many of the banks further explained their performance by stressing the fiscal disadvantages to which they are subject, a topic discussed more fully in section 9, 'Competition and regulation'. It should be noted in passing, however, that some of these defences look rather thin when the alleged pricing disadvantages are examined in detail.

There are two major reasons why consumers have tended not to favour the banks in investing their savings. Firstly, throughout the 1960s and 1970s they offered a very limited deposit-taking service. Most of them only provided the single savings facility of the seven-day deposit. The validity of this criticism was accepted by one of the London clearers in its submission to us. 'A personal customer with less than £10,000 to deposit with a bank two years ago would have been almost totally restricted to a seven-day deposit account.' At a time when there was an observable trend towards longer-term savings instruments, the banks generally failed to come up with attractive schemes. Secondly, and this brings us right back to access; the banks, unlike the building societies and the post office, were just not open at times which were convenient to personal depositors. This caused them to lose ground which it may be hard to recover.

It is artificial to separate current account costs completely from the profitable activities associated with such accounts, principally lending services. Personal lending, after money transmission and deposit taking, is the third category of business to which the viability of branch banking must be related. Because of the high costs of money transmission and the weight of competition for personal savings, the banks aim to sustain reasonably high levels of lending to the personal sector to boost the overall profitability of their retail operations as a whole. Personal lending is extremely profitable to the banks, even though relatively few current account customers are involved.

Substantial bank lending to the personal sector is, nevertheless, a comparatively recent phenomenon. Previously, the banks hinged their lending and borrowing operations on the old principle that the personal sector saves so that the business sector may borrow. Bank lending to the personal sector has at times been heavily constrained by monetary policy, though few branch managers were traditionally keen on marketing their lending facilities in a retail sense even when there was money to lend. The professional distaste of bankers for anything that smacked of salesmanship no less than the straitjacket of Treasury credit controls has been a factor in the banks' performance in consumer credit markets. Nevertheless, the lending ceilings imposed by the Bank of England in the 1950s and 1960s were sufficiently restrictive to prevent the banks from competing effectively against direct retailer credit agencies and finance houses and were, consequently, much resented. In order to increase their penetration of a profitable market, from the 1950s onwards the banks began to buy into the finance houses, and ultimately to take them over completely. The most recent stage in this process was the purchase of United Dominions Trust by the Trustee Savings Banks. The other major finance houses are all now bank owned: Lombard North Central by National Westminster; Mercantile Credit by Barclays; Chartered Trust by Standard Chartered; Lloyds and Scottish by Lloyds and the Royal Bank of Scotland; Forward Trust by Midland; and North West Securities by the Bank of Scotland.

With the introduction of Competition and Credit Control in 1971, the banks were freed from the constraints of the interest rate cartel and began in response to develop a range of new personal lending techniques as a means of advancing into different sections of the UK credit market. The overdraft was already a well-established form of borrowing and personal loans had been introduced at the end of the 1950s. Budget accounts were introduced during the 1960s, but other forms of personal lending, including the credit card boom, revolving credit loans and, more recently, mortgages, all came after the relaxation of credit controls in the early 1970s (10).

In explaining their relatively weak performance in the consumer credit market, the banks have tended to emphasise the monetary restrictions placed upon them rather than their local managers' lack of enthusiasm for selling money. In spite of the operation of 'the corset', for most of the 1970s, these arguments are unconvincing. As late as 1979, by which time government-inspired lending constraints were minimal, one of the London clearing banks was reported to have a personal loan portfolio of only £150 million, roughly equivalent, or so it was claimed, to what Citibank Trust was lending in Britain at that time. Citibank had about thirty branches in Britain and no captive customers at all; the London clearer in question had over two thousand branches and around three million personal account customers to sell to (11). This comparison illustrates the extent to which the banks appeared to be failing to sell their most attractive products at what were (and are) competitive rates.

Table IV.2   Consumer credit outstanding: end-June 1982

	£ million	%
London and Scottish clearing banks	8 314*	55.3
Other monetary sector (including finance houses)	4 980*	33.1
Insurance companies	324	2.2
Retailers	1 416	9.4
Total	15 034	100.0

Source: Derived from *Financial Statistics*

* Clearing bank figure is average of 19 May and 18 August; rest of monetary sector obtained by subtracting clearing bank figure from monetary sector total.

The performance of the banks in the credit market has improved, largely at the expense of retailers and insurance companies, but we can see from Table IV.2 that in mid-1983 finance houses and retailers still had a large share of the market whilst offering what was in terms of cost (if not necessarily of convenience) an inferior product.

These figures begin to look less flattering to the banks when related to the current account markets available to them. None of the major clearers has succeeded in selling personal loans to more than 14 per cent of their current account customers, a peak reached by one of the London banks between October 1980 and March 1981. Since that date, all the banks have begun to market their personal loan facilities with unprecedented vigour in conditions of intensifying competition. Nevertheless, because of the impact of the recession, the percentage of current account holders who have personal loans has fallen back amongst the big banks to around the 8/9 per cent mark, though the Yorkshire Bank has a very much higher percentage among its current account holders.

Again, these figures are critical to the debate about the future of branch networks. They may be interpreted in two ways. Because the banks charge significantly higher rates of interest to their personal customers than they pay out on deposits, personal lending business makes a major contribution to retail profits and helps sustain branch networks. On the other hand, banks which sell personal loan business to less than ten per cent of their customers are failing to spread the cost of branch overheads and money transmission business, even allowing for additional income from overdrafts and other ancillary services. It seems probable that the future size of individual branch networks will depend in part upon the degree of success enjoyed by the banks in spreading those overheads still

Table IV.3 Main sources of housing loans outstanding: end-June 1982

	£ million	%
Building societies	52 210	76.8
London and Scottish clearing banks	6 652*	9.8
Other monetary sector	1 218*	1.8
Insurance companies and pension funds	2 283	3.4
Local authorities	4 254	6.3
Other public sector	1 326	2.0
Total	67 943	100.0

Source: Derived from *Financial Statistics*

* See note to Table IV.2.

further by winning larger shares of this expanding market. The banks' entry into the mortgage market was one major milestone in this effort, though this form of lending appears to be less profitable than personal loans, for example, partly because lending rates are effectively set by the building societies. This may be one of the reasons why, at the time of writing, the banks had reined back sharply on new home loans. The clearers' share of this market at mid-1982 is indicated in Table IV.3.

It is instructive, as the banks and the building societies move into more direct competition with each other, to note the relative strength of the building societies in the total personal lending market (consumer credit plus housing loans). By aggregating the data in Tables IV.2 and IV.3 we can calculate the following:

Table IV.4 Total personal lending outstanding: end-June 1982

	£ million	%
Building societies	52 210	62.9
London and Scottish clearing banks	14 966	18.0
Other monetary sector	6 198	7.5
Local authorities, etc.	5 580	6.7
Insurance companies, etc.	2 607	3.1
Retailers	1 416	1.7
Total	82 977	100.0

Source: Tables IV.2 and IV.3

The building societies, strong in deposit-taking, strong in mortgage lending and as yet unencumbered by expensive paper-based money transmission services, may be better placed to preserve their branch networks than the traditional clearing banks.

References to Appendix IV

1. D. Vander Weyer, 'The economics of branch banking in the future', speech to St Andrews summer school for young bankers, June 1982.
2. For a more detailed analysis see Patrick Frazer, 'How not to measure bank productivity', *The Banker*, August 1982, pp. 103–5.

3. This view reflects a comparatively limited definition of access, of course; see section 4 for a fuller discussion.
4. However, the techniques used for measuring these costs appear to differ from individual bank to bank.
5. *Financial Times*, 23 September 1982.
6. *The Banks and Information Technology*, Banking Information Service, 1982, p. 4.
7. *Economist*, 8 December 1979. Special supplement on retail banking in the UK.
8. There is some evidence from the latest figures (1982/3) to suggest that the underlying upward trend may now have been reversed.
9. Dimitri Vittas and Patrick Frazer, 'Competition in retail banking', *The Banker*, February 1980, p. 47. See also section 8.
10. Barclaycard was launched in 1966 but credit cards did not really take off until the 1970s.
11. *Economist, op. cit.* We have not been able to verify this information as regards the bank concerned.

Appendix V / Letter to Dr Gerard Vaughan, MP, Minister of State for Consumer Affairs, from Mrs Rachel Waterhouse, Chairman of the NCC Banking Services Working Party

Letter to Dr Gerard Vaughan MP, Minister of State for Consumer Affairs, from Mrs Rachel Waterhouse, Chairman of NCC Banking Services Working Party, 3 September 1982

Dear Dr Vaughan,

Review by the Director General of Fair Trading of exemptions from the consumer credit advertisements and quotations regulations

I am writing to you as Chairman of the National Consumer Council Working Party which is carrying through the work on the banking remit which your predecessor gave us.

We have seen the Review by the Director General of Fair Trading of Exemptions from the Consumer Credit Advertisements and Quotations Regulations. This is a matter which has been raised by a number of organisations in response to a request from us for evidence for the banking remit. Our Working Party has considered the Director General's Review. We agree with his recommendations and hope that you will put them into effect.

I write now because we believe that this is a matter on which the Government could usefully take action without waiting until the conclusion of our review.

I am sending a copy of this letter to Sir Gordon Borrie.

Yours sincerely

Mrs Rachel Waterhouse (signed)

Appendix VI / Cashless pay: the NCC's response to the Department of Employment's consultative paper

CASHLESS PAY

Response by the National Consumer Council to the Department of Employment's consultative paper

1. The consultative paper raises two main issues:

    (i) the way in which wages are paid;
    (ii) deductions from pay.

    The NCC has no view on deductions from pay, an issue on which it is appropriate for those representing the interests of employees to speak.

2. We do, however, have views on cashless pay. These are from two main sources:

    (i) our report *Consumers and Credit*, published in December 1980, in response to a remit from the government;
    (ii) the review we are currently engaged in, again in response to a remit from the government, of the banking services available to consumers.

3. In *Consumers and Credit* we suggested that there were advantages in having a bank account which made cashless pay on a monthly basis more attractive to employees than weekly cash pay, and that trade unions should take this interest of their members into account when negotiating with employers about modes of payment. One major advantage is that people with bank accounts have at least the possibility of easier access to cheaper forms of credit than those without. This allows them to get better value when buying goods and services by credit. Secondly, the increasing pattern of payment of bills on a monthly basis, including the introduction of instalment payments for gas and electricity, sets up budgetary constraints on those who are paid weekly by cash.

4. We recognised, however, that a transition from weekly pay by cash to monthly pay by money transfer would cause problems for some people used to weekly budgeting. The implications of cashless pay for education in personal money management are considerable and are not properly addressed in the consultative paper.

5. The terms of the remit which the government has given us on banking are as follows:

    'to collect and consider evidence on the banking services available to consumers in the United Kingdom; and, as appropriate, to make recommendations'.

    The report is nearing completion and will soon be submitted to the Minister for Consumer Affairs. Two major issues discussed in the report are competition in the provision of banking services and perceptions of banking services both among those who are currently bank customers and among the unbanked. Both these issues are in different ways relevant to cashless pay. They are dealt with at length in the report so we shall not cover them in detail in this response. However, no consideration of reform of wage payment law can be complete without some reference to them.

6. The changing pattern of competition has encouraged deposit-taking bodies other than banks, including large building societies, to offer limited money transmission services. These developments are still in their infancy though the pace of change is rapid. Clearly employees are more likely to find cashless pay attractive if they are able to have their wages credited to accounts in the financial institutions they most like to deal with.

7. Our research confirms that many customers perceive building societies to be more accessible than banks. If there were to be any reform of Truck and Payment of Wages legislation, it would greatly enhance the acceptability of change if employees were to be given the right to have their wages transferred, whether weekly or monthly, *to an account held by any recognised deposit-taking institution of their choice*. We recognise that the realities of collective bargaining in the introduction of cashless pay tend to favour the High Street banks, particularly the bank or banks with which the company concerned holds its own accounts. There may well be advantages for some individuals in such arrangements; nevertheless we believe that these pressures should be counteracted by the provision of the greatest possible freedom of choice for employees at the point at which arrangements for automated payment transfers are negotiated.

8. Current arrangements for administering automated credit clearing in the UK are subject to the control of five shareholding banks. A number of other banks, known as sponsoring banks, enjoy equality of service with the shareholding banks. The facilities offered by Bankers' Automated Clearing Services [BACS] are open to any employer organisation or financial institution which can provide or receive payment instructions on magnetic tape, but the terms and conditions of the availability of the service on the processing side vary as between the shareholding and sponsoring banks and their non-BACS client institutions [whether bank or non-bank]. In practice an additional one or two days' delay between transfer authorisation by a company and the crediting of an employee's personal account takes place if the account holder's banking business is with a non-BACS institution. Clearly, non-BACS institutions are at a disadvantage under these arrangements. Insofar as this puts the financial institutions preferred by individual employees at a disadvantage, this may make progress towards the acceptance of cashless pay more difficult.

9. There appears to be some confusion in the Government's mind about obstacles, means and ends. The role of the Truck Acts and related legislation in inhibiting the rate of changeover to cashless pay is often exaggerated [e.g. paragraph 9 of the consultative document]. The historic preference for cash payment has far more to do with traditional bank attitudes towards manual workers, working class suspicion of banks and the attractions to people on low incomes of cash-based patterns of income management, than with the survival of antiquated legislation. There is good evidence that a substantial minority of the population have, rightly or wrongly, regarded having a bank account as unnecessary, inconvenient and expensive. It is therefore significant that the banks themselves, now engaged in unprecedented competition for the accounts of hitherto 'unbanked' workers, are actively opposed to repeal of the Truck Acts. The Committee of London Clearing Bankers [CLCB] takes the view that the protections afforded by legislation are a necessary ingredient of the relationship of trust that it is claimed has been established with employee organisations in recent years, and that continued progress would actually be jeopardised by removing these protections. We agree with the view that the willingness of employees to accept cashless pay is to a large extent a reflection of their perceptions of the benefits and disbenefits of having to deal with banks; statutory protection appears to us to be a marginal consideration.

10. This is particularly important at a time when itemised bank charges and the propor-

tion of current account holders paying charges have both risen sharply. We are concerned that some employees on low incomes may be forced into bank accounts which they cannot manage. Some will slip into overdraft and a few will ultimately find themselves excluded from cash access to their wages.

11. For some people there remain other disadvantages to cashless pay, particularly as regards geographical and temporal access to cash. General access to cash has undoubtedly improved dramatically in recent years with the rapid expansion of bank automated teller machine [ATM] programmes. But the gradual net decline in the branch networks of all the major banks, coupled with the maintenance by most banks of limited opening hours, means that getting cash can still be difficult for some, particularly for people living in less densely populated areas in which the installation of ATMs, or so we have been informed, would be uneconomic. Our evidence clearly shows that the overwhelming majority of employees who have adopted cashless pay do not revert back to cash payment arrangements; nevertheless, the knowledge that they are free to do so for any of the reasons to which reference has been made, appears to be reassuring.

12. This is not necessarily an argument for doing nothing, but rather for seeing the legislative issues in their true perspective. We do not believe that the repeal of the Truck Acts is necessary to achieve a greater rate of progress towards cashless pay. However, there clearly is a commonsense case for removing some of their more archaic and anomalous provisions; but if this is to be done by legislative modification the basic statutory right of employees to be paid in cash should be preserved. No employee should be obliged to accept a particular mode of payment as a condition of employment [i.e. a compulsory bank account with a particular bank]. Indeed, no person should be *forced* to have a bank account in any circumstances. That would be an unacceptable restriction on the individual's freedom of choice.

13. The consultative paper declares:

> 'The payment of wages by cheque or direct debit transfer [rather than in cash] brings important benefits – not just to employers and employees but to the community as a whole.'

14. We agree with this view: as we have said, we see advantages in having a bank account to employees and their families in their role as consumers. We believe, therefore, it is right for government to support and encourage the growth of payment into bank accounts. We believe it would be wrong for government to enable such payment to be enforced.

15. We therefore recommend that, in any reform of the payment of wages legislation, the government should adopt two criteria against which any proposals can be tested for acceptability:

   (i) employees should have a statutory right to be paid in cash if they so choose;
   (ii) employees should have the right to have wage payments transferred to any recognised deposit-taking institution of their choice.

16. Finally, particular considerations apply in Northern Ireland. There, unlike England, Wales and Scotland, the four commercial banks appear not to be keen to recruit a relatively large market of cash-paid workers. We have been informed that the four Northern Ireland clearing banks cannot profitably process low credit balance current accounts generating significant volumes of paper vouchers before they have completed their respective computerisation programmes. Clearly it would be wrong to force employees in the Province to bank with financial institutions who appear not to be ready to deal with their business.

National Consumer Council
18 Queen Anne's Gate
London SW1
1 June 1983

Appendix VII / Organisations which were consulted or gave written and/or oral evidence

Many finance houses and building societies chose to submit evidence through the Finance Houses Association and the Building Societies Association respectively. In the case of some finance houses, evidence was submitted by their parent companies. We also received a large amount of unsolicited correspondence from individual consumers.

Key: * organisations invited to give oral evidence (following written submissions)
** organisations consulted (but who did not give written evidence)

Abbey National Building Society*
Advertising Standards Authority**
Alliance Building Society
Allied Irish Banks
American Express Company**
Association of Management and Professional Staffs
Association of Scientific Technical and Managerial Staffs
Bankcard Holders of America, Washington DC**
Banking Insurance & Finance Union
Bank of Baroda
Bank of Canada**
Bank of Cyprus (London)
Bank of England**
Bank of India
Bank of Ireland*
Bank of Scotland*
Barclays Bank
British Legal Association
Building Societies Association*
Building Societies Members Association
Chequepoint
Cheshire Building Society
Civil Service Building Society
Clearing Bank Union
Clydesdale Bank*
Commission for Racial Equality
Committee of London Clearing Bankers*
Committee of Scottish Clearing Bankers
Confederation of British Industry
Consumers' Association (UK)

Consumers' Association of Canada**
Consumers' Union of United States Inc**
Co-operative Bank*
Co-operative Union
Coutts & Co.
Department for National Savings
Department of Consumer & Corporate Affairs, Canada**
Derbyshire Building Society
Diners Club International
Disabled Living Foundation
Equal Opportunities Commission
Federal Reserve System, Washington DC**
Federal Trade Commission (Bureau of Consumer Protection), Washington DC**
Finance Houses Association
First Co-operative Finance
Halifax Building Society*
HFC Trust
HongKong & Shanghai Banking Corporation
Independent Broadcasting Authority**
Inland Revenue (Finance Division)**
Institute of Consumer Affairs
Institut National de la Consommation, France**
Law Society
Leeds Permanent Building Society
Leicester Building Society
Lloyds Bank
Lombard North Central
London & South of England Building Society
Marsden Building Society
Metropolitan Police**
Midland Bank*
National Association of Citizens Advice Bureaux
National Council of Women of Great Britain
National Federation of Consumer Groups:
    Aberdeen Consumer Group
    Consumer Association of South Humberside
    Preston Consumer Group
    Winchester Consumer Group
National Federation of Women's Institutes
National Girobank*
National Housewives Association
National Westminster Bank*
Nationwide Building Society
Northern Rock Building Society
Office of Fair Trading*
Publix Super Markets Inc, Florida, USA**
Registry of Friendly Societies**
Royal Bank of Scotland*
Royal National Institute for the Blind
Skipton Building Society
Strathclyde Police**
HM Treasury**
TSB Group*
Verbruikersunie (Consumers' Association), Belgium**

West Bromwich Building Society
Western Trust & Savings
Williams & Glyn's Bank*
Woolwich Equitable Building Society*
Yorkshire Bank*
Yorkshire Building Society